CASTROISM

Theory and Practice

CASTROISM
Theory and Practice

THEODORE DRAPER

FREDERICK A. PRAEGER, *Publishers*
New York · Washington · London

FREDERICK A. PRAEGER, *Publishers*
111 Fourth Avenue, New York 3, N.Y., U.S.A.
77–79 Charlotte Street, London W.1, England

Published in the United States of America in 1965
by Frederick A. Praeger, Inc., Publishers

© 1965 by Theodore Draper
Library of Congress Catalog Card Number: 65-18072

Printed in the United States of America

To My Son
ROGER

FOREWORD

THIS BOOK had its genesis in a paper which I was asked to write for the conference on "A Hundred Years of Revolutionary Internationals," sponsored by the Hoover Institution on War, Revolution, and Peace, at Stanford University, California, in October, 1964. The subject of this paper, "What Is Castroism?," and its relative brevity forced me to crystallize my thoughts on the nature of Castroism and its relationship to the Communist movement. Of necessity, the primary aim was analytical, though I thought it best to give the analysis a historical framework. In general, however, I was less interested in telling the full story in chronological order than in diagnosing and seeking the essential elements or characteristics of Castroism.

After finishing this paper, I decided to go on and en-large the scope of the analysis. The Hoover paper was lim-ited, for reasons of space and time, to the distinctive fea-tures of Castroism as a revolutionary force. This led me, for the most part, to emphasize its tactical side. But I had long been dissatisfied with current theories on the social nature of Castro's revolution, such as the theory of the "agrarian revolution." I therefore decided to examine this and re-lated theories in order to arrive at a "social interpretation" of Castroism more consistent with the make-up of Cuban society and the known facts of recent Cuban history. In this search for a more tenable social theory, however, I have not always attempted to follow any chronological his-torical order. I have rather explored aspects of Cuban so-ciety or cited various events and statements as the need for them arose to clarify or support some point in the social analysis of the revolution. I hope that I have made the his-torical context sufficiently clear to enable the reader to find his way without too much difficulty.

The third chapter makes the transition from theory to practice. I have focused my attention on Castro's changing economic policies and their practical results, but here again my purpose has not been wholly economic. It has seemed to me to be necessary to seek the red thread or threads that run through the entire development of Castro-ism, before and after taking power, in revolutionary tactics and in economic policies. Thus this is not a book of his-tory, sociology, or economics, though there may be a good deal of history, sociology, and economics in it. It is perhaps more an essay, in part historical, sociological, and eco-nomic, that attempts to define a living political phenome-non which by its very nature does not yet lend itself to easy definition.

I have not tried to deal with such matters as education or culture because they pose special problems. In education, for example, the Castro regime announced that its anti-illiteracy campaign in 1961 had reduced illiteracy to the vanishing point. Yet, on March 14, 1964, Minister of Industries Ernesto Che Guevara revealed that so many illiterates were left that it was necessary to prohibit their employment in all the units controlled by the Ministry. The original claim was based on no more than a first-grade level of literacy, which may explain why the *analfabetos* were not equipped to do much more than they had done previously. In any case, this is a field in which qualitative evaluations are at least as important as quantitative statistics, and I have no way of checking on either the claims or the criticisms. For the subjects with which this book is primarily concerned, it is more relevant to note that "Marxism-Leninism" has become the official ideology of the Cuban educational system, taught at all levels in one form or another, and this may be taken into consideration in any effort to place the Castro regime politically.

Of much greater bearing on my main theme is another aspect of Cuban policy with which I have not tried to deal at length—the relations of Cuba, Soviet Russia, and Communist China. The reader will, I think, find allusions which will convey my general belief that Castro's Cuba has pursued its own ends within the Communist world, that it is not a replica of any other Communist power, and that its external relations with other Communist countries have been a mixture of practical dependence and independent ambitions. But Cuba's relations with Soviet Russia, Communist China, and other Communist powers would require an extremely detailed, exacting, and lengthy study to do much good. I have not been able to undertake this task within the confines of this book, though I have touched on some aspects of the problem.

I have chosen to use traditional historical documentation that anyone can check or study for himself. In this hotly controversial field, it has seemed best to tell both the serious student and the interested reader what my sources are, even at the risk of burdening the pages with footnotes. I have also given much of the evidence on which my conclusions rest because so much of the source material is not yet easily available even in our largest libraries. Unfortunately, very few, if any, of our Latin American scholars had specialized in Cuba before the present revolution, and very few, if any, have given it any special attention since then. The field has largely been left to the journalists, who, with the best will in the world, do not have the time or the training for painstaking and intensive research.

The subjects in which I happen to be interested require something more than a trip to Cuba for a few days or a few weeks of personal interviews, guided or haphazard tours, and kaleidoscopic impressions. I have made such a trip to Cuba and elsewhere myself, and I do not wish to scorn it. We cannot wait for the historians to tell us what is happening in the present. In a sense, the Cuban revolution is already too old for journalists to grasp as a whole and not old enough for historians to deal with in scholarly fragments. Yet we are caught up in it and must try to understand it with the materials at hand, no doubt inadequate from the viewpoint of a decade or two hence. Nevertheless, it is not too soon to begin to make the transition from journalism to history. The deeper questions, it seems to me, can be pursued meaningfully only by trying to take in the revolution as a whole, through its different, seemingly contradictory stages, and by linking the moving present with the receding past. The more we have to push back into the past, the less can interviews, tours, and impressions in the present tell us.

Fidel Castro, for example, has said so many different things at different times that it is no longer possible to think of him in terms of anything he may have said at any one time. There is no short cut to understanding what he is or was; no substitute, alas, for the formidable task of studying, or at least reading, his miles of uncollected speeches. They may not tell us all we want to know but they tell us far more than he may want us to know. The reason is simple: He could not anticipate in 1953 or 1957 or 1960 what might be indiscreet or compromising years later. He could not foretell which manifestoes and declarations, once sent forth into the world with such apparent sincerity and even innocence, would have to be banished to a historical limbo because they did not fit into the changing line and circumstances.

This book has also given me the opportunity to restudy and rethink aspects of the Cuban problem on which I had already written at much closer range. New material and a longer perspective have made me change my mind about some things. For example, Castro seemed to have turned over the main levers of power to the old-time Communists in 1961. And so he had, as he has admitted, but it was only a phase. We know much more about it now than we could know at the time; the problem is not only why it came to pass but why it passed. On the other hand, I feel fortunate in that I have not needed to change my basic view of Castroism.

I concluded my very first article on Cuba, in *The Reporter* of May 12, 1960, with the words: "Castro once spoke of his revolution as 'liberty with bread and without terror.' If he continues to push too hard, too fast, and too far, Cuba may yet have more terror without either bread or liberty." I have never regretted expressing this foreboding. In an article completed in December, 1960, and published in *Encounter* (London) and in *The New Leader*

(New York) in March, 1961, I called the Cuban revolution
a "variant" in the Communist "family" of revolutions,
comparable to the Yugoslav and Chinese "variants." The
more I have studied and thought about the Cuban experience, the more firmly have I held this conviction.

In a sense, then, this book is the distillation of five years
of study and thought about the Cuban revolution. I could
not have devoted so much time to it if I had not received
so much help and benefited from so much forbearance.
For varying periods during these five years, the following
institutions have made it possible for me to carry on my
work:

The Rockefeller Foundation, and especially Dr. Gerald
Freund.

The Russian Research Center at Harvard University,
and its former Director, Professor Merle Fainsod.

The Research Institute on Communist Affairs at Columbia University, and its Director, Professor Zbigniew
Brzezinski.

The Hoover Institution on War, Revolution, and Peace,
of Stanford University, and its Director, Dr. W. Glenn
Campbell.

But the actual writing of this book was done at the
Hoover Institution, where, as a Senior Research Fellow, I
have been able to work in complete freedom and independence, as was true of all the institutions previously
mentioned.

The first chapter, as I have noted, was originally written
for the conference at the Hoover Institution in October,
1964. The second chapter was written especially for this
book. About half of the third chapter was published in
Commentary magazine. I have added a revised and en-
larged version of two articles in *The New Leader* evoked
by Senator J. William Fulbright's speech of March 25,
1964, as an Appendix, because it does not directly concern

Castroism as such but rather U.S. policy in Cuba. I have included it, however, because it touches on vital issues indirectly relevant to the main body of the book.

Finally, to Antonio de la Carrera, I can only express the gratitude of one who has found him an unfailing counselor and friend. I am also indebted to Joaquín Godoy for invaluable assistance. I owe a great deal to the support and fortitude of Phyllis Freeman, who suffered all the way. And most of all, I have been helped and sustained by my wife. I am, of course, solely responsible for the views expressed in these pages.

CONTENTS

CASTROISM

Theory and Practice

I

WHAT IS CASTROISM?

THE QUESTION "What is Castroism?" inevitably leads to the question "What is the relationship between Castroism and Communism?" We must get to it sooner or later, and perhaps the sooner the better. The answer is a relatively simple one for two totally opposed schools of thought. One maintains that Fidel Castro is and always was a Communist; the other insists that he is not and could never be a Communist. The problem is far more complex for those who, like myself, think that Castro was not a Communist for all practical purposes before he took power but decided to cast his lot with the Communists sometime afterward.

Whatever position one may hold, however, the relationship between Castroism and Communism remains a problem. The first school must explain the open disagreements and bitter rivalries between Castro and the Communists until well into 1959; the second, why Castro and his closest associates now call themselves Communists and regard themselves as an integral part of the world Communist movement; and the third, why they were different in their origins and how their paths came together. Indeed, the fact that we can intelligibly ask whether or how Castroism is related to Communism already presupposes some distinction between the two, if only the distinction between a species and a genus.

For the immediate purpose of defining Castroism, and its relationship with Communism, the history of Castroism may be distinguished from the history of Fidel Castro. The movement could not exist without the man, but neither can it be reduced to the man. It exists, in varying degrees and forms, in Latin America as a whole, and its influence has even been felt in Europe, Africa, and elsewhere. Fidel Castro was born about a quarter of a century before Castroism came into existence, and therefore, he is older and in some ways more complex than his movement. Here we are primarily interested in the political phenomenon, Castroism, rather than in the personal history of Fidel Castro as a whole.

The 26th of July Movement

Historically, Castroism did not exist before July 26, 1953, the date of the unsuccessful attack on the Moncada army post in Santiago de Cuba, seventeen months after Batista's seizure of power. This act enabled Castro to emerge for the first time as an independent political figure with his own personal following. To it the "26th of July Movement" owed its *raison d'être* as well as its name.

The conception of the movement appears to have been worked out concretely during Castro's imprisonment on the Isle of Pines from October, 1953, to May, 1955. It was in this period that he actually wrote, in its present form, the "History Will Absolve Me" speech, originally delivered at his trial in October, 1953. According to Melba Hernández, Castro asked her and Haydée Santamaría, the two women who participated in the Moncada attack, to take the first steps to organize the new movement. As a basis for this task, they asked him to provide them with a "program of action."* Castro, it seems, had already conceived of dramatically casting such a "program" in the form of his defense speech at the trial. He wrote a letter to Melba Hernández in April, 1954, in which he mentioned "a pamphlet of decisive importance for its ideological contents and its tremendous accusations," and it was clandestinely published in June, 1954.† There is, therefore, reason to believe that the pamphlet was far more "programmatic" than the speech, which had not been delivered with the same purpose or audience in mind.‡

Politically, the pamphlet promised restoration of the 1940 Constitution and a "government of popular election," though not without a disturbing proviso for the immediate post-revolutionary period. In agriculture, it mainly advo-

---

* Francisco de Armas, "Como se editó en la clandestinidad la Primera Edición de La Historia Me Absolverá," *Hoy,* July 21, 1963, section 2, pp. 2–3. The author attributes the information in his article to Melba Hernández.

† Luis Conte Agüero, *Cartas del Presidio* (Havana: Editorial Lex, 1959), p. 37. The author of these letters was actually Fidel Castro.

‡ At least two different and seemingly contradictory stories have been told about the genesis of *History Will Absolve Me* in print. The first one claimed that it had been based on "shorthand notes" or the "record of the shorthand reporters" at the trial. A later version, given in the article by de Armas above and in the Appendix to the 1964 edition, says that it was a "reconstruction" made "little by little," with no mention of help from shorthand notes, which, presumably, would have made a lengthy, piecemeal "reconstruction" unnecessary (Havana: Editora Política, 1964, pp. 205–6). Unless the original transcript is produced, it will be impossible to tell how closely the "reconstruction" resembles it.

cated a land reform to restrict large holdings and increase the number of smaller ones. It made only marginal reference to the encouragement of "agricultural cooperatives," by which it clearly meant service organizations for independent landowners, rather than organs of state control. The most radical note in the speech—but not to Cuban ears— was perhaps a brief reference to the "nationalization" of the U.S.-owned electric and telephone companies. None of these points was new or startling. The pamphlet as a whole was little more than an anthology of familiar ills and cures, long the staples of Cuban politics, especially as practiced by the late Eduardo Chibás, founder of the party to which Castro at that time still nominally belonged.*

As Cubans understood it, *History Will Absolve Me* represented a program of radical social reform well within the framework of traditional Cuban left-wing politics. For at least twenty years, there had been a well-defined "left wing," even a "revolutionary left wing," outside of and opposed to the Communists. There was virtually nothing in the social and economic program of *History Will Absolve Me* that cannot be traced at least as far back as the 1932 program of the ABC—the largest of the anti-Machado organizations—or the 1935 program of Dr. Grau San Martín's Auténtico party, let alone the later propaganda of Chibás.

The 1932 program of the ABC had contained a seventeen-point economic plan that, among other things, had

---

* Chibás had been one of the student leaders in the struggle against the Machado dictatorship in 1927–33. In 1947, Chibás split the ruling Partido Revolucionario Cubano, founded and headed by then President Ramón Grau San Martín, and organized an opposition group, the Partido del Pueblo Cubano. The two parties were usually referred to as the "Auténticos" and the "Ortodoxos," respectively. Chibás committed suicide in 1951. Fidel Castro became active in the party about 1950 and ran for one of the houses of the Cuban Congress on the Ortodoxo ticket in 1952, but the election was never held owing to Batista's coup on March 10 of that year.

proposed the following: development and protection of small rural property holdings, gradual elimination of the *latifundios* (large landed estates), limitation on the acquisition of land by U.S. companies and measures leading to their nationalization, producers' cooperatives, nationalization of the public services, advanced social legislation, and preferential treatment for Cubans in commercial and industrial activities. The same program had put forward five fundamental principles: new men, new ideas and procedures, reconquest of the land, political liberty, and social justice.* The 1935 program of the Auténtico party had been based on the political trinity of "nationalism, socialism, anti-imperialism."†

After Castro had won power in 1959, it became customary to cite the "History Will Absolve Me" speech, or rather pamphlet, as if it were the only significant document in the whole period of his struggle for power. Some pro-Castro writers have even labored to show that it foreshadowed Castro's later Communism. Curiously, however, Castro himself has felt the need to explain why it had not been more radical. He had written the document "with care," he later said, in order to set forth a number of fundamental points without making the movement he wanted to build "very small and very limited." He intimated that his published words had not been as radical as his private thoughts. "If we had not written this document with care, if it had been a more radical program—though here it is certain that many people were a little skeptical of programs and often did not give them much attention—the revolutionary movement against Batista would not, of course, have gained the

* See Carlos G. Peraza, *Machado, Crímenes y Horrores de un Régimen* (Havana: Cultural, S.A., 1933), pp. 215–50, for the text of the ABC program.
† Ramón Grau San Martín, *La Revolución Cubana ante América* (Mexico City: Ediciones del Partido Revolucionario Cubano, 1936), p. 104.

breadth that it obtained and made possible the victory."*
On another occasion, Castro pointed out that *History Will
Absolve Me* owed its permanent value to its "vivid de-
nunciation of all the horrors and crimes of Batista's tyranny" rather than to its "theoretical value from an
economic and political point of view."† He was undoubtedly right.

But he wrote something else in 1954, far less well known,
which affords a much greater insight into his motivation.
In that year, he sent a number of letters to Luis Conte
Agüero, an Ortodoxo leader and popular radio commenta-
tor, to whom he appealed for aid in organizing his campaign for amnesty and to whom he confided some of his
innermost thoughts about his nascent movement.

"I ought," he wrote on August 14, 1954, "to organize the
men of the 26th of July and to unite into an unbreakable
body all the fighters, those in exile, in prison, and in the
street." They would constitute, he explained, "a perfectly
disciplined human nucleus" and provide "the force necessary to conquer power, whether it be by peaceful or by
revolutionary means." Then he went on, with rare candor:

"The indispensable conditions for the organization of a
true civic movement are: ideology, discipline, and leadership. The three are essential, but leadership is basic. I don't
know if it was Napoleon who said that one bad general in
battle counts more than twenty good generals. It is not
possible to organize a movement in which everyone believes
that he has the right to issue public statements without consulting anyone else; nor can anything be expected of one
made up of anarchic men who at the first disagreement take
the path they consider more convenient, breaking and
destroying the machine. The apparatus of propaganda and
of organization should be such and so powerful that it

---

* *Revolución,* December 2, 1961.
† *Ibid.,* March 28, 1962.

would implacably destroy anyone who tries to create tendencies, cliques, schisms, or rebels against the movement."*

Of the three conditions, Castro obviously concerned himself with ideology the least. What really interested him were the other two conditions, "discipline" and "leadership," especially the latter. His axiom *"La jefatura es básica"* ("Leadership is basic") was far more closely related to "leadership-principle" movements such as fascism and Peronism than to an ideology-and-party-conscious movement such as Communism. It is hard to imagine a Communist using the language of Castro in this extraordinarily revealing letter to Conte Agüero.

After Castro was released from the Isle of Pines, in May, 1955, he stayed in Cuba for only six weeks, after which he went to Mexico to prepare for his coming invasion of the island. On July 19, less than two weeks after his arrival in Mexico, he called a meeting of his adherents and formally decided to launch the 26th of July Movement.† It is common practice in Latin America to name new movements after dates of symbolic events, but it is not without significance that Castro should have decided to follow this pattern. His date symbolized a heroic act or gesture, not a political philosophy or revolutionary tradition. The act or gesture was all his own, something that no one could ever take away from him, the bedrock of his *jefatura.*

In August, 1955, Castro sent a message to a congress of "militants" of the Ortodoxo party in Havana in which for the first time since its formal inception he tried to explain publicly what the new movement stood for. He called it "Manifesto No. 1 of the 26th of July to the People of Cuba," and in substance, it closely followed the line of *History Will Absolve Me.* It invited the support of all Cubans who wished "to re-establish political democracy

* Conte Agüero, *Cartas del Presidio,* pp. 60–61.
† René Ray, *Libertad y Revolución* (Havana, 1959), p. 11.

and implant social justice." It undertook to realize all "reforms" within the spirit and letter of "our advanced" Constitution of 1940. It contained a fifteen-point program of these reforms, from "distribution of the land among peasant families" to "confiscation of all property of all grafters." Yet, in this manifesto, Castro made clear that he was still an Ortodoxo, "faithful to the purest principles" of Chibás, and hopeful of getting the support of the "best Ortodoxos." In order to stay within the party but organize his own movement outside it, he carefully explained that "we do not constitute a tendency within the party; we are the revolutionary apparatus of Chibasismo." In effect, he did not claim to represent a political tendency as much as a more effective *"aparato"* to overthrow the Batista dictatorship.* Inasmuch as Chibás himself had been a consistent, militant anti-Communist, anyone who claimed to be his loyal disciple, as Castro did, was bound to have some of Chibás' reputation rub off on him.

At the end of 1955, the Ortodoxo leadership decided to participate with other opposition groups in a final effort to reach agreement with Batista for a peaceful transition to constitutional government. As soon as the negotiations had broken down, Castro seized the occasion to make a final break with the Ortodoxo party. In his letter of resignation of March 19, 1956, however, he continued to take the position that he was breaking away organizationally, not politically. "For the Chibasist masses," he wrote, "the 26th of July Movement is not something distinct from the Ortodoxia." On the contrary, he insisted that the 26th of July

---

* From a copy of this manifesto in my possession. It apparently has never been reprinted in full, but excerpts may be found in Luis Conte Agüero, *Los Dos Rostros de Fidel Castro* (Mexico: Editorial Jus, 1960), pp. 104–7, and in . . . *y la luz se hizo: declaraciones del Comandante Fidel Castro Ruz, Primer Ministro del gobierno revolucionario, en el juicio contra el ex-Comandante Hubert Matos, Ciudad Libertad, December 14, 1959* (Havana: La Secretaría de Propaganda de la Confederación de Trabajadores de Cuba, n.d.), pp. 86–90.

Movement was the true repository of the Ortodoxo faith, the authentic embodiment of Chibasismo. Ostensibly, then, the 26th of July Movement came into the world to fulfill, not to betray, the true Ortodoxo political mission. (After the victory over Batista, Castro made a pilgrimage to the tomb of Chibás, where he declared that the 26th of July Movement "was the continuation of the work of Chibás, the harvest of the seed that he planted in our people.") *

Thus, Castroism as a movement may be said to have been created in four stages. It was given its initial impulse and *raison d'être* by the attack on the Moncada army post on July 26, 1953. Its conception matured during Castro's imprisonment on the Isle of Pines, from October, 1953, to May, 1955. It was officially launched in Mexico on July 19, 1955. And it severed its last ties with any other movement, to strike out entirely on its own in March, 1956.

Programs in Limbo

It is impossible here to analyze, or even to touch on, all the programmatic statements made by Castro from March, 1956, to the end of 1958. Yet, it is noteworthy that, in this period, the 26th of July Movement continued to feel a need for a full "program," and various efforts were made to fill the vacuum, though they have been relegated to a historical limbo since the fall of Batista. At least two important documents were not composed by Castro himself—the "Tesis Económica del Movimiento Revolucionario 26 de Julio" ("Economic Thesis of the Revolutionary 26th of July Movement"), written by Felipe Pazos and Regino Botí, first published in Mexico City in the magazine *Humanismo,* in January and February, 1957, and the pamphlet *Nuestra Razón: Manifiesto-Programa del Movimiento 26 de Julio (Our Cause: Manifesto-Program of the 26th of*

* *Bohemia,* January 18–25, 1959, p. 103.

July Movement), published in Mexico City in the summer of 1957 and written mainly by Mario Llerena. Probably the most important single document, however, was the "Manifesto of the Sierra Maestra," drafted by Castro and signed by him, Felipe Pazos, and Raúl Chibás on July 12, 1957.* This was actually the first and only formal program to which Castro ever put his name, if we exclude *History Will Absolve Me* as such a program. Unlike the latter, the Castro-Pazos-Chibás manifesto was published in Cuba's most popular magazine, *Bohemia,* in the issue of July 28, 1957, and thus reached many more Cubans than any previous programmatic statement by Castro's movement.† In any event, the "Manifesto of the Sierra Maestra" was taken

---

* The "Tesis Económica" and the "Manifesto of the Sierra Maestra" may be found in Fidel Castro, *La Revolución Cubana: Escritos y Discursos,* edited by Gregorio Selser (Buenos Aires: Editorial Palestra, 1960), pp. 119–24 and 393–422. I have been told by Raúl Chibás, brother and political heir of Eduardo Chibás, that the manifesto was written mainly by Castro. Felipe Pazos, who had been President of the National Bank of Cuba, had resigned immediately after Batista's coup, in 1952. He again served in the same post in 1959. Regino Botí was Minister of Economy in Castro's government from 1959 to 1964.

Nuestra Razón may be found in Enrique González Pedrero, *La Revolución Cubana* (Mexico: Escuela Nacional de Ciencias Políticas, 1959), pp. 89–130. This pamphlet is dated November, 1956, but I have been assured by Dr. Llerena that this date was put on it for reasons of expediency and that it was not actually published until after he had arrived in Mexico City, in June, 1957.

† The reader may wonder how it was possible for the most popular magazine in Cuba to publish such a manifesto in the midst of the civil war. The answer is that the Batista regime was much too repressive for democracy and not repressive enough for efficient dictatorship. Magazines such as *Bohemia* and newspapers such as *Prensa Libre* maintained a high standard of political independence throughout the Batista regime. *Bohemia* in particular provided a forum for all political groups, published letters and statements by Castro himself, and distinctly favored the anti-Batista side. After violent actions, such as the Moncada attempt in 1953 and the Directorio Revolucionario's attack on the Presidential Palace in 1957, the regime established press censorship for limited periods. During these months, *Bohemia* refused to publish any political articles whatever in order to avoid the appearance of political control. Batista subsidized and suborned many Cuban papers, which, as a result, few readers could take seriously; his partial control of the press was then "exposed" to provide a justification for Castro's total control.

to be an expression of Castro's more mature views in the heat of the civil war, and Castro himself directed attention to it as the basic document of the period.* He issued several other political statements and gave interviews in the next year and a half, but they were not intended to serve the same purpose.

It is not hard to understand why the "Manifesto of the Sierra Maestra," despite its exalted title, has never been cited as evidence that Fidel Castro made the kind of revolution that he said he would make. This document was primarily a plea for the unity of all the anti-Batista forces. It sought to close the breach between those who had hoped to get rid of Batista by means of peaceful elections and those who believed that he could be overthrown only by violent methods. To allay suspicions that Castro himself was not exactly a passionate devotee of democratic elections, the manifesto stated that they were precisely what the entire struggle was about. "Is it true that the rebels of the Sierra Maestra do not want free elections, a democratic regime, a constitutional government?" it asked indignantly. And it answered: "We have been fighting since the 10th of March, 1952, because they deprived us of those rights. We are here because we desire them more than anyone else." The manifesto then proceeded to spell out in detail the steps to be taken to achieve the desired objective. It insisted on only one condition: "truly free, democratic, impartial elections." It urged that "a provisional, neutral government" should preside over the elections. To lay the basis for such a government, it proposed the formation of a Frente Cívico Revolucionario (Civilian Revolutionary Front), made up of representatives of all

* In his "Carta a la Junta de Liberación Cubana" ("Letter to the Council of Cuban Liberation"), dated December 14, 1957 (Selser, *op. cit.*, pp. 130 and 138); and in the "Manifesto of March 12, 1958" (*ibid.*, p. 144). It is significant that *History Will Absolve Me* was never mentioned in this period.

opposition parties and groups. It also told the future Frente what was expected of it: choice of an impartial, nonpolitical Provisional President; rejection of any foreign mediation or intervention and a request for suspension of all arms shipments to Cuba during the civil war; nonacceptance of any kind of military junta to replace Batista; commitment "to dissociate the army from politics"; and a "formal promise that the provisional government will hold general elections for all national, provincial, and municipal offices at the end of one year according to the standards of the Constitution of 1940 and the Electoral Code of 1943." In addition, the authors of the manifesto demanded that the provisional government should commit itself to a ten-point program that included "absolute guarantees of freedom of information, of the spoken and written press, and of all the individual and political rights guaranteed by the Constitution," an intensive campaign against illiteracy, and agrarian reform based on distributing barren lands and converting all renters and squatters into owners, with prior indemnification to the former owners, a "sound financial policy," "acceleration of the process of industrialization, and creation of new jobs."

It should be noted that the future provisional government chosen by the still unformed, all-embracing Frente Cívico Revolucionario was not asked to consider this program; it was told what its program would have to be—a peculiar beginning for a constitutional democracy, irrespective of the program's desirability.* It should also be more understandable why there was so much concern about the holding of elections in 1959 after the fall of Batista. Castro himself had encouraged the widespread belief that the central issue in the struggle was the in-

---

* The expression used was "el gobierno provisional deberá ajustar su misión al siguiente programa" ("the mission of the provisional government will have to conform to the following program").

violability of "truly free, democratic, impartial elections." If he could not be trusted to carry out this "formal promise," which he had demanded of the proposed Frente Cívico Revolucionario, it was hard to know what to trust in the first months of his regime.

As one reads Castro's succession of statements in 1956–58, the most striking thing about them is their increasing "moderation" and constitutionalism. For example, he had called for nationalization of the public utilities in *History Will Absolve Me* and again in "Manifesto No. 1" of 1955, but he withdrew this demand on at least two occasions in 1958.* In virtually every document of this period, he reiterated his determination to live up to the "full enforcement" of the 1940 Constitution, including on one occasion the rights of "free enterprise and invested capital" as much as all the other constitutional rights. For the most part, he guaranteed elections in no more than a year after the fall of Batista and, to show that he meant to restore a traditional constitutionalism, gave assurances that he intended to convert the 26th of July Movement into a regular political party that would, after the revolution, "fight with the weapons of the Constitution and the Law."† His last important commitment came in the "unity pact" of July 20, 1958, which called for a common strategy of "armed insurrection," a brief provisional government leading to "full constitutional and democratic procedure," and a minimum government program guaranteeing "the punishment of the guilty, the rights of the workers, order, peace, liberty, the fulfillment of international agreements, and the economic, social, and institutional progress of the

---

* In the article signed by Fidel Castro in *Coronet,* February, 1958, and in his May, 1958, reply to the questionnaire of Jules Dubois, *Fidel Castro* (Indianapolis: Bobbs-Merrill, 1959), p. 263. Significantly, the text of Castro's reply to Dubois was included in Selser's semiofficial, pro-Castro anthology, pp. 147–51.

† Dubois, *op. cit.,* pp. 264–65.

Cuban people."* Significantly, Castro made very few programmatic statements in the second half of 1958, when
Batista's regime was crumbling. The most important in
this period was "Law No. 3 of the Sierra Maestra on Agrarian Reform," dated October 10, 1958, which he signed
with Dr. Humberto Sorí Marín. It was a detailed working-
out of the principle that those who cultivate the land
should own it, and made no mention of "cooperatives" or
"state farms."†

As far as most Cubans were concerned, Castroism was
what these manifestoes, programs, pamphlets, and assorted
declarations said it was. They had no way of looking into
Castro's mind or analyzing his personality to know his real
ambitions, motivations, and latent tendencies. Castroism
was the creation of Fidel Castro, but he created and re-
created it, partly in his own image and partly in the image
of those whom he wished to win over.

Public and Private

Castro and his closest associates have clearly admitted,
and even boasted, that there was some difference between
Castro and Castroism, between what the man thought
privately and what he made the movement stand for publicly, especially during the struggle for power.

We have already noted Castro's explanation of why *History Will Absolve Me* was carefully written in order that it
should not appear to be too radical. In effect, he said that
he had made it only as radical as could be politically effective or as a large number of Cubans would be willing to
accept.

The 1954 pamphlet was not the only case of political
double bookkeeping. This practice started at the beginning

* Selser, *op. cit.*, pp. 152–55.
† González Pedrero, *op. cit.*, pp. 139–56.

of the movement, and became more marked as it developed.

For example, Castro came dangerously close to implying that he had been something of a "Marxist-Leninist" in the Sierra Maestra but had consciously concealed it. "Of course," he said, "if we had stopped at the Pico Turquino [a height in the Sierra Maestra], when there were very few of us, and said: 'We are Marxist-Leninists,' possibly we would not have been able to get down to the plain. Thus we called it something else; we did not broach this subject; we raised other questions that the people understood perfectly."*

President Osvaldo Dorticós once played a variation on this theme. Soon after Castro had proclaimed the advent of the "socialist revolution" in Cuba, on April 16, 1961, Dorticós interpreted this act to mean that Castro had merely given "a name to the facts which had already occurred." When this comment aroused some speculation, Dorticós explained: "In other words, to a large extent, an integral revolutionary theory was not formulated previously for strategic reasons, wise strategy, and because it would have required a great effort of ideological training, and this effort could be avoided because the best ideological teaching that the Cuban people have received has been the incontrovertible teaching of the events themselves."† These words suggest that the *timing* of the proclamation of "socialism" was purely "strategic" in the sense that Castro waited until he thought that he had enough popular support to put it over. Castro himself has often resorted to the factor of "objective conditions" to explain why he said or did something at one time and not at another. The implication has been that he wanted to do it earlier but had waited until "objective conditions" made it feasible.

* *Revolución*, December 22, 1961.
† *Verde Olivo*, June 25, 1961, p. 29.

But the occasion for these "confessions" must be held in mind. They were made in the year that Castro professed himself to be a "Marxist-Leninist," and it was in his interest at this time to make his present seem to be a logical development of his past. None of Castro's statements on this delicate subject can be accepted or understood standing alone, and it is necessary to view all of them in their contexts and in relation to each other to get a reasonable facsimile of the truth. As I have tried to show elsewhere, Castro has given so many different versions of his evolution toward "full" Marxism-Leninism that it is foolhardy to jump to any conclusion on the basis of one or two quotations that, in any case, are open to more than one interpretation.* But the fact remains that Castro himself has encouraged the belief that he was guilty of dissimulation.

As we have seen, the "Manifesto of the Sierra Maestra" of July, 1957, was one of the key documents of the civil war and particularly encouraged confidence in Castro's democratic convictions. Did Castro really believe in its pledges of "free elections," freedom of the press, and all the rest, or did he merely subscribe to them for purely opportunistic reasons? If we may trust Che Guevara—who should know, since his close association with Castro dated from the Mexican period—the latter was the case. According to Guevara, precisely the "democratic" provisions of the document were virtually forced on a reluctant Castro by Pazos and Chibás (though he does not explain why Castro subsequently reiterated most of them independently, as in the *Coronet* article or in the reply to Jules Dubois's questionnaire). The only thing that Guevara praises unequivocally is a short passage which called the Sierra Maestra "an indestructible bastion of liberty." Otherwise, he complains that "we were not satisfied with the agreement," that it

---

* Theodore Draper, *Castro's Revolution: Myths and Realities* (New York: Frederick A. Praeger, 1962), pp. 144-54.

"limited our effort," and that it was "a small halt on the road." Castro signed the manifesto, Guevara explains, because it was "progressive at that moment" to get such support, though it "could not last beyond the moment." He justifies Castro's failure to live up to the manifesto, or as he put it, the need "to break the inconvenient fetters," on the ground that a "tacit pact" recognizing the "authority of the Sierra"—apparently to determine the future revolutionary government—was later broken. Guevara had to make the pact a "tacit" one because he could not point to anything in the document itself to bear out such an understanding. In Guevara's authoritative version, then, Castro had really resented the "democratic" points in the manifesto because they might have tied his hands, and the only thing that had really interested him had been the alleged recognition of his future "authority."*

That power was the determining factor is even more strikingly demonstrated in Castro's explanation of his letter of December 14, 1957, to the Junta de Liberación Cubana, denouncing the "unity pact" which his representatives had signed in Miami.† Ironically, Castro's main

---

* Ernesto Che Guevara, *Pasajes de la Guerra Revolucionaria* (Havana: Ediciones Unión/Narraciones, 1963), pp. 100–105.

† The text of the letter may be found in Selser, *op. cit.*, pp. 125–40, and an English translation in Dubois, *op. cit.*, pp. 188–206.
The Junta de Liberación Cubana (Council of Cuban Liberation) had been formed on November 1, 1957, by representatives of seven anti-Batista groups, including Dr. Felipe Pazos, Dr. Lucas Moran, and Lester Rodríguez for the 26th of July Movement. It was, in part, a response to the demand for a similar "united front" that Castro, Pazos, and Raúl Chibás had made in their "Manifesto of the Sierra Maestra" on July 12. The founders of the Junta signed a "Document of Unity" that embodied most, though not all, the points raised in the manifesto. Castro's letter of December 14, 1957, repudiated the action of his three representatives and withdrew the 26th of July Movement from the Junta. At the time, it was generally believed that the main difference between Castro and the Junta had been over the choice of the future Provisional President. The Junta had selected Dr. Pazos, who, as a signer of the manifesto and outstanding nonpolitical public figure, seemed a logical choice. But it seems to have infuriated Castro, probably because he knew that he could not dictate to Pazos. In his letter of December 14 denouncing the Junta, Castro uni-

pretext for rejecting the December, 1957, pact had been its failure to include some of the provisions of the July, 1957, manifesto. After his victory, however, Castro told a different story. He revealed that he had not been interested in broad unity in December, 1957, because he had had only 120 armed men and, therefore, was not strong enough to dominate unified action. Later, when he was much stronger, he confided, he favored unity because he could dominate it. He even went on to say that he had actually decided to prevent any broad unity until the end of the war (though he signed just such an agreement in July, 1958) because he could not get the official Cuban Communists accepted by the other groups.*

A peculiar light has also been cast on Castro's agrarian-reform program of late 1958 by the Communist representative in the Sierra Maestra and later head of the Instituto Nacional de Reforma Agraria (INRA), Dr. Carlos Rafael Rodríguez. In the discussion on agrarian reform, according to Rodríguez, "some who were apparently extremist" had proposed eliminating *latifundismo* completely. But Fidel, "with an extraordinary tactical and strategic clarity," had rejected the proposal on the ground that it would "range us against all the landowners of our country and the foreign imperialists" at a time when the fundamental task was the overthrow of Batista's regime. After he took power, however, Castro went ahead with his second step, "the liquidation of the internal enemy in agriculture," postponing the third step, against the "imperialist *latifundio*," until still later. For this reason, it appears, "Law No. 3 of the Sierra Maestra on Agrarian Reform," of October 10,

laterally proposed Dr. Manuel Urrutia as head of the future provisional government. One wonders whether something important, which has not yet come out, happened between July 12 and December 14, 1957, to explain Castro's sharp change of attitude, from seeming to want broad unity at all cost, to wanting it only on his own terms or not at all.

* *Revolución*, December 2, 1961.

1958, did not provide for wholesale expropriation. "It was necessary to conquer the enemy piecemeal," Rodríguez observed admiringly.* (Like Felipe Pazos and Raúl Chibás, the co-signer of Law No. 3, Dr. Humberto Sorí Marín, who was Castro's first Minister of Agriculture, realized that he had been used for purposes which he had never intended, suffered disillusionment, and apparently went into the underground opposition, but less lucky than the other two, he was caught and executed.)

Thus Castro has suggested that he did not privately believe in principles and programs which he had publicly espoused, and he has suggested that he could not afford to espouse principles and programs which he privately believed in. He has intimated that he was much closer to "Marxism-Leninism" than he had ever let on, and he has confessed to his past political innocence, whichever seemed to suit his purpose best at the time. On the whole, he has been far more convincing in his efforts to show that he was not what he had pretended to be than what he actually had been.

The Road to Power

Thus far, we have been considering Castroism before its assumption of power in terms of its "programs." There is reason to believe, however, that they were not the main source of Castro's power or influence. They were not different enough from others' to make Castro stand out, and in fact, he deliberately cast his ideas in a fairly traditional mold in order to gain a mass following. If a graph were charted of the "radicalism" of his public statements from 1953 to 1959, it would go almost steadily downward.

What made Castroism distinctive was something else. For the most part, Castro's road to power was based on

* *Obra Revolucionaria*, August 31, 1962, p. 6.

tactics, not on ideas. And his tactics were, by Cuban standards, at least partially different.

After Batista's coup in March, 1952, the opposition had split into two main camps, the "insurrectionist" and the "electoralist." The former believed that armed struggle was the only way to get rid of the usurper; the latter wished to use peaceful methods, leading somehow to new general elections. Castro was one of the "insurrectionists," but far from the only one. He was not even the first to plan an uprising. Castro had been anticipated by Rafael García Bárcena, leader of the Movimiento Nacionalista Revolucionario (MNR), whose conspiracy was foiled by the police on April 5, 1953, on the eve of the planned uprising, more than three months before Castro's Moncada attempt. Aureliano Sánchez Arango's "Triple A" was based on armed struggle, as were many other groups in the next six years.

In general, however, the others aimed their blows at the center of Batista's power—at the main military base near Havana, Camp Columbia, or at Batista himself. García Bárcena in 1953 and Colonel Ramón Barquín in 1956 both tried to overthrow Batista by getting the backing of a part of the armed forces to take over Camp Columbia. The attack on the Presidential Palace in Havana by the predominantly student Directorio Revolucionario on March 13, 1957, was planned to get rid of Batista personally in the expectation that his regime could not survive without him. The Directorio's slogan was *Golpear Arriba* ("Strike at the Top"), even after it had begun to wage small-scale guerrilla warfare in the Escambray Mountains early in 1958.*

Castro departed from these more traditional tactics. In 1953, he chose to attack the second largest encampment in

* From *Proclama del Directorio Revolucionario Desde la Sierra de Escambray: Al Pueblo de Cuba,* dated February 25, 1958 (copy in my possession).

Oriente Province, farthest from the capital.* Like the others, he did not contemplate and was not prepared for a long campaign; he also thought in terms of a spectacular pronunciamento and heroic act to set off a popular uprising in Santiago de Cuba, at the eastern end of the island, rather than in Havana. His unorthodox move at first caught the army garrison by surprise, but he was unable to gain much advantage from it because the soldiers, once alerted, fought for Batista instead of quickly going over to Castro's side. This was the risk which Castro took as a result of another unorthodox aspect of his Moncada tactics—an attack on the regular army from the outside rather than a conspiracy to win over a portion of the army from the inside.

Castro's second military plan—his "invasion" of Cuba from Mexico in December, 1956—was basically a variation of his first one in 1953. He intended to have his boat, "Granma," disembark near the port of Niquero, again in Oriente Province, where he expected reinforcements; after attacking Niquero, he was supposed to make an assault on the larger city of Manzanillo; at the same time, his supporters were to stage an uprising in Santiago de Cuba; and a country-wide campaign of sabotage and agitation was to culminate in a general strike.† So little did Castro envisage long-drawn-out guerrilla warfare in the Sierra Maestra that he had not made any effort to study the geography of the region or to try to set up any kind of organization there.‡ The 1956 plan misfired because, as one of its participants, Faustino Pérez, put it, "everything went wrong." Of the eighty-two men in the "Granma," only a handful—the number varies from as few as five to as many as twelve—

* There were actually two attacks in July, 1953, the main one against the Moncada army post in Santiago de Cuba and a smaller one against the army post in the town of Bayamo in the same province. The latter, equally unsuccessful, has been largely ignored.

† Faustino Pérez, *Bohemia*, January 11, 1959, p. 38.

‡ Fidel Castro, *Revolución*, December 2, 1961.

were able to strike out for the nearby mountains of the Sierra Maestra to escape capture.* In its conception, this plan was far more complex than the Moncada attack, inasmuch as it attempted to coordinate a landing near Niquero with an uprising in Santiago de Cuba. But in its essential, it was but another way of winning an urban base in Oriente Province from which to attack the main stronghold of the Batista regime.

Castro, in effect, backed into guerrilla warfare after all his other plans had failed. Yet this is what set him apart from the other anti-Batista conspirators. They would have withdrawn from Cuba to prepare another invasion or uprising. Castro and a few of his most trusted men went into the mountains to suffer privation and danger, slowly building up a small guerrilla force. In 1957 and the first months of 1958, however, no one, *including Castro,* thought that Batista could be overthrown by means of guerrilla warfare. In February, 1957, the pro-Castro urban-based Resistencia Cívica was organized, and victory seemed so far away in the Sierra Maestra that Castro expected the main blow to come from the urban resistance in the form of a general strike. In the manifesto of March 12, 1958, he still publicly affirmed that "the strategy of the decisive blow is based on the revolutionary general strike, assisted by armed action."† Thus, until the failure of the general strike the following month, Castro himself believed that guerrilla warfare was a subordinate, if indispensable, tactic.

Batista tried to follow up the failure of the general strike by launching an offensive in May, 1958, to wipe out Castro's band in the Sierra Maestra. This offensive was the beginning of the end of Batista's regime. For this battle, Castro had only about 300 men, about 60 of them so poorly

* Twelve became the legend. But Castro has also said that the first survivors of the "Granma" numbered as many as "the fingers of one hand" (speech of July 26, 1963).

† Selser, *op. cit.,* p. 144.

armed that they were almost useless.* After 71 days, Batista's offensive collapsed, at the end of July. The secret of Castro's victory must be sought in the next five months. Despite Batista's setback, his losses were relatively small and restricted to the eastern end of the island. Physically, the regular army was virtually intact. Morally, however, it had begun to crumble from top to bottom. The collapse of Batista's army was far more a political and psychological than a military phenomenon. Batista has charged that he was deserted by his military commanders, and they have accused him of quitting on them.† Batista's end came so suddenly that even Castro was surprised, for it was more a capitulation to a hostile people than a defeat by a superior enemy force. To a large extent, Castro cashed in on the cumulative effect of all the opposition efforts to overthrow Batista. The failures of the many contributed to the success of the one. Without Castro's military pressure, Batista's regime would not have fallen; but Castro's military pressure was far from enough to bring about Batista's fall.

Paradoxically, Castro did not start fighting with any thought of guerrilla warfare; he did not believe that guerrilla warfare was the key to victory until almost the end of the struggle; and guerrilla warfare as a theory of Latin American revolution was born, or at least propagated, after Castro's victory, not before. Guevara has insisted at least three times that the Cubans were not inspired by the Chinese example and that they knew nothing of Mao Tsetung's doctrine of guerrilla warfare while they were still fighting Batista.‡ The Cuban theory was an *ex post facto* rationalization of an improvised response to events beyond

---

* Fidel Castro, *Revolución*, December 2, 1961.

† Fulgencio Batista, *Respuesta* (Mexico, 1960), esp. pp. 91–145; José Suárez Núñez, *El Gran Culpable* (Caracas, 1963), pp. 155–74; Colonel Esteban Ventura Novo, *Memorias* (Miami, 1960), p. 25; Colonel Florentino E. Rosell, *La Verdad* (Miami, 1960).

‡ *Obra Revolucionaria*, August 25, 1960, p. 16; *Revolución*, August 21, 1963; *ibid.*, November 23, 1964.

Castro's control. The response itself owed much less to the example of Chinese or other Communists than to Cuba's own revolutionary tradition—every Cuban schoolboy knew that the Cuban "war of independence" in the nineteenth century had been largely a guerrilla struggle in the very region of Oriente which became Castro's sanctuary.

Thus, armed struggle—away from the center of Cuban political and military power; against rather than inside the regular army; with the ultimate aim of stirring up a mass, general rebellion against the existing regime rather than merely eliminating its head—was the distinctive mark of Castroism during the struggle for power.

From Antagonism to Alliance

Ideologically, then, Castroism had never lived a life of its own. Tactically, as a form of armed struggle, it had something all its own. And as such, it could attach itself to different ideologies.

Until 1956, Castro attached himself to the ideology, such as it was, of Chibasismo. In 1961, he publicly attached himself to the ideology of Marxismo-Leninismo. The transition from one to the other was a protracted, tortuous process, only the main lines of which can as yet be clearly drawn.

After the attack on the Moncada barracks in 1953, the Partido Socialista Popular (PSP), as the official Cuban Communist Party was called, issued a statement that said in part: "We repudiate the putschist methods, peculiar to bourgeois political factions, of the action in Santiago de Cuba and Bayamo, which was an adventuristic attempt to take both military headquarters. The heroism displayed by the participants in this action is false and sterile, as it is guided by mistaken bourgeois conceptions." The statement also condemned the repression which followed the attack, because the PSP paid most heavily for Castro's failure.* Its publications were immediately suppressed and the party itself was subsequently outlawed.

The Communists, in effect, did not regard Castro's tactics as basically different from those of other middle-class groups that wanted to overthrow Batista by force. "Putschism" was, by Communist standards, *ipso facto* "bourgeois," and a "putsch" in Santiago de Cuba was for them no better than a "putsch" in Havana. An official Communist organ referred to the Moncada operation as "dangerous and sterile" as late as October, 1956.†

During his imprisonment in 1953–55, Castro was never taken to be a Communist; not only did he claim to be an Ortodoxo, but the Ortodoxos were glad to claim him as their own. He was embroiled for the first time in a bitter public controversy over the charge that he was a Communist in July, 1956. It flared up as a result of an article in the Cuban magazine *Bohemia* by a Spanish Republican exile, Luis Dam, reporting the arrest of Castro and twenty-one others in Mexico. According to Dam, the Mexican police had obtained confirmation that "Fidel is a member of the Communist Party and leader of the 'Soviet-Mexican Cultural Institution.' "‡

Castro handled this accusation in a curious way. He cited a Mexico City newspaper denying the report attributed to the Mexican police, and he charged that the whole incident

---

* *Daily Worker* (New York), August 5, 1953. This statement could not appear in the Cuban Communist organ *Hoy,* which had already been suppressed. The name of the Cuban Party has changed three times. It was called the Partido Comunista de Cuba at its inception, in 1925; it became the Unión Revolucionaria Comunista in 1940; and, finally, the Partido Socialista Popular in 1944.

† *Carta Semanal,* October 10, 1956 (quoted by Andrés Valdespino, in *Bohemia,* June 26, 1960, p. 43, in a controversy with the Communist leader Carlos Rafael Rodríguez, who did not challenge it). This periodical became the chief Communist organ from 1953 to 1958. It was easily obtainable but not openly sold.

‡ *Bohemia,* July 8, 1956, p. 87.

was a plot against him by the Batista regime and the U.S. Embassy. But he also, indirectly, hit out at the Cuban Communists: "What moral right, on the other hand, does Señor Batista have to speak of Communism when he was the Presidential candidate of the Communist Party in the elections of 1940, when his electoral squibs hid behind the hammer and sickle, when his photographs hung next to those of Blas Roca and Lázaro Peña, when half a dozen of his present ministers and confidential collaborators were outstanding members of the Communist Party?"*

It is, I think, hard to imagine a Communist, open or concealed, defending himself in this way. The most unfriendly thing one could do to the Cuban Communists at that time was to remind them of their old partnership with Batista or, even worse, spread the word that they were still in collusion with the dictator. Apparently, in striking back at Batista, Castro could not resist striking out at the Communists.

Years later, however, Castro was quoted by an American correspondent as saying that he had made contact with the "old Communists" after he had left prison in 1955, and that "there was contact and collaboration" with them "especially when we were preparing in Mexico." Castro also stated that the Communists had agreed to "collaborate" with his group "when we started from Mexico."† This may

* Fidel Castro, "¡Basta Ya de Mentiras!," *Bohemia*, July 15, 1956, p. 84. Blas Roca was the Communist General Secretary and Lázaro Peña the Communist trade-union leader.

† Barnard L. Collier, *New York Herald Tribune*, August 23, 1964. According to Juanita Castro, the sister of Fidel and Raúl Castro, "the scheme to Communize Cuba was incubated in Mexico in 1955." She says that Fidel first "contacted" Soviet diplomats and the PSP leader Lázaro Peña in Mexico around the end of 1955 or the very beginning of 1956. She seems to attribute these alleged moves to the influence of Guevara, who, in that case, had worked very quickly, since he had known Fidel for only a very short time. But Juanita Castro did not have any direct knowledge of these events; she says that she later heard "many of the anecdotes and stories of this episode in conversations my brother had with his 'bosom' pals in

very well be true, but it is far from being the whole truth
or even the essential part of it. For one thing, if Castro first
made contact with the Communists in Mexico and some
form of collaboration began after that, the theory that he
had always been a Communist or Soviet agent as far back
as his university days must be given up. For another, Castro
had never before believed in putting all his political eggs in
one basket, and he did not do so in Mexico. He made
contact and sought to collaborate with every possible anti-
Batista element in Mexico, but by 1964 he chose to emphasize only the Communists. In 1956, he had appealed to and
obtained funds from such anti-Communist sources as Dr.
Justo Carrillo Hernández, leader of the Montecristi Group,
and former President Carlos Prío Socarrás. After all, he
had bought the "Granma" with Dr. Prío's money, not the
Communists'. Nevertheless, if we may trust this statement,
Mexico may be considered the starting point of the Castro-
Communist "collaboration." But it still had far to go to
become a full-fledged alliance, judging from Castro's un-
flattering allusions to the Communist leaders in *Bohemia* in
midsummer of 1956 and their subsequent reaction to his
invasion of Cuba.

For the Communists did not approve of Castro's
"Granma" expedition any more than they had approved
of his Moncada adventure. They stated their position most
clearly in a *Letter of the National Committee of the Popular Socialist Party to the 26th of July Movement,** dated

Cuba." These statements were made by Juanita Castro in a speech in New
Orleans on January 18, 1965 (I have quoted from the English transcript).
Yet Lázaro Peña was one of the two Communist leaders mentioned so un-
flatteringly by Fidel as late as July, 1956, in *Bohemia*. The problem seems
to be not whether Castro and the Communists or Soviet representatives
made some "first contacts" in Mexico but how far they went in reaching
a full understanding, and whether Mexico was the beginning or the culmination of Castro-Communist collaboration.

* *Carta del Comité Nacional del Partido Socialista Popular al Movimiento 26 de Julio.*

February 28, 1957, though not published until the following June. In this key document, the Cuban Communists
expressed their "radical disagreement with the tactics and
plans" put forward by Fidel Castro. They paid tribute to
his group's "valor and sincerity," but insisted that armed
action was the wrong tactic. They argued in support of
"resisting the government with every peaceful expression
of the popular will." They deplored the terrorism, sabotage, and burning of sugar cane which Castro was then
encouraging. Yet, the Communists noted, their disagreement with Castro was primarily over "methods and tactics."
Among the existing political groups in Cuba, the *Letter*
went on to say, the 26th of July Movement "came closest"
to the Communists' "strategic conception," though it ironically complained that the 26th of July Movement had not
yet taken a strong enough stand against "imperialist domi-
nation." Despite the tactical disagreement, then, the Communist leadership made a bid to the 26th of July Movement
for a "closer understanding" based on a "coincidence" of
strategy.

The tactical divergence was emphasized in another
document of this period, a letter dated March 17, 1957,
from the titular head of the PSP, Juan Marinello, to the
American journalist Herbert L. Matthews. "At the present
time, and with reference to the assaults on barracks and
expeditions from abroad—carried out without depending
on the people—our position is very clear: We are against
those methods," Marinello wrote sternly. After mentioning the 26th of July Movement by name, he added: "We
think that this group is inspired by noble intentions but
that, in general, it is following erroneous tactics." The
right tactics, the Communist spokesman said, would be "to
mobilize the masses" through "strikes, demonstrations,
civic protests of every kind." The culmination of such
activities, he assured Matthews, would be "elections," for

which he advocated a Frente Democrático de Liberación Nacional (Democratic Front of National Liberation) to form a government representing the workers, peasants, urban petty bourgeoisie, and the national bourgeoisie, all "under the leadership of the proletariat."*

If Castro and the Communists were still so far apart in the spring of 1957, after Castro was already fighting in the Sierra Maestra, it would appear that any "collaboration" which they may have arranged in Mexico a year or two earlier had not gone very far.

But, by February, 1958, the Communists decided to make a "half-turn" in their own tactical approach. In brief, they adopted a dual policy of simultaneously supporting both "the armed struggle in the countryside and the unarmed, civil struggle in the cities."† This decision apparently reflected a split in the Communist leadership and a compromise between the opposing factions.‡ In any case, the PSP ordered a number of young Communists to join Castro's forces in the Sierra Maestra.§ An old-time Communist, Osvaldo Sánchez Cabrera, was sent to Castro's headquarters as the first go-between.¶ Nevertheless, these overtures did not mean that the Fidelistas were ready for a full alliance with the Communists. The abortive general strike

* This letter is quoted, in a somewhat different translation, by Herbert L. Matthews, *The Cuban Story* (New York: George Braziller, 1961), pp. 51–52. The original letter is now in the Columbia University Library. I have cited some passages not used by Mr. Matthews.

† Aníbal Escalante, *Fundamentos*, August, 1959, p. 12. The February, 1958, "turn" was also mentioned by Carlos Rafael Rodríguez, in *Hoy*, April 15, 1959, p. 3.

‡ At the trial of Marcos Rodríguez in March, 1964, Carlos Rafael Rodríguez remarked that he had opposed the line of Aníbal Escalante (*El Mundo*, March 25, 1964). The indications are that Carlos Rafael won out when the Party Secretary, Blas Roca, went over to his side.

§ Two of the young Communists sent to the Sierra Maestra, Pablo Ribalta and Hiram Prats, were named at the Marcos Rodríguez trial (*El Mundo*, March 25, 1964).

¶ His role was revealed only after he was killed in an airplane accident in January, 1961 (*Verde Olivo*, January 22, 1961, p. 79, and July 2, 1961, p. 12).

of April 9, 1958, was carried out by the 26th of July Movement without Communist backing. The Communists blamed the failure of the strike in Havana on the "unilateral strike call" issued by the 26th of July leadership "without counting on the rest of the opposition or on the workers themselves."*

It is quite clear that an internal struggle took place inside both the 26th of July Movement and the Communist PSP before they were able to get together. In the 26th of July Movement, the struggle was waged between the civilian leadership of the *llano* (plain), which was anti-Communist, and the military leadership of the *sierra* (mountain), which was pro-Communist. The failure of the April, 1958, strike served to discredit the former and give the latter a free hand. In the PSP, the struggle raged between the old-line partisans of peaceful, "electoral" opposition and the new-style believers in armed, "insurrectionary" struggle. As late as June 28, 1958, the National Committee of the PSP put out a statement advocating an end to violence and settlement of the strife "by means of democratic and clean elections, respected by all, by which the people can effectively decide by means of the vote and the results of which would be honorably respected."†

But by this time, Batista's offensive in the Sierra Maestra was petering out, and the odds were changing in favor of Castro. A turning point in Castro-Communist relations apparently took place in June–July, 1958, or thereabouts. While Castro was negotiating with the other opposition groups for the "unity pact" which was signed in Caracas on July 20, he was simultaneously negotiating with the Com-

---

* *Declaraciones del P.S.P.: Las Mentiras del Gobierno Sobre la Huelga y la Situación,* leaflet signed by the Comité Nacional del Partido Socialista Popular, dated April 12, 1958.

† "Srs. Miembros de los organismos dirigentes del 'Movimiento 26 de Julio,' del PRC (a), de la Organización Auténtica, del Directorio Revolucionario, del grupo 'Montecristi,' del PPC (O) y del PNR," signed by the National Committee; Juan Marinello, President; Blas Roca, General Secretary.

munists and surreptitiously moving toward a second "unity pact" with them—surreptitiously because the democratic opposition groups would have nothing to do with the Communists. The former did not know, and even when they were told, would not believe, that Castro had accepted the Communists as allies.*

On June 5, 1958, the Communist leader Carlos Rafael Rodríguez sent an article from Havana to the French Communist organ *La France Nouvelle* in which he made known that negotiations were going on for a trade-union agreement. He named several groups, including the 26th of July Movement and the Communists.† Castro then invited the opposition groups to send representatives to the Sierra Maestra, but only the Communists and the Directorio Revolucionario responded.‡ Rodríguez himself went to the Sierra Maestra in July, and a younger Communist leader, Luis Más Martín, the following month.§ The trade-union negotiations, which must have been initiated at the end of May or the beginning of June, evidently did not go too smoothly because an agreement was not reached until October, over four months later.¶ This agreement took the form of enlarging the Frente Obrero Nacional (FON), which had been a united front of the non-Communist opposition groups, into the Frente Obrero Nacional

* Letter from Angel del Cerro to Theodore Draper, September 2, 1962. According to del Cerro, who then represented the Montecristi Group in Havana, Carlos Rafael Rodríguez returned from his first trip to the Sierra Maestra and told the "Caracas pact" representatives in Havana that Castro wanted the Communists included, but no one believed him—and he was not accepted.

† "Entre la Colère et la Peur," *La France Nouvelle*, July 17–23, 1958.

‡ Testimony of Carlos Rafael Rodríguez at the Marcos Rodríguez trial, *El Mundo*, March 25, 1964.

§ *Hoy*, January 11 and 15, 1959.

¶ Joaquín Ordoqui, *Elementos para la Historia del Movimiento Obrero en Cuba* (Havana: Secretaría de Divulgación de la CTC-R, 1961), p. 35, gives the date as October, 1958. The Communist trade-union leader Ursinio Rojas stated that the negotiations were initiated in "June and July, 1958," and concluded in "October and November" of that year (*Fundamentos*, March, 1959, p. 22).

Unido (FONU). The FONU symbolically accepted the Communists into the trade-union united front, but apparently this amounted to little more than a gesture.*

The Castro-Communist alliance, then, was first realized sometime in 1958. This does not mean that some Castroites and some Communists did not work for such an alliance before 1958. But as movements, they were inhibited from working together as long as an important section of the 26th of July Movement was anti-Communist in principle and the Communist leadership was anti-insurrectionist in practice. By the summer of 1958, however, the former had suffered an irreparable blow by virtue of its own failure to win power through the general strike, and the latter had immeasurably increased its maneuvering power by backing, at least partially, an "insurrectionary" policy. The dividing line between Castro and the Communists had increasingly narrowed down to a single issue—"armed struggle." The Communists had to cross this line and go over to Castro's side to make a full alliance possible. But whereas "armed struggle" was the *raison d'être* of Castroism, it was a purely tactical question, not a matter of principle, for the Communists. They could concede the point to Castro without, in their own minds, having made a more serious mistake than that of having misjudged the "objective circumstances" and the "relation of forces." The Castro-Communist alliance left the Communists' ideology intact. It did not leave Castro's ideology, or whatever he had professed to be his ideology, intact.

From Alliance to Fusion

First there was the Castro-Communist alliance, then there was the Castro-Communist fusion. About two years passed

* *Bohemia*, February 15, 1959, p. 88.

between the first stage and the second, and again only the main lines of the process can be clearly drawn.

We now know that Castro had decided on "fusing" with the Communists by the end of 1960, though the decision was not made public for another half year. On December 2, 1960, Castro presided at a meeting setting up the Escuelas de Instrucción Popular to train cadres for the future "united party." According to Lionel Soto, the Communist Director of these schools, this meeting was the "first formal manifestation" of the "integration of the revolutionary forces."*

This decision to fuse with the Communists was of such import and magnitude that it could not have been taken without long forethought and preparation. We will be able to interpret the events of 1960 far more realistically when we know more about the actual genesis of this decision and not merely its "first formal manifestation." One of the most striking aspects of this entire process was, and still is, the reluctance of the Cubans to tell much about it. Few Cuban secrets have been so well guarded as this one, as if the truth were still likely to be too upsetting. The Cuban leaders have preferred to pursue a policy of facts first and names afterward, in Dorticós' words, or to rationalize their actions by depicting them as reactions, as if they had never done anything to encourage precisely those actions to which they wished to react.

In many ways, the process of Castro-Communist fusion was similar to the process of Castro-Communist alliance. In both cases, struggles took place within both the 26th of July Movement and the Communist Party. In the former, the struggle between the pro-Communist and anti-Communist factions occupied most of 1959. Almost all the internal crises in the Castro regime that year—the defection of Major

---

* *Cuba Socialista*, February, 1963, p. 30.

Pedro Díaz Lanz, the first head of the Air Force, in June; the dismissal of Dr. Manuel Urrutia, the first President, in July; the arrest of Major Hubert Matos, the commander of the Rebel Army in Camagüey Province, in October; Castro's personal intervention to save the Communists from total rout at the trade-union congress in November; the removal of two ministers, Faustino Pérez and Manuel Ray, who refused to go along with Matos' arrest, in November; the replacement of the President of the National Bank, Felipe Pazos, by Che Guevara, in the same month; and the oppressive sentencing of Matos to a twenty-year prison term in December—all turned on the issue of Communism. It is significant that the Communist organ *Hoy* had launched a campaign against Urrutia as early as March and against Matos in June of that year.* Invariably, the days of those attacked by the Communists were numbered, and events bore out the direst forebodings of the anti-Communists.†

In the Communist leadership, the main struggle was over the balance of power in the new "united party." In order to achieve fusion, the Fidelistas had to pay homage to the old-time Communists' ideological pre-eminence, and the old-time Communists had to pay tribute to the Fidelistas' tactical superiority. Yet, in practice, the question remained whether the new party should be based on those who had been the long-time guardians of the orthodox ideology or on those who had been the long-derided executors of the successful tactics. In 1961, the pendulum swung in favor of the former, as indicated by Castro's humble admissions of ideological backwardness, his pledge of allegiance to the "collective leadership" of the party, and the original staffing of the new party's training schools almost exclusively with

---

* *Hoy*, March 5 and June 12, 1959.
† Others whose fate was foreshadowed were Treasury Minister Rufo López Fresquet and Luis Conte Agüero (*Hoy*, May 5 and June 30, 1959).

old-time Communists.* In March, 1962, with the purge of the old-time Communist leader Aníbal Escalante, the pendulum swung the other way. Thus there have been different phases in the relationship of Castroism and Communism, before and after fusion, in their former names and in their latest incarnations as "new" and "old" Communists.

Again the question arises how Castro's private beliefs accorded with his public utterances. On the surface it would seem that, in the first few months of his regime, he was torn between conflicting tendencies within himself and his movement. At different times he encouraged both the pro-Communist and anti-Communist wings of the movement and managed to give each of them reason to believe that he was merely waiting for an opportune moment to take a strong stand against the other. He characterized Communism in a way which would soon become a crime in anyone else's mouth. On April 23, 1959, for example, he classified fascism, Peronism, and Communism as different kinds of "totalitarianism."† On May 21, 1959, he talked of Communism as a system "which solves the economic problem, but which suppresses liberties, the liberties which are so dear to man and which I know the Cuban people feel." He said that the Communist states "sacrificed" man as "pitilessly" as did the capitalist states. He accused the Cuban Communists of complicity with "counterrevolutionaries" in stirring up unrest.‡ Yet, a few months later, it was political suicide in Cuba to say anything against the Communists, and Castro himself led the campaign in their behalf.

* Interview with Castro, *L'Unità* (Rome), February 1, 1961; *Revolución,* March 26, 1961; *Revolución,* December 2, 1961; Lionel Soto, *Cuba Socialista,* February, 1963, pp. 62–63.
† *Guía del pensamiento político-económico de Fidel* (Havana: Diario Libre, 1959), p. 30.
‡ *Revolución,* May 22, 1959.

Had it been a hoax or the real thing? In practical effect, it hardly matters. Castro succeeded in allaying the apprehensions of the anti-Communist wing of his movement as effectively one way or the other. Just as he had said that he could not have come down from the Sierra Maestra to the plain if he had called himself a "Marxist-Leninist," it might also be said that he could not have gained the time he needed to consolidate his personal power if he had prematurely called himself a "Marxist-Leninist" in 1959. Still, it is again hard to imagine a covert Communist choosing to characterize the Communist movement in general and the Cuban Communists in particular in the terms used by Castro in the first months of 1959. And, in his "I am a Marxist-Leninist" speech of December 2, 1961, Castro found it necessary to allude to these past transgressions and to beg indulgence for them on the ground that he had been a victim of "imperialist propaganda."

In the struggle for power, as we have seen, Castro never tried to give his movement a distinctive doctrine or ideology. After he took power, however, Castro did make one attempt to put forward an embryonic doctrine or ideology which he could call his own. This phase of Castroism was summed up in the term "humanism," which for a time served as the trademark of his revolution. Its background and fate are most revealing.

Ever since 1950, there had been, in Cuba, a "humanist movement," founded by a well-known intellectual, Rubén Darío Rumbaut.* This movement was an offshoot of what was known as the Catholic Left, and its promoters hoped that it would prepare the way for a Cuban Christian Democratic Party. They were inspired by, among others, the French Catholic social philosopher Jacques Maritain. But the movement never took fire, and "humanism" did not

---

* Rubén Darío Rumbaut, *Bohemia Libre*, January 1, 1961, p. 58.

amount to much politically until Castro suddenly appropriated the term, which he apparently used for the first time during his visit to New York in April, 1959.

For Castro, "humanism" seemed to be an alternative to both "capitalism" and "Communism," a third way. "Neither dictatorships of men, nor dictatorships of classes, nor dictatorships of groups, nor dictatorships of caste, nor oligarchies of class: government of the people without dictatorship and without oligarchy, liberty with bread and without terror—that is humanism," he said in New York on April 24, 1959.* "We believe that there should not be bread without liberty, but neither should there be liberty without bread," he said in Montreal a few days later. "We call that humanism. We want Cuba to be an example of representative democracy with true social justice."† In this period, he also said that "capitalism may kill man with hunger" and "Communism kills man by wiping out his freedom."‡

At first the Cuban Communists tried to avoid a clash with the new "humanist" vogue.§ But when a section of the 26th of July Movement took up the new slogan—for it was little more than that—as the long-awaited independent and indigenous Fidelista doctrine, and especially when the 26th of July trade-union section swamped the Communists in union elections on a humanist program, the Communists decided to fight back. Aníbal Escalante criticized it as "ideological confusion,"¶ perhaps one of the derelictions which Castro never forgave him. At the time, however, Escalante prevailed. Castro dropped the term and never used it again. Its life span was only about two or three months.

* *Guía del pensamiento político-económico de Fidel*, p. 48.
† *Hoy*, April 28, 1959.
‡ *Revolución*, May 22, 1959.
§ Blas Roca, *Hoy*, May 10, 1959.
¶ *Hoy*, June 30, 1959.

Thus, the one and only attempt by Castro to enunciate an ideology—or only the slogan of an ideology—of his own was characteristically unoriginal and pathetically short-lived.

"Armed Struggle" or "Peaceful Transition"

After the purge of Aníbal Escalante, in March, 1962, however, Castro made one notable attempt to assert his individuality within the world Communist movement. The occasion was provided by the "missile crisis" of October, 1962, which was resolved by Soviet Premier Nikita Khrushchev and President John F. Kennedy at some cost to Castro's pride and influence. Unable to relieve his feelings at the expense of the Soviets, Castro took out most of his rage on the Latin American Communist leaderships, which, with few exceptions, had been resisting following the Cuban "example," while profiting from it. In a speech on January 16, 1963, Castro paid them back and made his most outspoken bid for the leadership of Latin American Communism. He accused some of his Communist brethren of spreading "false interpretations" and distorting the "historic truths" of the Cuban revolution in order to justify their policy of "peaceful transition." He maintained that the "objective conditions" for revolution already existed in most of Latin America, and that only the absence of the "subjective conditions," or lack of revolutionary will, held it back. He accused other, unnamed Latin American Communists of such egregious vices as "conformism" with imperialism and "fear of revolutions."

In the same speech, Castro instructed the Latin American Communists on how to make the revolution. His ideas may be summed up in four points:

1. "The masses make history," but they must be

"launched into the battle" by "revolutionary leaders and organizations."

2. The Cuban masses had been launched into the struggle by "four, five, six, or seven" guerrillas.

3. The "objective conditions" for such a struggle exist in "the immense majority of Latin American countries" and only the "subjective conditions"—that is, the "four, five, six, or seven" willing to launch the armed struggle—are lacking.

4. "Peaceful transition" may be "possible," but there is not a single case of it on record, and in any event, armed struggle must take place in most Latin American countries.

Thus, the true face of Castroism showed itself within the Communist movement at a moment of crisis. In effect, on the single issue of "armed struggle," Castroism reasserted itself, this time inside the Communist movement. It had distinguished Castro from the official Cuban Communists before 1958, when they did not think that armed struggle could overthrow Batista, and now it distinguished him from most Latin American Communist leaderships, which did not think that they could overthrow the existing regimes in their countries through armed struggle. The basic issue was the same; only the context—all of Latin America instead of Cuba—had changed.

Castro did not have an easier time convincing most of the old Latin American leaderships than he had had convincing the Cuban Communists. Since 1962, the only countries in which he could induce the local Communist Parties to adopt his tactics—mainly through influence on youth and student sections—were Venezuela and Guatemala. Elsewhere, Castroism threatened the Parties with factional struggles.

In Argentina, for example, at the Twelfth Congress of the Communist Party, February 22–March 3, 1963, the main resolution of the Congress did not fail to pay tribute

to the Cuban revolution for having "qualitatively changed the character of the freedom revolution in Latin America." As for immediate tactics in Argentina itself, however, it chose "to conquer power by the peaceful road" through a "National Democratic Front" of workers, peasants, students, progressive professionals and intellectuals, the petty bourgeoisie, and even sectors of the "national bourgeoisie."*
In February, 1963, the outstanding Brazilian Communist leader, Luis Carlos Prestes, journeyed to Moscow and then flew directly to Havana. It was Prestes' first visit to the Cuban capital—the major established Latin American Communist leaders did not hurry to make the pilgrimage—and what had brought him there was clearly intimated in an interview published in the old-time Cuban Communist organ *Hoy*.

"There are persons," said Prestes, without naming names, "who mistakenly believe that the initiation of an armed struggle in Brazil to depose the government would constitute the best support for Cuba. In the present conditions of Brazil, this would be completely wrong. It would isolate the Communists from the masses and facilitate the work of those who are pressing the government in the direction of breaking relations with the Cuban Government." Prestes added, in case some "persons" might imagine that he was speaking only about Brazil: "For Marxism-Leninism, revolution is not synonymous with violence; it is fundamentally a change of classes in power; and that is possible, in certain countries of Latin America, in present conditions, without civil war and without armed insurrection."†

One of the problems that Castro took with him to Soviet Russia, where he arrived on April 27, was undoubtedly the growing tension between the Cuban and other Latin Amer-

* *XII Congreso del Partido Comunista de la Argentina: Resolución* (Buenos Aires: Editorial Anteo, 1963), pp. 4 and 9.
† *Hoy*, March 9, 1963.

ican Communist Parties. The outcome was a joint statement signed by Castro and Khrushchev on May 23 in which
one passage related directly to the intra-Communist dispute
in Latin America and obviously represented a compromise
formula. The key sentence on this subject reads: "The
PURS [Cuba's Partido Unido de la Revolución Socialista,
or United Party of the Socialist Revolution] and the CPSU
[Communist Party of the Soviet Union] consider that the
question of the peaceful or nonpeaceful road toward socialism in one country or another will be definitely decided by
the struggling peoples themselves, according to the practical correlation of class forces and the degree of resistance of
the exploiting classes to the socialist transformation of society." Another relevant phrase stated: "The working out
of the concrete forms and methods of the struggle for
socialism in each country is the internal affair of the people
of each country."* In short, the Cubans were to stop telling
the other Latin American Communists how to make a revolution as part of the price of the general agreement reached
by Khrushchev and Castro at this time.

This *modus vivendi,* Communist-style, lasted about six
months. In August, 1963, even Major Ernesto Che Guevara
assured a group of Latin American sympathizers that "armed
struggle" was to be undertaken only when and where the
necessary "objective conditions" existed, and the decision
was up to the revolutionaries of each country.† In the September, 1963, issue of the Cuban theoretical magazine
Cuba Socialista, Guevara raised the question: "Is the
method of guerrilla warfare the only formula for taking
power in all America? Or will it be, in any case, the predominant form? Or will it simply be one more formula
among all those used for the struggle?" He still insisted

---

* "Declaración conjunta soviético-cubana," *Cuba Socialista,* June, 1963,
pp. 17–18.
  † *Revolución,* August 21, 1963.

that "there are fundamental arguments that, in our view, determine the necessity for guerrilla action in America as the central axis of the struggle." But he conceded that "the peaceful struggle" could succeed in "special situations of crisis." In his book *Guerrilla Warfare,* one of the basic premises had been that all the conditions for making a revolution were not always necessary because the "insurrectional focal point" (*"el foco insurreccional"*) could create them.* Now he advised that "violence should be unleashed exactly at the precise moment when the leaders of the people have encountered the most favorable circumstances." At one point, he tried to generalize as follows:

"An analysis of the foregoing, taking a panoramic view of America, would have to come to the following conclusions: In this continent, there exist in general objective conditions which impel the masses to violent actions against the bourgeois and landlord governments; there exist crises of power in many other countries and some subjective conditions also. It is clear that, in the countries in which all the conditions are given, it would even be criminal not to seize the opportunity to take power. In other countries in which this is not happening, it is permissible that different alternatives should present themselves and that the decision applicable to each country should emerge from theoretical discussion."†

* Che Guevara, *La Guerra de Guerrillas* (Havana: Departamento de Instrucción del MINFAR, [1960]), p. 11. This point will be discussed more fully in the next chapter.

† "Guerra de guerrillas: un método," *Cuba Socialista,* September, 1963, pp. 1–17. The entire article, as may be seen, lends itself to different interpretations depending on which sentence is emphasized, which may have been Guevara's intention. The passage quoted above, however, has had an even more complicated career in translation. Unfortunately, the only publicly available English translation appeared in the *Peking Review,* January 10, 1964, pp. 14–21. At key points, this version significantly changed Guevara's meaning. For example, Guevara had used the expression *"las siguientes conclusiones,"* which became, in the Chinese Communist organ, "the inevitable conclusion" instead of, simply, "the following conclusions." More seriously, Guevara wrote: *"En este Continente existen*

It seems clear, from this rather tortuous and highly qualified line of reasoning, that Guevara was attempting to hold onto his original, extreme line in principle, while modifying it considerably in practice. As long as each Party could decide for itself what conditions required what tactics, the Cuban "road to power" could be honored more in the breach than in the observance.

Two months later, in December, 1963, the *World Marxist Review,* the international organ of the pro-Soviet Communist Parties, published an article by the Chilean Communist leader Luis Corvalán entitled "The Peaceful Way—A Form of Revolution." Whereas Guevara had made grudging admissions that the "peaceful road" might be applicable in some circumstances, Corvalán made grudging admissions that the "violent road" might be equally applicable. For Corvalán, the important thing was the coming Chilean elections, in which the Communists had succeeded in putting together a "Popular Front" based on a "peaceful," "democratic" approach to the Chilean electorate. Thus Corvalán was concerned with preaching against "adventurism," denigrating the importance of violence or armed struggle, extolling maximum flexibility in tactics, and emphasizing that both objective and subjective conditions had to be "ripe" for a successful revolution.

The Chilean leader was especially wrathful because the Chinese Communist Party had sent the Chilean Party a letter which had sharply contrasted Corvalán's "peaceful way" with Castro's "revolutionary way." In reply, Corvalán cited the Khrushchev-Castro declaration of May 23 on

---

en general condiciones objetivas," etc. The Chinese translated this as follows: "There exist everywhere in this continent the objective conditions," etc. By using the term "everywhere" for Guevara's *"en general"* ("in general"), the Chinese translation significantly distorted the meaning of the original, even though the sentences immediately following belie the intention of Guevara to assume objective conditions for violent action in every Latin American country.

"forms and methods" being the business of each individual Party. Thus Castro had temporarily put himself in a position of being used by both sides. "No Communist Party which accepts the thesis concerning the peaceful way repudiates the way of armed uprising *a priori,*" Corvalán protested. He also made it clear that, if the Chilean Communists ever won power, one way or the other, Chile would end up as another Cuba anyway. Still, on the burning question of tactics, there was no doubt where Corvalán stood: "In upholding the peaceful way our Party aims at solving the tasks of the revolution without civil war or armed uprising. On the other hand, whether a struggle is revolutionary or not is not determined exclusively (and often not even mainly) by the number of violent actions, by the predominance or absence of armed struggle."*

By the end of 1963, then, it was quite clear that the Moscow formula of May had worn somewhat thin. Both sides were using some of the same language to say quite different things. Still, as long as each Party was permitted to make up its own mind without interference or reproach by other Parties, the formula avoided open clashes and served a useful purpose. But the Cubans could not hold their fire for long. Early in 1964, Guevara was his old self again. To an Italian correspondent in Havana, he said in January of that year: "I maintain that the war of liberation will necessarily assume a violent form in almost every one of these [Latin American] countries—in almost all, I say. There is no other way. Violence is the only form in which their political will can manifest itself."†

Castro himself was somewhat more cautious. In an important interview with foreign correspondents during the celebration of the ninth anniversary of the Moncada affair, he was asked to comment on Chile just before the election.

---

* *World Marxist Review,* December, 1963, pp. 3–10.
† Gianni Corbi, "I Niños Malos," *L'Espresso* (Rome), January 26, 1964.

"In general, the political and revolutionary leaders of each country do not ask anyone what to do, and we ourselves do not ask anyone about anything," he replied in the spirit of the Moscow agreement. "But on the theoretical level, I will say that there is no one road to make the revolution; I believe that there is more than one road, and that these roads are determined by circumstances."

He went on: "In some countries, as, for example, Chile, where legal methods of struggle are open, I believe that the road which they are following in Chile, the constitutional and legal road, is a correct road. In those countries where all legal methods are closed and objective conditions exist for making the revolution, then it is necessary to have recourse to the methods of armed struggle in order to conquer revolutionary power. And if I were a Venezuelan, and if I were a Colombian, that is what I would do."*

All of which seemed quite fair and reasonable. But no sooner had the Communist-backed Popular Front in Chile suffered a setback in the September, 1964, elections than Castro changed his tune. He quickly held forth again on "the inevitable road of revolutions, in many circumstances the inevitable road of armed revolutionary struggle."†

Thus, until the Moscow agreement of May, 1963, the Castroite position on the question of "armed struggle" versus "peaceful transition" had clearly favored the former. Then began a period of over a year in which Castro apparently modified his position to approach closer to that of the major Latin American Communist Parties, of Argentina, Brazil, and Chile. Even if Guevara seemed to undercut the new line by making essentially superficial concessions, he did make some effort to broaden his approach and, in any event, it could be said that only Castro spoke officially and conclusively for Cuba. But the circumstances of the shift,

---

* *La Tarde* (Havana), July 29, 1964.
† *Obra Revolucionaria,* No. 20, 1964, p. 24 (speech of September 10, 1964).

and the hasty Cuban reaction to the disappointing Chilean elections, showed that the motivation had been practical rather than doctrinal. The Venezuelan Communist movement had already paid a heavy price for its terrorist tactics; the Castroite tendency in Brazil had virtually fizzled out; the Chilean elections made it imperative for the largest Communist Party in Latin America to muffle the Castroite chorus in its rear. The lack of suitable theaters of action for "armed struggle" in Latin America and Cuba's own overriding economic needs in 1963 made it necessary for Castro to tone down his previously contemptuous references to "peaceful transition." Ironically, the Castroite obsession with violence and terrorism—and, as Venezuela showed, all that the revolutionary rhetoric of "armed struggle" really boiled down to in practice was sheer terrorism—had threatened the unity and force of the larger Latin American Communist Parties more than it had the existing regimes.

But, after the Chilean elections, circumstances again changed, and with this came another change of line. Despite the opportunistic moderation of 1963–64, it was never a secret that "armed struggle" had remained the distinguishing characteristic and most strident war cry of Castroism within the Communist movement of Latin America, wherever, as in Venezuela, the Castroite tendency controlled Communist policy. If it did not have that, Castroism would lose its identity in the Communist mass. That is why, as long as Castro wishes to assert himself as an independent force within Latin American Communism, he can temporarily modulate, but he cannot abandon, his basic position.

Power and Ideology

Historically, then, Castroism is a leader in search of a movement, a movement in search of power, and power in search of an ideology. From its origins to today, it has had the same leader and the same "road to power," but it has changed its ideology.

If Castroism were merely an extension of its leader, it would belong to the traditional *caudillo*-type movements of Latin America in which power is its own justification. But Castro is not a traditional *caudillo;* he is a new type of *caudillo* with a need to justify his power ideologically.

Yet Castro's ideology has never come out of himself. He has only produced a "road to power," which has attached itself to different ideologies. He won power with one ideology and has held it with another. This is perhaps the most peculiar aspect of the Castroite phenomenon.

The three schools of thought mentioned at the outset explain this phenomenon in different ways. The first contends that there was no change in ideology, at least in Castro; that he was always a Communist, but a secret one. The second maintains that there was a natural, consistent development from his pre-Communist to his post-Communist ideology. The third—at least as I understand it—believes that Castro did not have an ideological core of his own and filled the vacuum in himself with different ideologies to serve his power in different ways at different stages of his political career.

Castro himself seems increasingly to have adopted the third view. For example, on January 2, 1964, he stressed the unpreparedness of both the Cuban leadership and the Cuban people for building socialism, and their lack of "organization, tradition, habits, customs, ideas, and mental attitude" for the new task. In a similar vein, Guevara had previously remarked that the revolutionary leaders had been "only a group of fighters with high ideals and little preparation."*

The old-time Communist leaders have agreed on a re-

* *Hoy,* July 16, 1963.

vealing formula to define Fidel Castro's "great historical merit." As one of the oldest and most authoritative of them has written, it has consisted essentially in his ability "to find the right road for achieving victory, that of the armed struggle of the people, the only possible road in the conditions of Cuba of 1952–58."* As late as January, 1964, the former Communist General Secretary, Blas Roca, paid tribute to Castro's "great historical merit" in virtually the same terms, always with emphasis on the fact that he had found the right road to power rather than what he had done with it.†

In effect, Castroism gave Communism total power in Cuba, and Communism gave Castroism an ideology of total power. In a previous period, Castroism might well have adopted a different ideology of total power. In this sense, Castroism has never been self-sufficient or homogeneous; it has been made up of elements from different traditions and movements; it has mainly contributed means and sought elsewhere for ends.

Thus, the reason for Castroism's coalescence with Communism can be explained less by what it was than by what it was not. It was not a movement with a serious political thought or a serious political thinker. It has had a leader with great gifts of popularization, demagogy, and dissimulation, with a contagious sense of mission and *jefatura,* with the physical attributes of a warrior-hero. But he has also had a deep, persistent feeling of intellectual inadequacy and inferiority, a tendency to depend on others for fundamental values or systematic theorizing, an inherent political superficiality and instability. Before taking power, he could put his name to fine democratic aims and principles, admittedly without believing in them, not because he was

* Fabio Grobart, *Cuba Socialista,* July, 1963, p. 55.

† Blas Roca, *ibid.,* January, 1964, pp. 11–12. Blas Roca used this formula for the first time in 1960 (Partido Socialista Popular, *VIII Asamblea Nacional: Informes, Resoluciones, Programa, Estatutos* [Havana: Ediciones Populares, 1960], p. 44).

profoundly committed to other beliefs but because he did not believe in anything very profoundly.

But it is only in Cuba that Castroism has gone through enough stages to make its relationship with Communism clearly visible and openly avowed. In other countries, one may detect Castroite tendencies which reflect earlier stages of Cuban Castroism and which still maintain a seemingly tenuous or ambiguous relationship with existing Communist movements. Thus, non-Cuban Castroite groups may resemble the Cuban Castroism of 1955 or 1957 much more than the Cuban Castroism of 1961 or 1965. The former may seem to be a revolutionary mood rather than a movement; it may be distinguished by its "pure" adherence to "armed struggle" or "direct action" without the (temporary) encumbrance of an ideology; it may even, like its progenitor, claim to be an alternative rather than a road to Communism. But it is much more difficult for any non-Cuban Castroism to pretend to be "democratic" and non-Communist, as Cuban Castroism once pretended to be, precisely because the latter has demonstrated what such professions were worth. The success of Cuban Castroism in turning itself into a Cuban form of Communism has, ironically, hindered Castroite groups elsewhere from achieving success in quite the same way. The hopes and illusions on which Cuban Castroism once fed can hardly be made to order for any other Castroite group, and we may even get a Castroite tendency somewhere which promises to avoid the mistakes and excesses of Fidel Castro.

There are, it seems to me, two main dangers to be avoided in any analysis of Castroism today. One is to separate it from the world Communist movement, and the other is to equate it with everything else in the world Communist movement. It is just as logical to say that Fidel Castro cannot be a Communist because he is a Castroite as to say that Mao Tse-tung cannot be a Communist because he is a Maoist or that Tito cannot be a Communist because he is a Titoist. On the other hand, it is just as illogical to deny the peculiar characteristics of Castro's Communism as to deny the peculiar characteristics of Mao's or Tito's or, for that matter, Khrushchev's or Khrushchev's successors'.

In short, Castroism today represents a tendency within the world Communist movement. There is no such thing as Castroism per se. Indeed, the term Castroism is not used in Cuba today, and Castro himself seems very coy about acknowledging the existence of Castroism. It is necessary to distinguish between the "ism" of the genus "Communism" and the "ism" of a species, such as Castroism. But, for better or worse, the different Communist tendencies are also called "isms," and this practice is not likely to be given up.

In this sense, Castroism may be distinguished from other Communist tendencies by its leadership, its history, its geographical sphere of influence, its language, and its "road to power."

1. The inspiration and source of authority of the Castroite tendency is Fidel Castro, not the Soviet leadership, Mao, or anyone else. Castro has his own personal cadre and independent following in Cuba, and to a lesser extent elsewhere, which have given him an increasing margin of maneuverability vis-à-vis the old-time Communists in Cuba and the other Communist states and Parties.

2. Castroism is the only tendency within world Communism which came into the movement from the outside and did not develop organically from within, as did Maoism or Titoism. In Cuba it has needed world Communism to give it a doctrine, a social and economic pattern, and material assistance, but it feels that world Communism needs it externally for expansion in Latin America.

Castro and his closest associates have repeatedly spoken of Cuba as the "example" which most of Latin America must follow to make the revolution. Many of the Communist Parties of Latin America date from the early 1920's (one, the Mexican, from 1919), and the old leaderships were brought up on the proposition that the "example" to follow with some modifications and adaptations was the Russian revolution and the Russian Party leadership. The "example" of the Chinese revolution was the first great challenge to the Russian prototype, but Castro hopes that the Cuban "example" will supersede both of them. The ultimate authority, of course, on who is and who is not correctly following the "Cuban example" will be found in Havana, not in Moscow or in Peking.

3. In effect, Castro has staked out for himself a Communist sphere of influence. He has, on occasion, made nothing less than a bid to be recognized as the Communist leader of Latin America, to be treated eventually on a par with the Soviet leadership and Mao Tse-tung. This may smack of delusions of grandeur for the leader of a country as small and weak as Cuba, but it is precisely Castro's point that numbers are not important. If a dozen men could start a revolution in Cuba, why should not little Cuba be able to set off the revolution in Latin America, or at least claim credit for it?

4. Guevara has pointed out that Cuba has "something" for Latin Americans which no other Communist power can match. "That something," he said, "which speaks to them in Spanish, in their own language, and which explains in a clear form what they have to do to achieve happiness, is called the Cuban revolution."* The same idea, less obtrusively, but no less unmistakably, has been publicly voiced by Blas Roca: "The Cuban revolution established the first socialist country in America and has made the first Marxist-Leninist revolution in the Spanish language. And that is

* *Revolución,* March 25, 1963.

for all time."* Language, in fact, reinforces and perhaps even outweighs geography as a factor in the Castroite sphere of influence. The language factor indefinably exacerbates and nationalizes whatever other differences may exist between the various Communist tendencies.

5. Finally, the Castroite "road to power" is not the traditional Communist one. In the orthodox Communist view of the past, revolutionary force or violence has been considered the last, not the first, stage of the revolutionary struggle. Objective conditions created the basis for armed struggle; armed struggle did not create objective conditions. As the veteran Argentine Communist Victorio Codovilla has said of the Chinese Communists, but which he might just as well have aimed at the Cubans, "they stake everything on armed struggle alone," and especially on "partisan warfare." Codovilla, who served for many years as a Comintern functionary, agreed that "in certain conditions partisan action as a component of the mass movement is a form of the popular struggle," and a "justified and necessary form," but, he insisted, armed force is only one of many admissible forms of struggle, and "if the objective conditions are not favorable for waging an armed struggle, partisan action will end in failure and in the long run will damage the revolutionary movement."† This is not the language of Castroism, which had previously advocated the use of force always and almost everywhere by a handful of guerrillas even in countries with a weak Communist Party or outside the Party altogether.

In view of the existing confusion in some quarters, it may be well to emphasize that the difference between Codovilla, an outstanding representative of the Communist "old

---

* *El Mundo* (Havana), October 14, 1964.
† Victorio Codovilla, in *Information Bulletin,* Supplement No. 3 to *World Marxist Review* (Ontario: Progress Books, 1963), pp. 33–34.

guard," and Castro, the exemplar of the Communist "new wave," is not one of "armed struggle" versus "peaceful transition" in principle. The difference is over when, where, and in what circumstances, it is necessary or advisable to use force. The "old guard," as in the case of Luis Carlos Prestes in Brazil, has painful memories of the heavy price paid years ago for the misuse of force and considers the stakes too high to be risked lightly. Soviet Russia and not Communist China has, after all, given Castro the material assistance and military equipment that have made his belligerence possible. The difference, then, is not one of abstract doctrine; thus far the "old guard" and the "new wave" have found it possible to live with it. Nevertheless, factional struggles in the Communist movement have flared up and have raged out of control for less cause. The antagonism between the "old" Communists and the "new" in Castro's Cuba should not be pooh-poohed. For historical, personal, and tactical reasons, it is one of the most divisive elements in Castro's regime and potentially one of the most explosive.

In historical perspective, then, Castroism represents a particular case of cross-fertilization, as yet difficult to assess with finality, of a Latin American revolutionary tradition and the European Communist tradition, just as Leninism represented a cross-fertilization of the Russian revolutionary tradition and the European Marxist tradition. It is "a particular case," because it is not yet certain that the Cuban phenomenon is typical or representative of Latin American Communism as a whole. It is as yet difficult to assess with finality because it is still of relatively recent vintage and in constant flux. If the Cubans should ever achieve their ambition and truly carve out for themselves a Latin American sphere of influence—which still seems to be a long way off—it will mark a further division of the Communist world into regional oligarchies. Castroism has given world Communism cause for both exhilaration and apprehension. It has created new opportunities and new tensions. It represents growing pains and growing contradictions. All that it is safe to say at present is that the end is not yet in sight.

II

THE DÉCLASSÉ
REVOLUTION

WHATEVER THE RELATIONSHIP between Castroism
and Communism may be, another question is
just as perplexing and inevitable: "What is the
relationship between Castroism and Cuban society?" To
put it another way, what kind of social interpretation—or
as Cuba's newly converted Marxists might prefer to say,
"class analysis"—can we give of Castroism?

For this purpose, it is necessary to retrace some steps and
look more closely at the struggle for power. As a starting

point, it is well to consider the leading theories that have appeared in Cuba. Much can be learned from them, if only for the problems they raise.

During the struggle for power and for about a year or two after power had been won, Castroism seemed to be a movement without a theory or ideology. It even made a virtue of an apparent necessity and impressed its friends and well-wishers with its nonideological character. "The Cuban revolutionary never generalizes," Jean-Paul Sartre was led to believe in the spring of 1960.* "We're practical men, not theorists—although some of us are getting more and more interested in theories," C. Wright Mills was told a few months later.† This ideological modesty was partly protective, partly genuine. By protesting that he was neither left nor right in May, 1959, Castro made himself much harder to attack from the left or right.‡ Yet, it would have been much more difficult for him to have acted the role convincingly if there had not been some truth in it. Castro himself did not have an ideological mind, and so long as he was almost the sole authoritative spokesman of his movement, it had to live on borrowed ideologies or none at all. Until the capture of power, the future ideologist-in-chief, Guevara, preferred to be known as a man of action rather than of words. Thus, as we have seen, it suited both Castro's temperament and tactics that the closer his movement approached power, the less ideological it seemed to become.

Most revolutionary movements have had what might be called "anticipatory" theories. Castroism has rather had only a "retrospective" theory, in the sense that only after taking power did it begin to ask itself what it had done and how it had been done. The usual process was reversed. We are accustomed to ideologies which are most dogmatic in their origins and become more and more amorphous as

* *Sartre on Cuba* (New York: Ballantine Books, 1961), p. 80.
† C. Wright Mills, *Listen, Yankee* (New York: Ballantine, 1960), p. 111.
‡ *Revolución*, May 9, 1959.

they grow older. Castroism was most amorphous in its origins and has become more and more dogmatic as it has grown older. Sartre and others were deceived into thinking that an aversion for ideology was an essential characteristic of Castroism. An increasing need for and attraction to theory or ideology in certain chosen areas was necessary for Castroism's self-realization. And Sartre might also have found, if he had listened less and had been able to read more, that the Cubans were not so averse to theory even by March, 1960.

In the first few months of 1959, Castro himself frequently referred to ideology, not to exclude it, but to insist that whatever the ideology of his revolution might be, it was a *Cuban* ideology. He generally made this point in order to deny that the Cuban revolution was Communist in ideology. "Now anything which is not reactionary is Communist," he complained on May 5 of that year. "Every people has the right to its own ideology. The Cuban revolution is as Cuban as our music."* Or, as he put it three days later: "When we say that our revolution is not Communist, when we show that our ideals do not belong to Communist doctrine, that the revolution is original, that it has its own philosophy, completely its own, that it is Cuban and entirely American, why then is there this determination to accuse our revolution of being something which it is not?"† In this period, in effect, he counterposed Communism and Cubanism as if one could not be compatible with the other. But when he tried in the same speech to define what this peculiarly Cuban ideology or philosophy was, he could do no better than: "We offer men not only bread but also liberty, and that is our ideological position." A careful reading of Castro's early speeches in 1959 would reveal all or most of the essential ideas later formulated by Guevara,

* *Revolución*, May 6, 1959.
† *Ibid.*, May 9, 1959.

such as the necessity for guerrilla warfare and the role of the peasantry. But they were hidden in the maze of Castro's stream-of-consciousness oratory, and did not emerge clearly until Guevara had put them together in some systematic and coherent fashion.

Birth of a Theory

Guevara began this task in January, 1959, the first month of the revolution in power. His first important theoretical effort came in a talk to a Communist-controlled "united front" cultural organization in Havana, Nuestro Tiempo (Our Time), at the end of the month.*

On this occasion, Guevara chose to sketch the political development of Castro's movement from the time that he had joined it, in Mexico, in 1955. In that period, he re-called, the social views of the group in training for the in-vasion had been such that, when he had once expressed the necessity for presenting a "revolutionary program" to the Cuban people, one of the Moncada survivors had ob-jected that it was necessary only to overthrow Batista and take power. Even in the Sierra Maestra, the members of the group were "for a long time" merely tolerant of each other's views, not politically "integrated." Little by little, however, the reserve of the local peasants toward the guerrillas had broken down; they began to be incorporated into the guer-rilla force; and "thus our army of civilians was transformed into a peasant army." With this change in the composition of the guerrilla force, Guevara averred, the "great magic words" Agrarian Reform surged forth.

Another turning point, according to Guevara, was the abortive strike in April, 1958. The first steps "to give a theory and a doctrine to the revolution began in the Rebel

* The Communist control of this organization was clearly brought out at the trial of the informer Marcos Rodríguez, in March, 1964.

Army" after this setback. In the next few months, "we were fully identified as a peasant movement closely linked with the land and with the agrarian reform as our banner." Guevara described the peasant as "the invisible collaborator" who did what the guerrillas could not do, such as providing information about the enemy and carrying urgent messages. In other passages, he referred to the "coalescence of the [guerrilla] leaders and the peasant masses" and to the "restructuring of the Rebel Army [into] an armed body of peasants and workers, many of them illiterate, uneducated, and technically untrained." In this talk, he also introduced the idea that "a small group of men," definitely supported by the people and without fear of death, could defeat a regular, disciplined army. And he concluded that "the revolution is not limited to the Cuban nation," that it was the first of a series of similar Latin American revolutions.*

Guevara's second noteworthy theoretical contribution appeared the following month, on February 19, in the form

---

* "Proyecciones Sociales del Ejército Rebelde," *Humanismo*, January–April, 1959, pp. 346–57. The talk was delivered on January 27, 1959; it is reprinted in Selser, *op. cit.*, pp. 427–36. This was, in its essentials, the same story told by Guevara in his article "Notes for the Study of the Ideology of the Cuban Revolution," originally published in *Verde Olivo*, October 8, 1960, pp. 10–14, most of it translated in *Studies on the Left*, I, No. 3 (1960), 75–78, the only version I have seen. In this article, Guevara described the pre-"Granma" mentality as "blind confidence in a rapid popular explosion, enthusiasm and faith in the power to liquidate the Batista regime by a swift, armed uprising combined with spontaneous revolutionary strikes, and the subsequent fall of the dictator." He definitely dated the entrance of the *campesinos* into the guerrilla war as coming after the early setback of the "Granma" invaders, which would be sometime in 1957. He then attributed the increasing role of the peasantry to two events: the "antagonism that the city people, who comprised the central guerrilla group, felt towards the *campesinos* was erased"; and the peasants lost their distrust of the guerrillas and decided to take refuge with them owing to "the bestialities of the army and all the persecution." He noted, however, that these two factors were "hardly important in terms of the number of combatants, but of great psychological value." Guevara seems to suggest that a more humane and sympathetic army policy toward the Sierra Maestra peasants, caught in the middle, might have deprived the guerrillas of much peasant support.

of an article entitled "What Is a 'Guerrilla Fighter'?" In it he came closer to what was to become his main theme.

Unlike the rest of the world, he began, only in Cuba had the term *"guerrillero,"* which at this time he used in preference to *"guerrilla,"* taken on "a repulsive meaning," owing to the guerrilla forces which had fought for Spanish rule in the nineteenth century. The truth, Guevara went on, was just the opposite—the *guerrillero* was "the fighter for liberty *par excellence,* the elect of the people, the latter's fighting vanguard in the struggle for liberation."

Thus Guevara's first exposition of guerrilla warfare took the form of defining and glorifying the aims and methods of the guerrilla. He proceeded to set forth his own ideas in the guise of correcting existing misconceptions. Guerrilla warfare was not limited to a small minority; the guerrilla fighter was rather the "armed vanguard" of the whole people. Guerrilla warfare required a new kind of discipline, extreme mobility, absolute knowledge of the terrain. The guerrilla fighter was a "social reformer," dedicated to the destruction of existing institutions. Because guerrilla warfare was most effective in "rural and little populated" areas, where the people's demands were almost exclusively for a "change in the social composition of the ownership of the land," the guerrilla fighter was "fundamentally and, before all else, an agrarian revolutionary." His "fighting banner" was agrarian reform, which Guevara here defined as the interpretation of the "desires of the great peasant mass to be owner of the land, owner of their means of production, of their animals, of all for which they have fought for years, of that which constitutes their lives and will also be their graves." Finally, Guevara hinted that the days of the 26th of July Movement might be numbered and that it would soon exhaust its usefulness. He did this by saying that the "historic mission" of the 26th of July Movement was to complete the agrarian reform, after which it would "perhaps have given up the reason for its existence." As usual, Guevara was a step ahead of events.*

This talk and this article early in 1959 clearly show that Guevara had come out of the Sierra Maestra with the rudiments of a theory. It was not yet an official or commonly accepted theory even in the 26th of July Movement, in which it was still possible to dispute whether the Rebel Army or the underground resistance had done most to achieve the victory.† This dispute, however, was by no means exclusively historical. It was intimately related to the more immediate struggle that took place in 1959 within the 26th of July Movement between the political representatives of the former guerrilla forces and the former underground resistance. As Guevara later admitted, the latter had revealed even during the fighting "a certain opposition to a *caudillo,* which they feared in Fidel, and to the 'militaristic' fraction which the people of the Sierra represented."‡ When the anti-*caudillo* and anti-militaristic resistance wing was politically and, in some instances, physically crushed by the end of 1959, it was necessary to denigrate the role that the resistance had played in the past. Thus, Guevara's little book *Guerrilla Warfare* celebrated the Castroite victory in two civil wars—one against Batista and the other against the civil, democratic wing of the 26th of July Movement.

Guerrilla Warfare

Guevara's book appears to be a practical handbook on the tactics, organization, and technical problems of guer-

---

* *Revolución,* February 19, 1959. The article was republished in *Temas en torno a la Revolución* (Havana: Editorial Tierra Nueva, 1959), pp. 67–73.

† This dispute was still voiced openly in March, 1960, to Sartre, *op. cit.,* pp. 52–53. By August of that year, the official line had hardened in favor of the Rebel Army and in this form was passed on by Mills, *op. cit.,* pp. 46–49.

‡ "Un Año de Lucha Armada," *Verde Olivo,* January 5, 1964, p. 33.

rilla warfare. But it is more than that. It also contains a revolutionary theory, which is all that concerns us here. Indeed, the theory is presented in the very first paragraphs, though a number of other theoretical points may be found scattered elsewhere in the text. Some of the key theoretical passages are taken word for word from Guevara's own article of February, 1959, of which the book in this respect is only an amplification.

Guevara's first sentence is a claim of theoretical ascendancy and a challenge to revolutionary competitors. "The armed victory of the Cuban people," he announces, has been nothing less than "a modifier of old dogmas about the conduct of the popular masses of Latin America, and has clearly demonstrated the capacity of the people to free themselves from a government that oppresses them by means of guerrilla warfare." A crucial word in this sentence is "modifier" ("*modificador*"), which I have translated literally because it best conveys Guevara's thought that the Cuban revolution did not create a new theory but only modified an old one.* But what and whose are the "old dogmas"? Guevara prefers to leave these questions unanswered. It is not too much to assume, however, that his more knowledgeable readers understood that he meant the "old dogmas" formerly held by, among others, the old-time Cuban Communists and still held by the old-time Latin American Communist leaders. In effect, Guevara implied that Castroism had come to "modify" the traditional tactics of the Communist movement, not to supplant it altogether.

Unlike Castro, Guevara rarely wastes words. In substance, the whole theory is set forth in the second sentence: "We consider that these are the three fundamental con-

---

* Guevara, *La Guerra de Guerrillas*, p. 11. Of the two existing English translations, the only one worth using is that by J. P. Morray, published by the Monthly Review Press, in 1961, but it is far from being without fault, and I would advise anyone seriously interested in the subject to consult the original. I have made my own translations in order to get as close to the original as possible.

tributions which the Cuban revolution has made to the mechanics [*mecánica*] of the revolutionary movements in America:

"1. Popular forces can win a war against the army.

"2. It is not always necessary to wait for all the conditions for a revolution to exist; the insurrectional focal point [*foco*] can create them.

"3. In underdeveloped America, the countryside must be fundamentally the locale of the armed struggle."*

Theoretically, the rest of the book is little more than an elaboration of these three points. Guevara hastens to tell us that the first two points "make war on" the "quiescent attitude" of "revolutionaries or pseudo revolutionaries" who refuse to fight against a professional army unless they have all the "necessary objective and subjective conditions." Who are these "revolutionaries or pseudo revolutionaries"? Again, Guevara restrains himself. No doubt they are closely related to those who, we have just been told, hold onto "old dogmas." In any event, it is well to keep in mind not only what Guevara says but against whom he says it.

Unexpectedly, Guevara at this point backtracks a little (and has probably regretted it ever since). Without "a minimum of the necessary factors," he cautions, the "focal point" of guerrilla warfare cannot be set up. That minimum is a popular recognition of the "impossibility"† of struggling

* Here again I have preferred a more literal translation, even if it seems somewhat awkward, to get closer to the original sense. Morray translates *"mecánica"* as "conduct," for which there is a perfectly good Spanish word (*conducta*) that Guevara could have used if he had wanted to do so. It may well be that Guevara deliberately chose "mechanics" instead of "conduct" in order to suggest that there was less basic change. More important perhaps, Morray translates *"el foco insurreccional"* simply as "the insurrection," for which there is also a perfectly exact Spanish equivalent (*insurrección*) that Guevara did not choose to use here. By using *"foco,"* Guevara refers specifically to the small guerrilla force, which may be only a part of the insurrection as a whole.

† Here Morray translates Guevara's term *"imposibilidad"* as "futility." It is hard to understand why Guevara would not have used the word *"futilidad"* or *"inutilidad"* if he had meant "futility." By changing "impos-

for social objectives by peaceful political methods. To make his meaning doubly clear, Guevara emphasizes: "Where a government has assumed power through some form of consulting the people, fraudulent or not, and maintains at least an appearance of constitutional legality, it is impossible to bring about a guerrilla uprising, inasmuch as the possibilities of peaceful political struggle have not been exhausted." In order to make war on the government of Venezuela, however, the Castroist movement has had to violate this clear injunction. Instead of waiting for the Venezuelan Government to give up even the "appearance of constitutional legality," it has striven to make the reality of constitutional legality appear impossible. The explanation for this inconsistency is probably twofold: Castroism has encouraged guerrilla warfare elsewhere in Latin America not according to its own precepts but according to the cadres which it happens to have in various countries; and as Castroism has become a more and more extremist expression of Communism, it has tended in practice to revert to the pre-1935 "ultra-leftist" Communist policy which made the liberal and social-democratic left the "main enemy."

The third point, as Guevara develops it, is another implied thrust at the "pseudo revolutionaries." The primacy of the countryside, he admonishes, "must be given heed by those who seek, in a dogmatic way, to center the struggle of the masses in urban movements," which happened to be the strongholds of the traditional Latin American Communist movements. Guevara's reason, however, for preferring the countryside to the city is of a purely practical nature—the greater difficulty of carrying on an armed struggle in the cities. Once he has posited the necessity of

---

sibility" to "futility," Morray has subtly altered the exact meaning in such a way as to make Guevara's concession to even the appearance of constitutionalism less extreme and thereby less embarrassing.

armed struggle, Guevara's entire analysis rests on the conditions best suited for it.

Thus, Guevara does not derive guerrilla warfare from the nature of an agrarian revolution; he derives the agrarian revolution from guerrilla warfare. The central concept is guerrilla warfare, and the role of the peasantry follows from it for, so to speak, technical or pragmatic reasons. His line of reasoning may be summed up as follows: Guerrilla fighters must operate in the most sparsely settled, rough, mountainous terrain; this terrain coincides with the most backward, rural areas; in these areas, it is a matter of life or death for the guerrillas to gain the support of the local inhabitants, who are, of necessity, peasants; to win them over, the guerrillas must promise them "agrarian reform," which at this stage means giving them what they want—their own land. If guerrillas could operate effectively in nonpeasant territory, the whole line of reasoning would break down.

Who and what is the "guerrilla fighter"? As in the February, 1959, article, Guevara calls him "above all an agrarian revolutionary." But this does not mean that he is a peasant himself. In one place, Guevara describes him as "a sort of guiding angel who has fallen into the zone, always to help the poor and to bother the rich as little as possible in the first period of the development of the war." These "guiding angels" are soon identified as the "directors" (*"directores"*), or leaders, who have initiated the guerrilla war. The "directors," Guevara says, "are not men who have bent their backs day after day furrowing the soil; they are men who understand the necessity for changes in the social treatment of the peasants but the great majority of whom have not suffered the bitter experience of this treatment." Guevara then makes a clear distinction between the "directors" and the "people," who at a later stage join the struggle. As he explains it, the "directors" first set in motion the "people"; then the "people" make the "directors" progressively more revolutionary by making them conscious of the necessity for agrarian reform. That in Cuba the "directors" had not been peasants or workers was elsewhere made clear by Guevara: "None of us, none of the first group who came in the 'Granma,' who established ourselves in the Sierra Maestra, and learned to respect the peasant and worker while living with them, had a worker's or peasant's background."*

How many guerrillas are necessary? Guevara answers that thirty to fifty are enough to initiate an armed struggle in any Latin American country, though only twelve did so in Cuba. In mid-1959, Castro once reduced the minimum figure to twenty.† This number has a direct bearing on the whole theory because, if so few are needed, guerrilla warfare can be started without delay and without initial mass support. The theory does not say that the guerrillas do not need mass support; on the contrary, Guevara insists that the guerrilla is only the "armed nucleus" and "fighting vanguard" of the people; the guerrilla struggle can be won only by giving an impetus to and becoming part of a "mass struggle." The cutting edge of the theory, however, concerns the problem of where, when, and by whom to *begin* an insurrection. The Castro-Guevara thesis in its most original and extreme form says: everywhere, at any time, and by a minimum number. Instead of waiting for the right "subjective" conditions, that is, the revolutionary organization and activity of the masses, the insurrectional *foco,* made up initially of a few handfuls of nonpeasant, non-working-class guerrillas, can "create" them. Given the necessary "objective" conditions, the "to be or not to be" of the entire Castroist revolution becomes the existence of a small guerrilla force, a desideratum so modest and attainable that it seems possible for a few young men to make a revolution just by deciding to fight and die for it.

* *Obra Revolucionaria,* September 16, 1960, p. 21.
† *Revolución,* May 6, 1959.

And so, step by step, Guevara worked out a theory whereby a few middle-class guerrilla fighters became "agrarian revolutionaries," and the revolution as a whole became, at least until 1960, "fundamentally agrarian," albeit with the support of the workers, the middle class, and even industrialists.*

How "original" was this theory? The revolutionary role of the peasantry was certainly not discovered by Guevara or Castro. It had been present in Lenin's thought as far back as 1907, and later became one of Mao Tse-tung's cardinal tenets. But for Lenin, the "peasant revolution" had not lived a life of its own; sometimes he viewed it as a form of the larger "bourgeois-democratic" revolution, sometimes as an adjunct of the "proletarian revolution," and always under the leadership of the proletariat. Mao, it seems, was first impressed by the leading role of the poor peasantry but later brought his teachings into line with more orthodox Leninist doctrine.† In Guevara's book, however, there is never any mention of a "bourgeois-democratic" phase of the revolution or of proletarian leadership. Guevara's leaders are clearly of bourgeois origin but they supposedly succeed in sinking themselves into the peasantry. In this respect, it appears, Guevara's "agrarian revolution" is either an incomplete or immature version of Lenin's and Mao's, or goes far beyond them.

Guevara's theory, however, strikingly resembles Mao's on two points—the primacy of the countryside as the most favorable revolutionary terrain, and the necessity for guerrilla warfare. Yet, as I have already mentioned, Guevara in particular has gone to some pains to establish that the Cubans were not indebted to Mao or to anyone else for

---

* This definition of the revolution as a whole was written by Guevara in an appendix early in 1960. The main body of the book was written in 1959.

† Arthur A. Cohen, *The Communism of Mao Tse-tung* (Chicago: The University of Chicago Press, 1964), pp. 29–53, has a most lucid discussion of this point.

these ideas. In an introduction to a Cuban edition of a book by General Vo Nguyên Giap, Defense Minister of North Vietnam, published at the end of 1964, Guevara did not fail to observe: "Cuba, without knowing these writings, nor others of the same kind which have related the experiences of the Chinese revolution, started out on the road of its liberation by similar methods, with the success that today is visible to all."* If the Cubans recognize the similarities, they still insist that they took the same road as the Chinese and North Vietnamese unwittingly and, therefore, without direct indebtedness. Guevara once made the same point about Marxism in general, as if the Cubans had also rediscovered its "roads" all by themselves.† The implication seems to be that Castroism may not have brought anything very new into the world, but it has gone its own way in the past and, inferentially, intends to do so in the future.

An "Agrarian Revolution"?

Guevara's theory, however, may be more useful for the problems it raises than for the problems it solves.

At best, and on its own terms, the theory of the "agrarian revolution" applies to only a single phase of the Cuban revolutionary process. This process began, according to the official Castroite version, at least as early as 1953, with the attack on the Moncada army post. For the next three years, there was admittedly no contact with the peasantry at all. The first peasant officially to join the guerrilla force in the Sierra Maestra was Guillermo García, in December, 1956.‡

* Comandante Ernesto Che Guevara, Introduction to General Vo Nguyên Giap, *Guerra del pueblo, ejército del pueblo* (Havana: Editora Política, 1964). The introduction was also published in *Revolución*, November 23, 1964.

† *Obra Revolucionaria*, August 25, 1960, p. 14.

‡ Juan Hidalgo, "Guillermo García: El primer campesino que se unió a Fidel en la Sierra Maestra," *Hoy*, July 21, 1963.

The reinforcements sent from Santiago de Cuba to the Sierra Maestra in March, 1957, were urban products, not peasants. Thereafter, for several more months, the peasant recruits increased slowly. According to Castro, the peasants "made our victory certain" by March, 1958, when the rebel force numbered 160 men with arms.* It may be assumed, then, that the peasant influx into the Rebel Army took place toward the end of 1957 or the beginning of 1958. But the influx was never very great. Castro has said that he had 300 men with arms in May, 1958, and that the "decisive battles" of the war were fought with "fewer than 500 armed men."† In his January, 1959, talk, Guevara himself implied that the guerrilla fighters had not fully identified themselves with the peasants until after the April, 1958, strike failure, only nine months from the end of the war.

In terms of the guerrilla force, then, the "agrarian revolution" did not gather much momentum until 1958. And by the middle of 1960, according to Guevara, industrialization had superseded agrarian reform as the main objective of the Castro regime, as a result of which "the peasants have fully completed the first historic stage," giving way, in effect, to the proletariat as the leading class in the revolution.‡ Thus, Guevara's "agrarian revolution" on its own showing can account for only about two and a half or three years out of at least seven. It is so wedded to guerrilla warfare that it seems irrelevant for the period before and after. At best, it is a theory of a portion or a phase of the Cuban revolution, not of the whole.

But even in this modified form, its validity may be questioned.

There is clearly a vast difference between the proportion of peasants in Castro's guerrilla force and the proportion of guerrillas in the Cuban peasantry. Even if the proportion

* *Revolución*, February 25, 1959.
† *Ibid.*, July 27, 1963.
‡ *Obra Revolucionaria*, June 16, 1960, p. 4.

of peasants in his guerrilla force was relatively large, the proportion of guerrillas in the Cuban peasantry was extremely small. There were 50,000 peasants in the Sierra Maestra alone, and at least 500,000 agricultural workers in all of Cuba. Besides the 500 or so peasants that may have fought with the guerrillas in the very last stage, there were some thousands more who helped the guerrilla cause in one form or another. Still, Castro's active peasant backing was so limited in terms of the peasantry or agricultural population as a whole that it can hardly serve to support the theory of an "agrarian revolution." Much more to the point than the proportion of peasants among the revolutionists would be the proportion of revolutionists among the peasantry.

Moreover, most of the peasant recruits came from the Sierra Maestra region and were, therefore, atypical and unrepresentative of the agricultural population. The *montuno* was notoriously the poorest, the most backward, the most illiterate of the Cuban peasants. He knew almost nothing, wrote the Castroite geographer Antonio Núñez Jiménez, "of the progress of the modern era: no radio, no newspapers, no television, no motor transportation, no electricity," and scraped out "a backward and miserable life."*

Ironically, the peasantry of the Sierra Maestra did not mean by "agrarian reform" what it came to mean for Castro and Guevara. "Cooperatives" and "state farms" were the last things in these peasants' minds. They merely wanted to own the land that they worked on, no more and no less. Later, Guevara tried to set the record straight: "The soldiers that made up our first rural guerrilla army came from that part of this social class which shows its love for the land and its possession most aggressively, that is, which

---

* *Cuba con la mochila al hombro* (Havana: Ediciones Unión/Reportaje, 1963), pp. 120–21.

shows most perfectly the petty-bourgeois spirit; the *campe-sino* fights because he wants land; for himself, for his sons, to manage it, to sell it, and to enrich himself through his work."* Agrarian reform, Sierra Maestra-style, was little more than the primitive yearning of the peasantry for the land, hardly a world-shaking discovery. A true agrarian revolution would have been based not on the atypical minority of Sierra Maestra peasants but on the sugar and tobacco workers who constituted the much more numerous majority of the agricultural population.

A glance at the available statistics shows how atypical the Sierra Maestra peasantry was:

The agricultural population, according to the census of 1953, was divided into 596,800 farm laborers and 221,900 ranchers and farmers. Of the former, about 400,000 were sugar laborers, who worked for wages and were not attached to any particular piece of land. Of the latter, renters and sharecroppers accounted for 50–60 per cent and "squatters" (*precaristas*) for 8–10 per cent. Ever since 1937, the renters had been protected by special legislation. But the "squatters," without any title to the land which they occupied, were most vulnerable to eviction, and agrarian reform in the sense of giving them title to "their" lands, usually less than an acre, was most meaningful to them. Over four-fifths of all the "squatters" in Cuba were located in Oriente Province, and they particularly abounded in the Sierra Maestra region. Yet they constituted a very small percentage of the total agricultural population and even of the farming population attached to an individual piece of land, however large or small.†

Obviously, too, the social or political nature of a revolu-

* *Verde Olivo,* April 9, 1961, p. 25.

† The estimates for the renters and squatters are based on the 1946 agricultural census; no later ones seem available. The different forms of Cuban land tenure are described in Lowry Nelson, *Rural Cuba* (Minneapolis: The University of Minnesota Press, 1950), pp. 162–68.

tion does not derive solely from numbers, especially from the number of peasants in a guerrilla force that never amounted to more than a thousand. If numbers were all that mattered, Batista's army was also made up largely of peasants, and more of them. An agrarian revolution implies a peasant party, a peasant leadership, and a peasant ideology, none of which the Cuban revolution had. It had peasant participation and support for a limited time, mainly 1958, and in a limited place, mainly the Sierra Maestra and Sierra Cristal, in Oriente Province. There was no national peasant uprising. Outside the immediate vicinity of the guerrilla forces, revolutionary activity in the country as a whole was largely a middle-class phenomenon, with some working-class support but without working-class organizations.

By themselves, the "magic words" agrarian reform could not determine the social nature of the revolution because there is more than one kind of agrarian reform. The nature of a system determines the nature of the agrarian reform, not vice versa. In the Cuban case, the type of agrarian reform put into effect was admittedly not the type the peasants of the Sierra Maestra wanted or had been promised. To the extent that the peasants supported the revolution in the struggle for power, they did so for what proved to be the "wrong" reasons. Castro himself has told how he was riding in an airplane, after taking power, when it suddenly occurred to him that the Cuban agrarian reform should be based on "cooperatives," not on an independent, land-owning peasantry.* Even some of his closest associates were not prepared for the abrupt change of line, but once Castro had made up his mind, the "cooperatives" became the pride and proof of the "agrarian revolution."

I saw the first of these cooperatives when I traveled in Oriente Province in March–April, 1960. The two I visited

* *Revolución*, December 22, 1961.

were not yet in operation; only the housing had been built, and the little three-room houses seemed centuries removed from the traditional huts of the peasant *guajiros*. I wrote at that time that "for the poor illiterate, landless, outcast *guajiros*, the cooperatives represent a jump of centuries in living standards."*

These lines have been quoted again and again by pro-Castro writers, as if they were my last words on the subject. Since the cooperatives were not yet in operation, and it was still not even clear whether they would be real cooperatives or not, what I wrote about them in the spring of 1960 tells more about my state of mind than about the actual record of the cooperatives. I was more than willing, at first glance, to give the Castro regime the benefit of the doubt, even if events proved that I was, in this respect, too generous. I may have been at fault in judging the cooperatives too hastily, but it was surely not my fault that the peasants became "allergic" to them by the end of 1961 and that they had to be transformed into "state farms" by the summer of 1962.

In the end, the peasants helped Castro to make *his* revolution far more than he helped them to make *their* revolution. There was nothing comparable in Cuba to the classic peasant revolutionary movement led by Zapata in Mexico in 1910. Without a peasant party or leadership, Castro could turn the Cuban "agrarian revolution" on and off, or define it one way in 1958 and another way in 1959. On one occasion, however, Castro praised the peasantry in such a way as to reveal what he really thought of them: "The peasant possesses a virgin mentality, free from an assortment of influences which poison the intellects of citizens in the city. The revolution works on these fertile intellects as it works on the soil."† It was this "virgin mentality," which

---

* "The Runaway Revolution," *The Reporter,* May 12, 1960.
† *Obra Revolucionaria,* March 7, 1961, p. 24.

could be "worked on" and manipulated, not the peasants' active, driving political force, that made them most useful to Castro.

But it was not long before the Castro regime stopped paying even ceremonial compliments to the peasants' "fertile intellects." In the Second Declaration of Havana, a basic document promulgated by Castro in February, 1962, the peasants were downgraded as follows:

"But the peasantry is a class which, because of the illiterate state in which it is kept and the isolation in which it lives, needs the revolutionary and political leadership of the working class and the revolutionary intellectuals, without which it could not alone engage in the struggle and gain the victory." *

This was, in Castro's own words, the death knell of the theory of the "agrarian revolution." It was, of course, a product of the "Marxist-Leninist" phase of the revolution, but if true, it applied to the earlier phases as much as to the later ones.

The Working Class

But if it was not an "agrarian revolution," what was it? One of the few things on which everyone seems to agree is that it was not, at least as far as the conquest of power was concerned, a "proletarian revolution."

In this respect, the Cuban revolution differed significantly from the Russian and Chinese revolutions. The Russian proletariat was relatively small and weak, but at critical moments it probably played a role proportionately greater than its weight or importance in Russian society. In China, an almost nonexistent proletariat played an almost nonexistent role. In Cuba, however, the working class was proportionately much larger and stronger than it had been

* *Cuba Socialista*, March, 1962, p. 23.

in Russia or China. According to the last census, in 1953, 327,208 Cubans were economically active in "manufacturing," 395,904 in "services," 232,323 in "commerce," 104,-003 in transport—a total of 1,059,438—and only 818,906 in agriculture. The Cuban trade-union movement also suggests the relative importance of the working class; it claimed about 1,000,000 members, an unusually large number for a country of fewer than 6,000,000 people in 1953.

In Cuba, then, a relatively large working class played a relatively small role, unlike Russia, where a relatively small working class played a relatively large role, and unlike China, where a relatively small working class played a relatively small role.

The question arises why the Cuban working class played such a minor role in the pre-1959 struggle. For one reason, it had long been oriented toward trade unionism rather than politics, and the trade unions, whether led by Communists or anti-Communists, had over the years gained enough concessions and benefits to make their members a relatively privileged class. About 1956, moreover, the Cuban economy under Batista began an upward swing, and 1957—the first year of the guerrilla struggle in the Sierra Maestra—was one of the best years economically in Cuban history.* Thus arose another paradox of the Cuban revolution—it was won in conditions of relative prosperity rather than of stagnation or decline.

The Middle Class

Much of the controversy over the Cuban revolution has centered on the role of the middle class.

As I have already pointed out, even if the Rebel Army may have had a largely peasant rank and file in its last year

* "During 1957, Cuba's economic activity attained the highest level registered since the war" (Department of Economic and Social Affairs, *Economic Survey of Latin America 1957* [New York: United Nations, 1959], p. 177).

or so, there is no doubt that the revolutionary activity in the country as a whole was predominantly urban and middle class. As long as the Batista regime could claim the allegiance of, or at least acceptance by, the bulk of the middle and working classes, it could not be overthrown. The Moncada attack in 1953 was a signal failure for social as well as for military reasons; it was launched in a social vacuum which precluded the slightest practical repercussions. For months, the guerrillas in the Sierra Maestra were similarly isolated and contained without too much difficulty for much the same reason. The general strike of April 9, 1958, failed because only the workers and trade unions could carry it off, and the middle-class resistance movement futilely tried to substitute for them. The necessary condition for Batista's overthrow was the mass desertion of the middle class, and Castro's entire political strategy in 1957 and 1958 was designed to encourage and hasten this process. It was a far more successful strategy than his later disdain for the middle class would lead one to believe.

The odd thing is that before it became fashionable to say that Cuba was a backward, peasant country, the Communists used to hold that the trouble with Cuba was that it was such a middle-class country. As far back as 1941, the rising young Communist intellectual Carlos Rafael Rodríguez noted: "On the eve of the Soviet revolution, V. I. Lenin defined Russia as a 'petty-bourgeois country.' The same could be said of Cuba."* It has been estimated that from one-fifth to one-third of the total Cuban population belonged to the middle class before 1958.† The Cuban trade-union move-

* "Las Clases en la Revolución Cubana," *Fundamentos*, April, 1941, p. 41.
  † Gino Germani, "The Strategy of Fostering Social Mobility," in *Social Aspects of Economic Development in Latin America* (Paris: UNESCO, 1963), p. 228, estimated Cuba's population in the middle and upper "strata" at 22 per cent. This figure was exceeded only by Argentina, with 36 per cent. Others were Chile and Colombia, 22 per cent; Peru, 18 per cent; Brazil, 15 per cent. Carlos Manuel Raggi Ageo had previously estimated at least 33 per cent of the economically active Cuban population

ment was partially middle class in character because it organized white-collar personnel in commerce, banking, and other fields, who regarded themselves as middle class in other countries. As a rule, the more "middle class" the union, the stronger was the Communist influence in it, a notable example of which was the union of bank employees. The "middle-class mentality" of a considerable part of the Cuban working class was a commonplace, and as the Communists sadly admitted, the "petty-bourgeois parties" had had since 1933 the greatest influence over the masses.* As late as 1962, Blas Roca lamented that there had existed in Cuba "a very numerous petty bourgeoisie and that the petty-bourgeois spirit infected even certain categories of workers and employees."† A considerable part of the 818,906 listed as agricultural in occupation in 1953 was upper or middle class in social and economic status, since about a quarter of the total consisted of owners and renters of farms. Cuba ranked high in typically middle-class possessions: 1 automobile for every 39 inhabitants (in Argentina, 1 for every 60; in Mexico, 1 for every 91; in Brazil, 1 for every 158), and 1 radio for every 5 inhabitants (second only to Argentina, with 1 for every 3). Cuban tourists used to spend more in the United States than American tourists spent in Cuba.

Until Guevara's book set a new official line, it was not considered particularly reprehensible in Cuba to stress the role of the middle class in the struggle against Batista as long as Castro's guerrilla force in the mountains was not neglected or underestimated. One effect, and perhaps one intent, of the theory of the "agrarian revolution" was to make all other theories "counterrevolutionary," and any-

---

in the middle class ("Contribución al estudio de las clases medias en Cuba," *Materiales para el estudio de la clase media en la América Latina* (Washington, D.C.: Pan American Union, 1950), II, 79.

* Blas Roca, *Fundamentos*, May, 1950, p. 772.

† *Cuba Socialista*, January, 1962, p. 50.

one who dared to murmur that the middle class might have had something to do with the revolution soon found himself denounced as *ipso facto* a reactionary.

If giving the middle class some credit for the revolution was reactionary, then the official Cuban Communists were among the worst reactionaries. All through 1959, they emphasized the role of the middle class and, in part, the upper class. At first, the determining factor for them was the "class character" of the government that came into power in January, 1959. According to the chief Party spokesman, Blas Roca, the power had "passed into the hands of the petty bourgeoisie and national bourgeoisie"—the latter, in Communist terminology, Cuban industrialists not dependent on or subservient to the United States.* In October, 1959, Blas Roca continued to take the line that the "most advanced elements of the radical sector of the petty bourgeoisie" still exercised "the hegemony of the revolution."† As late as June, 1960, Juan Marinello wrote: "It was clear that the triumphant revolution was directed by the 'radicalized' urban petty bourgeoisie—students, members of the liberal professions—with important participation by the national bourgeoisie, which was not compromised with imperialism, and strong intervention by the peasantry and proletariat."‡

By "the most advanced elements of the radical sector of the petty bourgeoisie" and the "'radicalized' urban petty bourgeoisie," Blas Roca and Marinello could only have meant, in the circumstances of late 1959 or mid-1960, Castro and his main associates. These formulas were, for the orthodox Communists, the highest praise that they could bestow on those with Castro's social background. The Communists had evidently not been impressed by Guevara's theoretical

* *Fundamentos*, February, 1959, p. 44.
† *Hoy*, October 7, 1959.
‡ *Démocratie Nouvelle* (organ of the French Communist Party), June, 1960, p. 67.

alchemy which had transformed the guerrilla leaders into "peasant revolutionaries."

The Question of "Exceptionalism"

The question that troubled and divided the Cuban Communists in 1959 was whether the Cuban revolution had conformed to the orthodox "Marxist-Leninist" doctrine or had been an "exception" to the prescribed rules. As Blas Roca later revealed, the "exceptionalists" had been strong enough to constitute a "tendency" within the Party, and two months had been spent in discussion before the problem was temporarily settled at the Party's Plenum in May of that year.*

An early attempt to find a solution was made by Aníbal Escalante, long the Communists' leading theorist. At the first post-Batista Plenum, toward the end of January, 1959, Escalante somewhat daringly asserted: "Rather than following the classic revolutionary road, the Cuban revolution has followed the 'road' according to which the movement began and developed in the far-off countryside and finally enveloped the cities, particularly the capital. In this experience, which broke with pre-established dogmas and rules, the vision of Fidel Castro and his general staff soared highest; it is similarly necessary to recognize the role unquestionably played by the Partido Socialista Popular to open the way for the 'Chinese road.' "† Curiously, then, it was Escalante and not Guevara who had first suggested that the Cuban "road" was related to the Chinese, though Castro and Guevara may not have appreciated Escalante's anxiety to claim so much credit for the PSP. Castro was at this time busy insisting that the Cuban revolution was not like

* *Hoy,* October 9, 1959, p. 7. A "plenum" was a conference of the entire Communist leadership, somewhat smaller, of shorter duration, and held more frequently, than a "congress."

† *Ibid.,* January 28, 1959, p. 4.

any other, and Guevara liked to remind people that the Cubans had never known of the "Chinese road" before taking power. In any case, Escalante may have rubbed important people the wrong way, because he was replaced as editor of the Communist organ *Hoy* by Carlos Rafael Rodríguez in April, 1959.

A striking example of the Communists' failure to anticipate Castro's policies and their willingness to adapt themselves to whatever they proved to be occurred in these first months of the regime. On February 27, 1959, the Communist top leadership adopted an eight-point program of agrarian reform which relegated "cooperatives" to eighth and last place. Even at that, it referred to them in this highly tentative form: "To promote the tendencies toward the creation of agrarian cooperatives, providing facilities and state aid to these institutions." But, as if this might be going too far, it added: "To try to impose agricultural cooperatives right now would be an error."*

Less than three months later, on May 17, Castro made "cooperatives" the cornerstone of his "agrarian reform." The following week, the Communists held their second Plenum that year. The document that resulted from the Plenum did not say that Castro's decision had been an "error." On the contrary, it came out in support of the May 17th program "without reservations."† For the Communists, in effect, the issue of cooperatives was somewhat like the earlier issue of violence—they agreed in principle but had disagreed in the timing. Once they decided to hitch their wagon to Castro's star, they would not permit another tactical difference to separate them.

At the May, 1959, Plenum, too, the first full-scale Communist theory of the Cuban revolution was unveiled, and it was clearly indebted to the Chinese Communist anal-

---

* "Resolución del Buró Ejecutivo del Partido Socialista Popular," *Hoy*, March 4, 1959, pp. 1 and 3.

† "Conclusiones del Pleno del Comité Nacional del Partido Socialista Popular" (May 25–28, 1959), *Hoy*, June 7, 1959, p. 8.

ogy. It borrowed from Mao Tse-tung the concept of the "four-class" bloc or alliance, made up of the middle class, peasants, workers, and national bourgeoisie, though not always in that order. It presented a catch-all formula of the Cuban revolution as "an advanced popular revolution, a patriotic, democratic, national-liberationist, and agrarian revolution," the beauty of which was that it had something for almost everybody. The Rebel Army received credit for having been the "fundamental factor" in the overthrow of Batista. But it could not have triumphed without "the support of the immense majority of the Cuban people." The armed struggle had been "nourished" by workers, especially agricultural workers, elements of the petty bourgeoisie and the great mass of poor peasants, but "the most radical sector of the petty bourgeoisie took the initiative and directed both the armed struggle and the subsequent course of the revolution." To display their orthodoxy, however, the Communists defended the honor of the Cuban proletariat as "the most consistent and profoundly revolutionary class of existing Cuban society"—unfortunately prevented by circumstances from demonstrating in action how revolutionary it was. They admitted that the Cuban revolution had been marked by certain "peculiarities"— the defeat of a professional army by a guerrilla force; the principal role played by armed struggle since 1957 and the merely auxiliary role of mass, urban activity, such as strikes; the directing role of the "most radical sector of the petty bourgeoisie" instead of the most radical sector of the proletariat; and the movement of the revolution, "as of the Chinese or the Cuban of 1895," from the countryside to the cities, from the provinces to the capital. But they warned against "exaggerating" these peculiarities.*

These pro-Soviet Cuban Communists permitted them-

---

* This Plenum was held May 25–28, 1959. The main resolution was published in *Hoy*, June 7, 1959. Two of the key sections may also be found in Blas Roca, *29 artículos sobre la Revolución Cubana* (Havana, 1960), pp. 19–29.

selves to lean so heavily on Chinese Communist theory in 1959 because they were still blissfully unaware of the full scope and intensity of the Sino-Soviet conflict. In September, 1959, it was still possible for Blas Roca to write a eulogy on the "human warmth, wisdom, and sincerity" of Mao Tse-tung, and to defend the success of the Chinese "communes."* Two years later, Blas was basking in the glory of Nikita Khrushchev from whom he was separated only by Ho Chi Minh of North Korea in Red Square on the forty-fourth anniversary of the Bolshevik revolution.

But the problem of "exceptionalism" would not go away. On the Communist side, Aníbal Escalante continued to struggle with it, trying to find just the right formulas to reconcile the "old," but not too old, and the "new," but not too new, in the Cuban revolution.

In March, 1960, he attacked the idea of Cuban "exceptionalism" as a form of that old disease—"revisionism." Instead of invoking the "Chinese road," as he had done the year before, he now thought it wiser to recognize only a single road—"forward or backward." According to Marxist-Leninist doctrine, he reminded everyone, the revolution in a "backward capitalist society," such as Cuba, had to be "bourgeois democratic," not socialist. Moreover, the doctrine also said that the "hegemony" of the proletariat was necessary to go from the bourgeois-democratic stage to the socialist stage.

It was here that Escalante, theoretically, collided with Guevara. The latter had just put out a book in which he had demonstrated, to his satisfaction, that this had been and was an "agrarian revolution" and that the peasantry had played the leading role in it. Escalante contended, on the contrary, that the "radical petty bourgeoisie" still exercised "the hegemonic role," as of March, 1960, though he granted that the influence of the "workers' and peasants' alliance"

* *Hoy*, September 4, 1959.

had increased. Moreover, Escalante insisted, it was possible to get to socialism only through the hegemony of the proletariat, not the peasantry. "Without the hegemony of the proletariat," he expounded, "of proletarian ideas, doctrines, philosophy, there can be no socialism." Compared to Guevara's rather simple schema of the "agrarian revolution," Escalante's theoretical apparatus was infinitely more complex—a four-class "union," a two-class "alliance," a "bourgeois-democratic revolution," topped off by the "hegemony of the proletariat." Escalante conceded that one of the characteristics of the period was the "interweaving of the old and the new," a large part of the new being the proved worth of guerrilla warfare. But, in the end, he was most interested in reaching the following orthodox conclusion: "The Cuban revolution is a process in which, in our opinion, the Marxist-Leninist analysis and prognosis of historical development have been confirmed."[*]

Communist theory was never quite able to catch up with events. The theory was again put to the test at the Eighth Congress of the PSP, in August, 1960, as the United States and Cuba were rushing to a head-on collision and the confiscations had already begun. Still reflecting the old line, Blas Roca said, as if nothing had changed or was about to change, that Castro's government "represents and executes the policy of the coalition of the proletariat, the peasantry, the petty bourgeoisie, and the advanced sectors of the national bourgeoisie"—the four-class theory. He spoke of elections as if Castro intended to hold them soon. He counseled that private enterprises were still needed in Cuba, that no economic purpose would be served by nationalizing many more in the near future, and that some already taken over might perhaps have been better left alone. Aníbal Escalante warned that the "national bourgeoisie" was filled with "a

[*] "El Marxismo-Leninismo y la Revolución Cubana," *Fundamentos*, May, 1960, pp. 44–64. This was a lecture delivered on March 11, 1960.

strong fear of the revolutionary changes" and efforts had to be made to keep it in the revolutionary camp. "We maintain," he declared, "the strategy of the alliance of classes with which the revolution originated." Referring to the nationalization of the first U.S. properties, on August 6 of that year, he assured his listeners that "there are going to be few more." To be ready for anything, however, he took out some insurance policies—the present stage of the revolution did not have to be "in all cases necessarily prolonged," and it would not be "improper" to refer to the future socialist stage of the revolution in the Party program.

But at least two Communist leaders, Carlos Rafael Rodríguez and César Escalante, the younger brother of Aníbal, spoke in a more "Castroist" vein. Though they paid lip service to the official Party line, they were clearly impatient to get to a more "advanced" stage of the revolution without and against the bourgeoisie. Rodríguez could only bring himself to admit that the small employers and medium merchants could still be useful, and César Escalante significantly omitted the "national bourgeoisie" from the "bloc" supporting the revolution. In the end, the Congress voted a resolution which said diplomatically that the revolution "objectively serves the historic interests of the working class, the peasants, the urban petty bourgeoisie, and the national bourgeoisie," but that "its motor forces and its leaders are, at present, workers, poor and medium peasants, and the radical wing of the urban petty bourgeoisie."*

Two months later, on October 13, the Castro regime nationalized 376 all-Cuban enterprises, and on October 24, 166 properties owned wholly or partially by U.S. interests. In a matter of days, virtually the entire Cuban bourgeoisie was wiped out. Later, the "socialist" stage of the revolution was traced back to October 13, 1960,† though Castro did

* Partido Socialista Popular, *VIII Asamblea Nacional*, pp. 92–93, 96, 177–80, 230–31, 242, 244–46, 321, 368, 423.

† Lionel Soto, *Cuba Socialista*, November, 1961, p. 29.

not officially baptize it as such until April 16, 1961. And at about this time, the decision was probably made to fuse Castroism and Communism organizationally. The youth divisions of the PSP and the 26th of July Movement were merged on October 28, 1960.

It is hard to believe that the PSP's Eighth Congress, its last, would have included the "national bourgeoisie" among the classes whose historic interests the revolution was still serving if the Communist leaders had known what was coming or even suspected that it might come. By 1960, Castro and Guevara had given up all thought of an "alliance" with the "national bourgeoisie." Elsewhere in Latin America, however, the traditional Communist parties continued to advocate the same kind of tactical alignment that the Cuban Communists had, at least in theory, supported until the summer of 1960. After using the bourgeoisie so advantageously in its own conquest of power, Castroism changed its line and moved toward the position that the "national bourgeoisie" in Latin America was hopelessly "under the tutelage of imperialism."* In effect, Castroism in power liquidated the "national bourgeoisie" and then made the policy retroactive to apply to the struggle for power in Latin America as a whole.

Those who think that the Cubans have merely taken over Chinese Communist theory and practice would do well to ponder this—for Communists—vital difference in attitude toward the "national bourgeoisie." In Mao Tse-tung's doctrine, not only is the "national bourgeoisie" an essential element in the struggle for power but it is given a role to play in the new revolutionary state. Chinese Com-

---

* In an interview in Algeria, Guevara made a distinction between Africa and Latin America. "We think that the bourgeoisie in Africa has a role to play today," he told Mme. Josie Fanon of the publication *Révolution Africaine*. "This is very different from Latin America, where the national bourgeoisie already has no other way out than to put itself totally under the tutelage of imperialism" (see *Revolución*, December 23, 1964, for the Spanish text of this interview).

munist theorists have even made the claim that Mao's most original contribution to the post-Leninist theory of the Communist state is the inclusion of the "national bourgeoisie" in the revolutionary dictatorship, albeit with the real power safely lodged in the Communist Party.* In this respect, the traditional Latin American Communists, not the Castroists, have been following the Chinese Communist line. Or, to put it another way, Castroism has taken a far more extreme position vis-à-vis the "national bourgeoisie" than the Chinese Communists have ever done. In some ways, Castroism is more extreme than any existing Communist tendency, and even Mao Tse-tung might privately consider it a "leftist deviation."

Behind the Great Reconciliation

Whatever theoretical differences there may have been between the Castroists and Communists before October, 1960, a great reconciliation took place afterward. Now that "socialism" had come to Cuba, even if a little more quickly than they had expected or advised, the old-time Communists volunteered their services as the only real, certified experts on the subject. The Communists quietly buried the "bourgeois-democratic revolution," and Guevara unobtrusively interred the "agrarian revolution." The proletariat was promoted to the role of the leading class, and the peasantry was demoted to the role of its chief ally.

All through 1961, Fidel Castro was stricken with unwonted modesty. Though he had virtually dragged the old-time Communists into "socialism," he now spoke of them

* Cohen, *op. cit.*, pp. 74–104. It should be noted that the concept of "national bourgeoisie" was not original with Mao; the term was used by Stalin as early as 1925. Cohen seems to use "national bourgeoisie" interchangeably with "small capitalists" (p. 86). But he also quotes from an Indonesian Communist manifesto of 1954 that equates it with "entrepreneurs" (p. 92).

with a respect almost amounting to reverence. On February 1, 1961, the Italian Communist organ *L'Unità* published an interview with Castro in which for the first time he confessed that the Communists had been right to be distrustful of the guerrilla leaders in the Sierra Maestra because the latter had been "full of petty-bourgeois prejudices and defects." Aníbal Escalante was given a key command in the new united party, the preparatory phase of which was called the Organizaciones Revolucionarias Integradas (Integrated Revolutionary Organizations), better known as ORI. In his famous "I Am a Marxist" speech on December 2, 1961, Castro referred humbly to "Marinello, Carlos Rafael, Aníbal, Blas" as having been Communists twenty years earlier, when he had still been a political "illiterate" and his brother, Raúl, had just finished learning how to read and write. Castro's deep-seated feeling of political inadequacy came to the surface, and he in large part turned over Cuban "socialism" to the old-time "Socialistas," as the PSP-ers had also been known, until the purge of Aníbal Escalante, on March 26, 1962.

Despite the official transformation of the "bourgeois-democratic" into the "socialist" revolution, however, the problem of "exceptionalism" continued to perturb the Cuban leaders in 1961. The subject was tackled anew by both Guevara and Aníbal Escalante.

In April, 1961, Guevara published an important article entitled "Cuba—Historical Exception or Vanguard in the Anticolonial Struggle?" Guevara, however, did not mean the same thing by "exception" that the Cuban Communists had meant in their earlier discussions. For the latter, the question had been whether the Cuban revolution had been "exceptional" in terms of the accepted Marxist doctrine. For Guevara, the question was whether the Cuban revolution had been "exceptional" in terms of the conditions prevalent in Latin America as a whole. Guevara's article was, in essence, a polemic against other Latin American parties and leaders who did not think that the Cuban methods could or should be applied in their own countries. The exceptionalists, Guevara charged, were talking about the differences between the Cuban revolution and "the lines of other progressive parties in America," thereby taking the position that "the form and paths of the Cuban revolution are the unique product of the revolution, and that the historical transition of the peoples in the other countries will be different." In effect, this article was aimed mainly at the Latin American Communist leaderships that were still reluctant to adopt guerrilla warfare as their immediate tactical policy.

Guevara agreed that every revolution in Latin America was bound to have "peculiar characteristics." The Cuban revolution, in his view, had had three of them. The first was "that telluric force," Fidel Castro, whose personality was so "tremendous," Guevara said, that he would have assumed command of any movement in which he might have chosen to participate. The second was the weakness of U.S. policy, which, as Guevara put it, "was disoriented and could never assess the true dimensions of the Cuban revolution." But Guevara warned that other countries could not count on this good fortune because "imperialism, unlike some progressive groups, learns from its mistakes." And the third peculiarity was the character of the Cuban peasantry, which, in most places, had been "proletarianized" by the "large, semimechanized capitalist cultivation" of the land—an unusual admission that Cuban agriculture, whatever else may have been wrong with it, had not been as hopelessly backward as Castro liked to maintain. It was in this connection that Guevara referred to the peasants of the Sierra Maestra as the most petty-bourgeois–minded in

Cuba, intent only on owning their own land—an exception to the exception.*

But on the main issue, whether the "Cuban road" was the right and only one for the rest of Latin America, Guevara refused to budge. He maintained that the basic Cuban conditions prevailed everywhere else, and that they called for the same tactics as the Cubans had used. Having paid his respects to Cuba's "peculiar characteristics," he went on to repeat, in summary form, all his old arguments in favor of guerrilla warfare. He again argued that "armed struggle" was the only way to take power; that the conditions in the cities were unfavorable for armed struggle; that the only alternative was guerrilla warfare; that guerrilla warfare could be waged only in a relatively unpopulated, mountainous terrain; and that it was, therefore, necessary for the guerrillas to join forces with the peasant masses. Against those, either on the right or left, who said that the Cuban revolution was "unique and inimitable," Guevara exclaimed: "Falsehood of falsehoods, we say—the possibility of the triumph of the popular masses of Latin America is clearly expressed by the road of guerrilla struggle based on a peasant army, in the alliance of workers and peasants, in

---

* Guevara seems to ignore the contradiction into which he has driven himself. In order to justify the original "agrarian reform" of promising the peasants their own land in the traditional fashion, the land-hungry, "petty-bourgeois" peasants of the Sierra Maestra must be invoked. In order to justify the subsequent "collectivization," the great mass of "proletarianized" Cuban agricultural workers must be brought forward. But if the latter far outnumber the former, as Guevara agrees, why did not Castro's movement advocate "collectivization" rather than traditional "agrarian reform" before 1959? The answer is, of course, that "collectivization" would have given the game away, whereas "agrarian reform" is sufficiently vague to appeal to the largest number. In effect, Guevara advocates the *slogan* of "agrarian reform" in the struggle for power, and the *reality* of "collectivization" after the capture of power. Or, to put it another way, these are two forms of "agrarian reform" so different socially and politically that Guevara cannot make them represent the wishes of Cuba's landless agricultural population as a whole. His argument resembles a sleight-of-hand trick in which the audience is supposed to look at one sleeve while he is hiding something in the other.

the overthrow of the [regular] army in frontal battle, in the taking of the cities by way of the countryside, in the dissolution of the army as the first step in the total rupture of the superstructure of the former colonialist world."*

Thus Guevara came down heavily against "exceptionalism" in order to insist on Cuba as the "vanguard in the anticolonial struggle." Yet by this time the context had changed markedly: The stage of "agrarian revolution" had given way to the "socialist," "proletarian" stage of the revolution. In this article, Guevara used the term "peasant army," not "peasant revolution," but the peasants were, for him, still the crucial factors in the victory. More than ever, then, the logic of his position flowed less from the social or political nature of the revolution than from the practical or pragmatic requirements of the struggle for power. There was now, even more sharply, a basic ambiguity, which Guevara never tried to clarify, between the "agrarian revolution" of an agrarian class or party and the "agrarian revolution" of a nonagrarian class or party, for which the "agrarian revolution" was only a means to an end, a tactical "stage," a weapon in the struggle for power.

Whatever may have been his previous ups and downs, Aníbal Escalante emerged with greater authority than ever in 1961. He spoke and wrote, not merely as an old-time Communist, but in the name of the new united party and, to most Cubans, of the Castro regime. Yet close listeners and readers might have detected the undercurrents of a theoretical rivalry with Guevara.

In May, 1961, a month after the appearance of Guevara's article on "exceptionalism," Escalante delivered a televised talk on "The Development of the Revolution and

---

* *Verde Olivo,* April 9, 1961, pp. 22–29. On one occasion, however, Castro spoke of the Cuban revolution as if it might have been "unique" in its origins. In his speech against Aníbal Escalante, he referred to the "conditions 'sui generis'" of the Cuban revolution (*Revolución,* March 28, 1962). Consistency has never been one of Castroism's strong points.

the Role of the Revolutionary Forces." In his opening remarks, Escalante launched into a criticism of what he
called "a simple-minded conception of the revolution."
Whose conception was it? The conception of those who say,
Escalante informed his listeners, "that a revolution is any
change which is more or less produced by violence, and
which substitutes a popular order for an unpopular one,
a democratic order for an antidemocratic one." Escalante
went on: "There is even a distorted conception of the
revolution which says that revolution is any violent action
to seize power." What was Escalante's conception of the
revolution? In his most schoolmasterish manner, Escalante
recited the orthodox formula: "Revolution is, clearly, a
radical and profound change in the economic structure of
society," etc. Just what role violence did play he did not say.

Guevara, of course, had never said anything so *simplista*
about violence. He had always advocated violence as a
form of struggle for a political and social revolution, not in
and for itself. Yet Castro had once talked about a kind of
revolution not too much unlike a violent struggle for a
popular, democratic order against an unpopular, antidemocratic one. And, if Castro and Guevara did not say
that violence alone was the determining mark of a real
revolution, they did say that no real revolution was possible
without violence, that what distinguished revolutionaries
from pseudo revolutionaries was the advocacy and employment of violence. In effect, Escalante chose to denigrate the
place of violence in an abstract definition of revolution,
whereas Castro and Guevara preferred to emphasize the
need for violence in the concrete struggle for power. The
difference was, to say the least, significant.

On one point, however, Escalante was willing to admit
another old-time Communist miscalculation. He was still
sure that the Cuban revolution had been "bourgeois democratic" initially in January, 1959, but he conceded that it

had already changed character in May, 1959. Yet, in the orthodox fashion, he attributed the change not to the peasantry, as Guevara had done, but to the working class, which, he claimed, "had been, as a class, the leader."*

An equally revealing theoretical article by Escalante, entitled "The True Breeding Ground of Communism," was published about two months later, at the end of July, 1961, in *Verde Olivo,* the official organ of the Cuban armed forces, where Guevara's articles were usually to be found. Escalante's thought again took a polemical form, this time against those who said that poverty was mainly responsible for the growth of Communism. If this were so, Escalante argued, the revolutionary movement would be stronger in Turkey than in Italy, or in Saudi Arabia than in Greece, which as everyone knew, was not the case. Escalante was even indiscreet enough to cite Cuba as an example:

"In fact, Cuba was not one of the countries with the lowest standard of living of the masses in America but, on the contrary, one of those with the highest [standard-of-living] index, and it was here that the first great patriotic, democratic, and socialist revolution in the continent burst forth and the imperialist chain was first broken. If the historical development had been governed by the false axiom expressed above, the revolution should have been first produced in Haiti, Bolivia, Colombia, or even Chile, countries of greater poverty for the masses than the Cuba of 1952 or 1958."

In this way, Escalante raised that most difficult of problems—the historical causation of revolutions. If, as he maintained, "the broad poverty of the masses is a spur to the revolution, but it is not the fundamental and decisive factor," what was that factor? Escalante himself answered in this article that it was "the capitalist system itself," so full of contradictions, injustices and inequalities that "the domi-

* *Obra Revolucionaria,* May 25, 1961, especially pp. 3, 5, and 8.

nant classes, for various reasons, can no longer hold back the revolutionary upsurge or maintain power in their hands." If a "socialist" revolution could take place in Cuba, with one of the highest standards of living in Latin America, he reasoned, it could take place anywhere. And, therefore, he was also able to reject the idea that the Cuban revolution was "an exceptional phenomenon."*

And so Guevara and Escalante came to the same conclusion about Cuban "exceptionalism" in Latin America, but by somewhat different routes. For Guevara, the question was essentially tactical—whether the Cuban methods of guerrilla warfare could be successfully applied in the rest of Latin America. For Escalante, the question was so abstractly theoretical that his answer had little bearing on the issues which concerned Castro and Guevara the most. They were much less interested in whether capitalism, rather than poverty, was the true breeding ground of the revolution than whether the time had come to make the revolution immediately, everywhere in Latin America, by a few armed men taking the initiative. And, to the extent that they were interested in Escalante's problem, they tended to handle it differently. While Escalante rightly pointed out Cuba's relatively advanced development, Castro and Guevara preferred to base their propaganda on Cuba's "underdevelopment," as if it were an absolute, applicable to the country *in toto.*

Another aspect of "exceptionalism" was touched on by Guevara at about this time. Soon after the Bay of Pigs, at the height of the Cuban euphoria, Guevara explained why Cuba had to be immune to the Soviet infection of Stalinism:

"There is no danger that we shall simply copy the Soviet Union slavishly, or that we shall slide towards what you call

* "El Verdadero Caldo de Cultivo del Comunismo," *Verde Olivo,* July 30, 1961, pp. 15–17.

Stalinist totalitarianism, for the good reason that the conditions which exist in Cuba are not the same as those in
Stalin's Russia. Stalinism was a historical phenomenon
provoked by the capitalist encirclement of the U.S.S.R. and
by the consequent necessity to create, by its own unaided
efforts, the basic industries required for its economic development and defence. Our situation is quite different.
We do not need to make such sacrifices to industrialize
because we can get all we want from the other Socialist
countries. For us, industrialization is a good thing which
will bring immediate benefits to the population and which
will enable us to liquidate unemployment, the chronic
scourge of Latin America. In addition, we have no agricultural problems. The creation of cooperatives has not only
aroused no resistance: it is one of our most popular revolutionary measures."*

Revealingly, even then, in the very act of appearing to
reject "Stalinist totalitarianism," Guevara did not have a
word of blame for Stalin himself. It had all been the fault
of "capitalist encirclement," rather than anything in the
Soviet system. Guevara's history of this "historical phenomenon" was, of course, mythological. Stalinism had
flourished in the 1930's long after the "capitalist encirclement" of the first years of the Bolshevik revolution had
fallen apart. The purge trials, for example, had started the
year after the United States, the last holdout, had established normal relations with Soviet Russia, and the purges
had become progressively obsessive during the period of the
Franco-Soviet pact, hardly an evidence of "capitalist encirclement." Moreover, the final and most pathological
stage of Stalinist totalitarianism had come in Stalin's last
years in power after the total defeat and collapse of the very

---

* To K. S. Karol, in *New Statesman*, May 19, 1961, p. 778. A similar
statement may be found in Mills, *op. cit.*, pp. 81–82, indicating that Guevara was not alone in this view.

powers necessary to "encircle" Russia and the latter's vast territorial expansion at their expense.

If Guevara had hit on a peculiarly unfortunate historical apologia for Stalinist totalitarianism, he was equally unlucky in his reasons for Cuba's immunity to it. In the months ahead, every one of his reasons for avoiding the Stalinist infection proved to be a forewarning of just the opposite. Cuba did need to sacrifice to industrialize. Cuba could not get all it wanted from the other socialist countries. Industrialization did not bring immediate benefits to the population. Even as Guevara spoke, Cuba's "nonexistent" agricultural problems were rapidly becoming, in a different form, more severe agricultural problems than Cuba had had before. In a matter of months, the cooperatives aroused so much resistance and became so unpopular that Guevara himself later referred to the situation as having been a "serious crisis." Guevara subsequently admitted that Cuba had simply copied East European economic methods slavishly. And three years later, he was not inhibited from quoting Stalin as one of his authorities, without apologies.

The Overdevelopment of Underdevelopment

As much as anything else, deeply rooted and widespread misconceptions of the nature of Cuban society have stood in the way of a more fruitful theory of the Cuban revolution.

One of the most prolific sources of misconception is the term "underdeveloped." As too frequently used, it covers such a wide spectrum of countries and societies that it has ceased to be a useful analytical tool. If, for example, both Ghana and Cuba are lumped together as "underdeveloped," the resulting image of both can only be ludicrously misleading to those who have never been to or spent much time studying either. The differences between them are so much greater than the similarities that the same word cannot do justice to both, even if it is modified by "more" or "less." The trouble is compounded if "Latin American" is added to "underdeveloped," and for much the same reason. Latin American countries differ so much that most generalizations merely reveal the ignorance or the bias of the generalizers.

The relativity of the whole concept of "development" is well shown by Cuba's place in the scale of per capita income, one of the most significant indexes. A study by Dr. Harry T. Oshima for the Food Research Institute at Stanford University, California, showed that the per capita income of Cuba in 1953, the year after Batista's coup, "was not less than $430." But 1953 was a very bad year economically in Cuba, and the per capita income rose about 25 per cent by 1957, a peak year. Compared with the per capita income in the United States of $1,870 in 1953, it was very low. But very few countries in the world compare favorably with the United States. The Cuban figure was approximately the same as that found for Italy and the Soviet Union. In Latin America, only Venezuela exceeded the Cuban mark in 1957. Dr. Oshima concluded: "Although Cuba's potentials for development clearly have not been fully utilized, these comparisons show that it is a mistake to think of Cuba as a seriously underdeveloped country."*

Pedro C. M. Teichert has pointed out, with justice, that

---

* *A New Estimate of the National Income and Product of Cuba in 1953* (Stanford: Food Research Institute Studies, reprint of Vol. II, No. 3, November, 1961, pp. 213–27). Dr. Oshima found that the official estimates of per capita income prepared by the Banco Nacional de Cuba were 25 to 35 per cent too low. The Bank's figures were $374 in 1957 and $356 in 1958. The figures for the twenty Latin American countries may be found in Grupo Cubano de Investigaciones Económicas de University of Miami, *Un Estudio Sobre Cuba* (Miami: University of Miami Press, 1963), p. 843, which states that Cuba was second in 1957 and third in 1958 (behind Venezuela and Uruguay). Argentina was sixth with $296, Chile seventh with $295, and Brazil fifteenth with $145.

average per capita income is not necessarily a true indicator of general economic development. He, therefore, added
nine other indexes to get a more meaningful estimate of
"real growth and wealth" in Latin America. His study
found that, for 1953, some countries went up or down in
ranking as a result of the additional criteria, but that Cuba
was the only one that remained in exactly the same place
—fourth in both per capita income and in the average of
all the other indexes.* Cuba was also ranked in fourth
place by Rev. Roger Vekemans and Rev. J. L. Segundo in
their attempt to work out a "socio-economic typology"
of the twenty Latin American countries on the basis of
twenty-four criteria, divided into five categories—economic,
social stratification, culture, standard of living, and ethno-
graphic.† It appears, then, that per capita income happens
to be an accurate indicator of general development in the
case of Cuba.

Felipe Pazos has suggested that "semideveloped" would
be a better term to apply to Cuba than "underdeveloped."‡
A similar conclusion was reached by Eugene Staley, who
has grouped countries by level of economic development
into "highly developed," "intermediate," and "underdeveloped," and has placed Cuba with five other Latin
American countries in the second level.§

It is instructive to compare Cuba and Mexico. I have

* "Analysis of Real Growth and Wealth in the Latin American Repub-
lics," *Journal of Inter-American Studies* (Gainesville, Fla.), April, 1959,
pp. 173–202. In this study, for example, Venezuela went from first place
in per capita income to ninth place in the other indexes.

† "Essay of a Socio-Economic Typology of the Latin American Countries," in *Social Aspects of Economic Development in Latin America*, pp.
67–93. Argentina, Uruguay, and Chile came out ahead of Cuba in both
this and the Teichert study.

‡ "The Economy," *Cambridge Opinion* (Cambridge, Eng.), No. 32, 1963
(issue devoted to Cuba), p. 13.

§ *The Future of Underdeveloped Countries: The Political Implications
of Economic Development* (Rev. ed.; New York: Frederick A. Praeger,
1961), pp. 16–17. The other five were Argentina, Chile, Puerto Rico, Uruguay, and Venezuela.

deliberately chosen the latter because Castro has said that Mexico has "a flourishing economy, an economy which advances with higher levels than any other Latin American country."*

	Cuba	Mexico
Per capita income	$356 (1958)	$263 (1959)
Illiteracy	23.6% (1953)	43.2% (1950)
Persons per physician	998 (1957)	1,896 (1956)
Persons per dentist	3,052 (1957)	20,345 (1956)
Daily average caloric intake	2,730 (1957)	2,250 (1956)
Newspaper circulation (per 1,000)	129 (1956)	48 (1955)
Salaried and wage employees	55.4% (1953)	45.9% (1957)
Economically active population in agriculture	41.4% (1953)	57.8% (1957)
Economically active population in manufacturing	12.5% (1953)	11.7% (1957)
Motor vehicles (per 1,000)	33 (1957)	19 (1956)
Telephones (per 1,000)	24 (1957)	13 (1956)
Radio receivers (per 1,000)	176 (1957)	84 (1956)
Population in localities of 100,000 or over	25.6% (1953)	15.1% (1950)

Sources: The per capita income figures have been taken from *Un Estudio Sobre Cuba*, p. 843, which uses the Banco Nacional de Cuba estimate rather than Dr. Oshima's for Cuba. All the other figures come from *Statistical Abstract of Latin America 1960* (Los Angeles: Center of Latin American Studies, University of California, 1960).

I have chosen a fair sampling of comparative economic and social data to give the reader a basis for judging the relative development of pre-Castro Cuba and Mexico. I could have drawn up another set of figures to demonstrate how far Cuba was behind the United States or Canada. My purpose has been twofold: to show that Cuba's "underdevelopment" has been, by Castro's own standards, absurdly exaggerated; and to suggest that there is no necessary correlation between revolution and development. All the theories based on Cuba's "underdevelopment" merely

* Speech of September 19, 1964.

make a mystery of the absence of revolution in dozens of less developed countries.*

"Monoculture" is another term that has bred a multitude of misconceptions. In its usual form, it means that Cuba was a one-crop country, producing sugar and little else. It evokes the image of an almost unending sugar plantation, and of a people devoted in the vast majority to the cultivation and milling of sugar.

Sugar has, to be sure, dominated the Cuban economy and all that depends on it for a century. But it has done so because sugar has represented about three-quarters or more of all Cuban *exports* and, therefore, almost its sole source of foreign exchange. Cuba has been, without doubt, a *mono-exporting* country. But producing and exporting are far from the same thing, especially in their effects on the make-up of a society. The social composition of the Cuban people does not conform to the pattern of a monoculture

* Even an East European writer has seen fit to disabuse his readers of the crude notion of Cuban "underdevelopment." In the *Literarni Noviny* (Prague), of August 8, 1964, Radoslav Selucky shared what must have seemed to him and his readers some daring discoveries:

"The notion prevails in our country that Cuba had no industry before the revolution, except sugar factories. This is false. Cuban industry employed one-sixth of the entire labor force. Sugar, nickel, and tobacco products were one category of industrial production where wages were on the level of the United States or in some cases (tobacco factories) above it. These three industrial branches, together with the cane plantations, supported the Cuban economy and were the basis of Cuban exports. Although the nickel and sugar industries lacked refinery installations, the technological standards of these two branches were above the world average.

"Industries producing for the domestic market belonged to a second category which was distinguished by high concentration. Here, too, wages were relatively high. This category included synthetic fibers, detergents, glass, refined oil, Coca-Cola produced under an American franchise, ginger ale manufactured under a Canadian franchise, and good beer and outstanding rum based on local recipes. These industries depended on U.S. maintenance services, and necessary components and spare parts were imported by air within twelve to twenty-four hours.

"Industries producing textiles, footwear, and minerals—except for nickel ore—formed a third category of production. Here wages were low, about 75 per cent below the American level" [translation in *East Europe* (New York), October, 1964, pp. 19–22].

for the simple reason that Cuba has not had a monoculture. Yet, in the popular view, an "agrarian revolution" suggests a largely agrarian society, and the myth of Cuban "monoculture" has tended to reinforce this misconception.

For our purpose, which is a clearer understanding of Cuban society, it is more important to know that the sugar industry, both in its agricultural and industrial segments, has accounted for only one-quarter to one-third of the national income. In 1954, for example, the entire sugar industry contributed exactly 25 per cent of the national income, although in that year, sugar accounted for 80.2 per cent of the national exports. If we break down the sugar percentage into its component parts, the agricultural side of the sugar industry contributed only 16 per cent of the national income; the industrial and commercial side, 9 per cent. In other words, 84 per cent of the Cuban national income derived from sources other than sugar cultivation.*

The distribution of the Cuban "labor force," or as it is also known, "economically active population," also fails to conform to the model of a "monoculture." In the first place, according to the last census, in 1953, 41.4 per cent, or a minority, were engaged in agriculture as a whole. Of these, little more than half were employed in sugar cultivation. Thus, this "monoculture" accounted for less than one-quarter of the total labor force.

It must be emphasized that the production and exportation of sugar have played a determining role in the fluctuations of the entire Cuban economy and that many other types of economic activity in varying degrees have serviced the sugar industry. But the fact remains that four out of five Cubans had nothing to do with the cultivation of sugar, and three out of five had nothing to do with agriculture as

* *Investment in Cuba* (Washington, D.C.: U.S. Department of Commerce, 1957), p. 6. This is one of the most authoritative and commonly accepted sources on the Cuban economy.

a whole. In fact, the whole concept of "monoculture" as applied to Latin America requires overhauling because it tends to encourage oversimplification and underestimation of most Latin American societies. Like Cuba, many Latin American countries depend on one or two commodities for the major portion of their exports. Venezuela is even more dependent on oil exports than Cuba is on sugar, but less than 1 per cent of the population derives its income from the oil industry.

In short, a social interpretation of the Cuban revolution must begin with a view of a Cuban society that is far more urban, far less agrarian, far more middle class, far less backward, than it has been made to appear. In Castroist propaganda and in the speeches of Castro himself, one of the most complex and advanced Latin American countries has been flattened out into a one-dimensional, hopelessly backward, agrarian fantasy that "had not developed economically or technically" for dozens of years.* In Cuba, the middle class, the working class, and the peasantry were roughly coordinate components of the society. Of the three, the middle class had long been the political class *par excellence,* and it was sociologically unlikely that either of the other two classes could muster enough strength by themselves to overthrow the Batista regime.

The Breaking Points

By itself, the social structure of Cuba cannot explain the specific form of the Cuban revolution. If it could, essentially the same social structure should have resulted in essentially the same kind of revolution in other countries, and that did not happen.

The operative factor, I think, is not the social structure as such but the *tensions* within that social structure. A

* Fidel Castro, *Revolución,* November 1, 1964.

country far less developed than Cuba may have fewer tensions than a country far more developed, and to that extent, the more developed country may be closer to a revolutionary crisis than the less developed one. In this sense, Escalante was certainly right in pointing out that, if "underdevelopment" or standard of living is made the decisive factor in the Cuban revolution, the revolution should have first taken place in sixteen or seventeen other Latin American countries.

It may be argued that certain types of social structure inevitably breed dangerous tensions. More probably, every known social structure contains its own built-in tensions which must be released in order to become dangerous. Tensions which seem to be held in leash in "normal" circumstances may perform a progressive function by forcing the existing order to lessen injustices and inequalities; the same tensions may become revolutionary if subjected to some shock or extreme dislocation. Cuba's economic development, for example, jumped ahead markedly in the 1950's, but that decade was far more revolutionary than the preceding one. It was not so much that the social structure had changed for the worse as that the tensions within the social structure had reached the breaking point.

One of the basic tensions in Cuban society was the disparity between the cities and the countryside. Whereas the rate of illiteracy was only 11.6 per cent in the urban areas, it was 41.7 per cent in the rural areas. Almost all available information about sanitation, health services, housing, and the like reveals similar or greater disparities. According to Dr. Oshima's figures, the per capita income in 1953 of the *nonagricultural* labor force was $1,600; the per capita agricultural income must have been very low to drive down the average to about $430.* The gap between the cities and the countryside was not, of course, a uniquely

* Oshima, *op. cit.,* p. 214.

Cuban phenomenon, and there are comparable examples in far more developed countries. In fact, the disparity suggests that it would be far more helpful to think of Cuba as an *unevenly* developed country, with a backward hinterland that lagged further and further behind, and a middle-class sector almost too large for the economy to sustain. In such a society, it is possible to manipulate statistics to emphasize extreme backwardness or extreme progressiveness, depending on which end of the scale is being manipulated. But the tendency to judge a country in terms of its least developed areas has even less to commend it than the tendency to judge it in terms of the most developed.

The rural-urban tension in Cuba was not, even by Guevara's account, one that could set off a peasant party or movement. At most, it enabled a small guerrilla force to obtain a few hundred recruits and a sympathetic environment in the most backward backwoods of Cuba. As a political phenomenon, the relative passivity of about 500,-000 "proletarianized" agricultural laborers was at least as significant as the relative activity of a fraction as many Sierra Maestra peasants under urban leadership. Yet the long neglect of the Cuban countryside was a major factor in Batista's defeat. Most of his army was made up of raw peasants, paid the munificent sum of $30 a month, who saw their top commanders use their positions mainly to enrich themselves.* The great mass of the agricultural population had so little stake in the existing regime that, once it began to show signs of weakening, they hastily abandoned it, and this, to a large extent, contributed to its military collapse.

The working class also had its share of tensions. At the top was a relatively large group of skilled workers, who, in 1953, numbered almost a half million, or almost a quarter

* Suárez Núñez, *op. cit.*, p. 92. This book was written by a former pro-Batista youth leader and editor with close ties to the military hierarchy. It is a devastating inside view of the corruption and incompetence at the top.

of the total labor force.* These workers benefited most from high wages, trade-union organization, and the social security system.† At the bottom was a floating population which was either totally or seasonally unemployed. Most of the unemployment in Cuba was directly traceable to the fluctuations and seasonal character of the sugar industry and was, therefore, another serious count against it. The *zafra,* or sugar-cane harvest, usually lasted only about three months a year, and for the rest of the time, in the *tiempo muerto,* or dead season, most agricultural workers and mill-hands were let out to fend for themselves. The fields and mills needed relatively few workers to prepare for the next *zafra.* Some sugar workers took odd jobs during the dead season, but their lot was on the whole precarious. Thus, even in 1956–57, a period of economic upturn, unemployment was estimated at 9 per cent of the labor force during the harvest and 20 per cent afterward. Another 10 per cent of "underemployed" worked fewer than 40 hours a week.‡ A human flotsam numbering about 200,000 at best and over 500,000 at worst could not be fully assimilated by the existing economic order and, for the most part, had a minimal stake in its perpetuation.

The key economic tension in Cuba may have resulted from the sluggish rate of growth rather than from over-all underdevelopment or general poverty. There is a vital difference between the level of economic development and the range of economic dynamism. Mexico may have been

---

* *Investment in Cuba,* p. 22. The total number was 447,391, or 22.7 per cent.

† See Carmelo Mesa Lago and Roberto E. Hernández Morales, *Social Security in Cuba* (Miami: Cuban Economic Research Project, University of Miami, 1964), for this subject before and after Castro.

‡ Consejo Nacional de Economía, *Symposium de Recursos Naturales de Cuba,* 1958. For an analysis of the 1952–53 period, see *Investment in Cuba,* pp. 23–24, with comparable results. Felipe Pazos says that, for the three decades before 1959, unemployment seldom dropped below 15 per cent and underemployment afflicted at least 30 per cent more (Pazos, "The Economy," *Cambridge Opinion,* p. 13).

behind Cuba in its general level of development, but it was far ahead in its dynamism. It has been calculated that the total product and per capita product of Mexico for the period 1950–58 increased 5.7 and 3.1 per cent, respectively; Cuba's total product increased by only 1.8 per cent and its per capita product decreased by 0.3 per cent.* From 1951 to 1957, the Cuban annual growth in per capita income was a very meager 1.3 per cent.† The Cuban economy had never fully recovered from the depression in the mid-1920's, primarily because the sugar industry had largely stagnated, and the gains registered in other fields were not sufficient to catch up with the inexorable increase in population.

For more than a century, a dangerous and sometimes explosive tension has also existed between Cuban and foreign economic interests. In the nineteenth century, the urban bourgeoisie was mainly Spanish, fiercely opposed to Cuban nationalism. After Spanish rule was overthrown in 1898, this business class was stripped of its political power and devoted all its energies to its economic survival. With the turn of the century, a new wave of Spanish immigration again gave Cuba an infusion of tradesmen, artisans, and petty entrepreneurs who helped enormously to build up the country but were not native to it. While Spanish, Chinese, and other immigrants became shopkeepers or opened small workshops, and U.S. investments poured into the sugar industry, railways, and public utilities, the only business in which Cubans had a monopoly was politics.

This is not the place to refight the old battles of U.S.-Cuban relations. But it cannot be ignored that they have been saddled with an almost crushing burden. For thirty-

* Jorge Ahumada, "Economic Development and Problems of Social Change in Latin America," in *Social Aspects of Economic Development in Latin America*, p. 117.

† Felipe Pazos, "Desarrollo insuficiente y depauperación económica," *Cuadernos* (Paris), Supplement No. 47, March–April, 1961, p. 47.

one years, from 1902 to 1933, Cuba's sovereignty was gashed by the so-called Platt Amendment, which permitted the United States to intervene in Cuban affairs. From 1898 to 1902, and again from 1906 to 1909, Cuba was directly ruled by the United States, and from 1909 to 1933 indirectly dominated. The circumstances were sometimes far more complex and double-edged than many suppose; the intervention of 1906, for example, was urged by Cuban President Estrada Palma against the better judgment of President Theodore Roosevelt. Nevertheless, generations of Cubans were brought up in the shadow of the hateful Platt Amendment, and grew to political maturity waging a struggle against it. The major, long-term U.S. investments were made in precisely this period and, therefore, reeked of old-style imperialism.

If there is one form of foreign ownership most wounding to the national consciousness, it is foreign ownership of the most elemental of natural resources—the land. In the case of Cuba, U.S. ownership of vast tracts of land was all the more politically vulnerable because they were not ordinary tracts—they were *sugar* lands, bearing the crop that was the sustenance and affliction of the people. Without sugar, Cuba would not have grown in population and wealth in the nineteenth century, but sugar was also largely responsible for Negro slave labor, for the devastation of magnificent forests, for the profit-hungry displacement of other crops, and for the attraction of so much foreign capital. The main U.S. investment was situated at the sorest and most vulnerable point not only of the Cuban economy but of the Cuban national psyche, and whatever was or had ever been wrong with the sugar industry was linked in the most direct and intimate way with U.S. capital and trade. Foreign ownership of public utilities runs foreign ownership of natural resources a close second in political offensiveness, and Cuba had an excess of both. U.S. investment in and trade with Cuba were somewhat like sugar in their effects—without them Cuba would have been far less developed, but Cuba might have developed in a far more balanced and harmonious way. Yet if one can imagine a Cuba without the presence of U.S. capital, technology, and organization, the choice might be a difficult one.

It was not a wholly one-sided bargain. The sugar mills and other U.S. plants were the most modern and efficient in Cuba. They paid the highest wages and made the best agreements with the Cuban trade unions. The largest part of the U.S. investment in Cuba could easily have been bought back with Cuban investments outside the country. The historic tendency of the main U.S. investment was its Cubanization; U.S. control of the sugar industry declined from about 70 per cent in 1928 to about 35 per cent in 1958. It has been estimated that the pre-Castro U.S. investment represented only about 5 per cent of the total Cuban valuation.* U.S. companies employed only about 70,000 of Cuba's total labor force of about 2 million.† Cuba was economically dependent on the United States, but if this is distorted to mean that Cubans owned almost nothing, made almost nothing, and employed almost nobody, the result is little more than a caricature.

It is noteworthy that there was less anti-Americanism in pre-Castro Cuba than almost anywhere else in Latin America, and that Cubans were not accustomed to the use of any derogatory term, such as *"gringo"* (a Mexican expression), for *norteamericanos*. Most Cubans recognized that a small, tropical island of about 6 million people, without vital raw materials, with a single export crop, could not help but be dependent on a great industrial

---

* José R. Alvarez Díaz, *Trayectoria de Castro: encumbramiento y derrumbe* (Miami: Editorial AIP, 1964), p. 11, gives the figures on which this percentage is based.

† *U.S. Investments in the Latin American Economy* (Washington, D.C.: U.S. Department of Commerce, 1957), p. 75.

power only 90 miles away, and that dependence on the United States was probably the least onerous of available options.

Nevertheless, past U.S.-Cuban relations and present U.S. investments in Cuba were still loaded with political dyna-mite. The tradition of the entire Cuban left, from Eduardo Chibás to the Communists, was doctrinally "anti-imperial-ist." Perhaps the worst thing that the United States did to too many Cubans was to give them a ready-made alibi for their own frailties.

Challenge and Tragedy

The middle class, I think, offers the greatest challenge to an understanding of Castroism.* In a sense, the middle class had most to gain and most to lose from it. No other class could let political power slip out of its grasp because no other class ever had such power. The main leaders, in-

* I am mindful of the fact that there is some dispute whether the term "middle class" is applicable to Latin America. Professor John J. Johnson has argued that "middle class" has a predominantly economic connotation, whereas social and cultural factors have tended to establish status in Latin America more than strictly economic ones (*Political Change in Latin America* [Stanford: Stanford University Press, 1958], pp. viii–ix). For this reason, he prefers to use circumlocutions such as "middle sectors," "groups," and the like. Be this as it may, it should be noted that Cuba would, by almost any standards, rank ahead of three of the five countries in his study in the importance of its "middle sectors"—behind Uruguay and Argentina, and ahead of Chile, Brazil, and Mexico. Another difficulty, I feel, comes from the word "middle," which implies something on top as well as at the bottom. Strictly speaking, a *petite* bourgeoisie needs an *haute* bourgeoisie, and while Cuba had a good deal of the former, it did not have too much of the latter. Yet, *clase media* and *pequeña burguesía* have been common us-age in Cuba, and Castro has used them repeatedly. There were enough small and medium businessmen, merchants, professionals, technicians, executives, government bureaucrats, intellectuals, and better-paid white-collar workers to constitute a substantial "middle class" even by purely economic stand-ards. If by "middle class" is meant a style of living as well as economic status, the phenomenon is perhaps much easier to recognize than to define. I do not feel that those in the United States or Western Europe who can recognize their own "middle class" would have too much difficulty recog-nizing their Cuban counterparts. Moreover, the Cuban middle class was notoriously more "Americanized" than any other in Latin America.

cluding Castro himself, belonged to, or at least came out of, that class. This revolution was literally led by a lawyer without clients and a doctor without patients. If there is some dispute which class was most instrumental in the victory, there is no question but that the anti-Batista struggle was initiated by middle-class elements and, for four or five years, was largely limited to them. It was throughout financed by middle-class supporters and even by some sympathizers among the very rich. The urban resistance movement was mainly middle class. Until 1957 or even perhaps 1958, the great majority of the leadership and a large part of the rank and file came from the middle class, especially if the revolution is viewed as a whole and is not narrowly confined to Castro's movement. The revolutionary center of gravity shifted from the *llano* to the *sierra* in 1958, but it quickly moved back again as soon as Batista was overthrown.

Yet this was not a revolution of the middle class. Middle-class leaders and leaders of the middle class are not the same thing. The class was too divided to be revolutionary or counterrevolutionary; it was something of both. The division was most noticeable between the younger and older generations. Many middle-class fathers were drawn into the anti-Batista struggle by their sons. Some of the richer businessmen contributed to both pro-Batista and anti-Batista causes.* Batista's coup in 1952 pleased many businessmen and merchants because, as one qualified American observer put it, they felt that "he would bring law and order to the country, stability that meant prosperity, and a sounder economy."† The same businessmen and merchants, especially those who took their lead from the United States, abandoned Batista

---

* J. Alvarez Díaz, A. Arredondo, R. M. Shelton, J. Vizcaino, *Cuba: Geopolítica y Pensamiento Económico* (Miami: Colegio de Economistas de Cuba en el Exilio, 1964), p. 377.

† R. Hart Phillips, *Cuba: Island of Paradox* (New York: McDowell, Obolensky, 1960), p. 260.

as soon as they thought they saw signs that the United States wanted to get rid of him, which is how they widely interpreted the U.S. arms embargo of March, 1958. For at least four decades, the middle class had provided the most adroit defenders of the *status quo* and the most passionate adepts of "the revolution." Parts of this class were just as capable of supporting a dictatorship of the right as a dictatorship of the left. Some gravitated toward political and bureaucratic careers; others traditionally considered politics degrading and dishonorable.

In July, 1960, I pointed out that, in countries like Cuba, "revolutions still issue out of the middle class but not in behalf of the middle class. The sons and daughters of the bourgeoisie dedicate themselves to the destruction of their own class in the name of nationalism and socialism."* These remarks apparently inspired a distinguished Cuban writer and editor, Lino Novás Calvo, to make a penetrating historical and sociological analysis of what he called "the tragedy of the Cuban middle class." Like many other students of Cuban society, he attached much importance to the difference between the old and the new Cuban middle class. The fathers may have been Spanish or other immigrants who made money in farming or business, but many of their Cuban sons flocked in large numbers to the liberal professions, to the government bureaucracy, or to the career of politics, which held out the quickest and largest rewards. Of the two main subdivisions of the middle class, the professional-political and the industrial-commercial, the former was far more popular with the younger generation than the latter. Yet the economy could not sustain so many professionals and would-be politicians, especially lawyers, and the latest aspirants, doomed to disappointment, turned in rebellion against the entire system. This rebellion was institutionalized in the Cuban high

* *The New Leader,* July 4–11, 1960, p. 3.

schools and universities, where the worst students often made the best agitators. According to Novás Calvo, then, the Cuban middle class was characterized by a kind of "schizophrenia," much of it resulting from the discontinuity and estrangement of fathers and sons.*

Fidel Castro, of course, conformed almost perfectly to these specifications. The son of a poor, illiterate Spanish immigrant who had grown rich in the sugar and lumber industries in Oriente Province, Fidel was brought up to escape from his father's economic and social environment. He was sent off as a child to the best private schools, first in Santiago de Cuba and then in Havana. Like the vast majority of ambitious but aimless young Cubans, who wished to study the least and prepare themselves for nothing or anything, he chose to enter the Law School of the University of Havana. Years later, he recalled guiltily: "I ask myself why I studied law. I still don't know. But I attribute it in part to those who said, 'He talks a lot, he has the makings of a lawyer, he is going to be a lawyer.' Because I used to argue and discuss, they made me believe that I was qualified to be a lawyer. Possibly, that was one of the reasons why I studied law, because they made me believe it."†

* "La Tragedia de la Clase Media Cubana," *Bohemia Libre* (New York), January 1, 1961, pp. 28–29, 76–77. It is, of course, impossible to do justice to the complexity and richness of the original in this short summary. Another acute analysis of the historical development and "social frustrations" of the Cuban middle class may be found in *Cuba: Geopolítica y Pensamiento Económico,* pp. 397–429.

† *Revolución,* April 10, 1961. This decision to become a lawyer seems so disturbing that Castro brought it up on two other occasions two years later in talks to students, once in Havana (*ibid.,* February 27, 1963) and again in Moscow (*ibid.,* May 22, 1963), both times blaming others.

The reader may wonder how it was possible for Fidel Castro to put a "Dr." in front of his name. The answer is that this Cuban "doctorate" is largely a fiction by U.S. or European standards. Fidel spent five years in all in the Law School, which he entered at the age of eighteen. Unlike similar U.S. institutions, it did not require a college degree as an entrance requirement; it was, in fact, little more than the equivalent of a college education. To graduate as a *Doctor en Leyes,* it was not necessary to take several years of post-graduate work, to publish a dissertation on original research, or to

As he himself has admitted, he was not a good student;* he belonged to those who "never went to class, never opened a book other than on the eve of examinations." In one of these self-revealing outbursts, Castro cried: "How many times have I deplored the fact that I was not forced to study something else!"†

There were, of course, more serious students at the University of Havana, even in the Law School, but they were goaded by greater economic or intellectual necessity. Fidel Castro was a classic case of the self-made rich man's son in a relatively poor country for whom the university was less an institution of learning or a professional-training school than a nursery of hothouse revolutionaries. He chose a field of study in which the standards were notoriously low, the pressure to study minimal, and his future profession already overcrowded. Since he did not have any real needs to satisfy in the school, did not respect his teachers, and could get by on his wits and retentive memory, he was easily tempted to get his more meaningful and exciting experiences in extra-school political adventures.

Yet the political lawyer was not a new Cuban phenomenon; a much more innovating and invigorating sector of the new—or perhaps, more accurately, the newest—Cuban middle class was a rising group of modern technicians, many of them wholly or partially trained in the United States. The emergence of this vital force in Cuban life was increasingly visible after World War II in business, the technical professions, and the governmental bureaucracy. For this new generation, the old shibboleths about the omnipotence of sugar, the impossibility of industrialization, and the dependence on foreign capital were spuri-

---

fulfill any of the other requirements for a doctorate in the United States. Most Cuban lawyers, equally entitled to sport the title, prefer to forget about it—or use it only to impress non-Cubans.

* *Ibid.,* March 7, 1964.

† *Ibid.,* March 14, 1964.

ous, antiquated, and exasperating. Government planning, a mixed economy of state and private initiative, and a fairer distribution of the national income held no terrors for them.* For the unemployed and underemployed, the low growth rate of the Cuban economy meant privation or hunger; for the more responsible and farsighted members of the middle class, it represented frustration and disaffection.

The most authoritative post-World War II study of the Cuban economy by a U.S. mission of experts was strongly impressed by all the favorable factors which should have put Cuba far ahead of its actual economic status. It was equally impressed by the fact that the chief obstacles were political and social rather than economic.† A dynamic, modern economy required an enlightened, determined, and efficient government policy of the kind that Cuba had never or rarely had. In Cuba, then, it was impossible to separate economic progress from institutional change; the only question was whether the change would be democratic or not. Economic frustration almost inevitably translated itself into political disaffection, not necessarily from the ideals of democracy, but from the oligarchies and vested interests that stood in the way of democratic progress. As the Presidential elections of 1952 approached, the new Cuban technical elite was preparing to play a far more promi-

* The most advanced expression of this thought may be found in the "Tesis Económica," by Pazos and Botí. It was, incidentally, published in *Revolución*, January 21–27, 1959, and thus seemed to carry over from the struggle for power.

† This conclusion was reached, in a somewhat guarded form, in the monumental *Report on Cuba*, sponsored by the International Bank for Reconstruction and Development (Baltimore: The Johns Hopkins Press, 1951), esp. pp. 77–78. It was spelled out by Eugene Staley, the chief economist of the Economic and Technical Mission that drew up the report, who used Cuba as an example of a country whose economic development was "caught in a mesh of vicious circles" of a political and social nature (*op. cit.*, pp. 208–10).

nent, if not a dominating, role in the next administration, whether it would have been Ortodoxo or Auténtico.

And so, the revolution owed as much to the untapped potentialities of the existing system as to its palpable vices. It was a child of both hope and hopelessness. But the existence of these social tensions and their eruption into a social revolution were two different things. To go from one to the other, a catalytic agent was needed.

That agent was Batista's coup in March, 1952. If anyone was responsible for opening the way to Castro's capture of power, that man was Fulgencio Batista. If there were gravediggers of the former social order in Cuba, they were all those, Cubans and Americans, who condoned the coup and supported the regime that came out of it.* Batista did not make a revolutionary out of Fidel Castro, who had long been engaged in revolutionary activities without notable success. But Batista made revolutionaries out of hundreds and thousands of others who could not reconcile themselves to a cynical usurpation of power and who, if forced to choose between Batista and Castro, would choose Castro, at least in his pre-1959 guise. Cuba was full of revolutionary conspiracies against Batista rather than with Castro; Batista, not Castro, was the indispensable revolutionary ingredient. It was precisely in the middle class, moreover, that Batista's havoc was greatest. This class, never a coherent body, was most fragmented by the divisiveness of the struggle. The

---

* The honorary pallbearers should certainly include those U.S. officials and perhaps others who decided to recognize Batista's regime about two weeks after the coup, and then sent an ambassador who was so pro-Batista that he made the veteran *New York Times* correspondent "think that at times he even embarrassed President Batista with his support"—no small feat (Phillips, *op. cit.*, p. 311). Even after Batista was overthrown, this ambassador, who spent most of the crucial years 1953–57 in Havana, was capable of telling a Senate subcommittee: "I don't think we ever had a better friend [than Batista]" (Testimony of Arthur Gardner, in *Communist Threat to the United States Through the Caribbean: Hearings Before the Subcommittee to Investigate the Administration of Internal Security Act and Other Internal Security Laws of the Committee of the Judiciary*, U.S. Senate, 86th Cong., 2d sess. [Washington, D.C.: Government Printing Office, 1960], Part 9, p. 665).

working class retained a large measure of apolitical cohe-
siveness as long as Batista's regime did not touch its economic perquisites and privileges. But the middle class had
been *the* political class, and now all politics was either
repressive or revolutionary. The tensions between the backward *sierra* and the more advanced *llano,* between the root-
less unemployed and the organized worker, between the
older middle-class generation and the younger, broke loose
from their accustomed moorings. In the last few months of
1958, the old order disintegrated even before the new forces
were ready to take over.

Poco a Poco

January, 1959, has become the official beginning of the
present Cuban revolution. In reality, however, it was not
the revolutionary dividing line between pre-Castro Cuba
and Castroism in power. It took several months for Castro
to feel his way and consolidate his power. Only after he
knew how far he could go did he go far.

Castro's first political line in power was a continuation
of the line which had served him so well in the struggle for
power—soothing moderation. One of his statements in the
first month will show how reassuring he was. At a press
conference in Havana, he declared that he wished to avoid
the "difficulties" that Mexico had had with the United
States as a result of the latter's oil expropriations in 1938.
"In our struggle for the recovery of our economy," he said,
"evolutionary" and not "radical" methods would be used.
He did not fear that the United States would retaliate with
an economic blockade because, he explained, "we are going
to take measures gently, not radically, because we will go
poco a poco."*

---

* *Revolución,* January 23, 1959. A French writer in Jean-Paul Sartre's
organ has taken the PSP leaders to task for their moderate statements
before 1959. She quotes from a PSP document dated December 10, 1958,

Gently, little by little—a better description of Castro's tactics in the first weeks of 1959 might be hard to find. But it took Castro only a few weeks to determine that there was no force in Cuba that could or would deny him anything. Whatever qualms Castro may have had about the Cuban middle class, they were soon dispelled by the ease with which its representatives could be used and discarded. The fate of the first post-Batista Prime Minister, Dr. Miró Cardona, and of the first President, Manuel Urrutia, told Castro all that he needed to know.

An eminent jurist, Dr. Miró Cardona had served as Secretary General of the Frente Cívico Revolucionario (Civilian Revolutionary Front), the coalition based on the "unity pact" of July 20, 1958, and he thus symbolized the broad anti-Batista struggle rather than the interests of the 26th of July Movement alone. But Castro rather than Miró Cardona controlled the latter's Cabinet, a majority of whom came from the 26th of July Movement, mainly from the former urban-based, middle-class Resistencia Cívica. Castro personally controlled the armed forces, and from the outset permitted no one else to act as political spokesman for the revolution, even as he disavowed all political ambitions. Dr. Miró Cardona took office on January 5 and offered his first resignation on January 17, only twelve days later, when he was outvoted on the issues of restoring the death sentence and making legal penalties retroactive,

not hitherto known to me, in which, among other things, the Communist leaders promised to do nothing to frighten the "national bourgeoisie" and protested that they were not proposing any "general nationalization" of foreign interests (Janette Habel, "Le Procès de Marcos Rodríguez et les Problèmes de l'Unité du Mouvement Révolutionnaire à Cuba," *Les Temps Modernes*, August–September, 1964, pp. 519–20). The idea seems to be that this was the original sin of the PSP. If the same writer took the trouble, she could make an anthology of similar statements by Fidel Castro well into 1959. Yet it is interesting that this kind of anti-PSP propaganda by a pro-Castro writer should come out of Havana toward the end of 1964, and come back to Havana via Paris.

both of which he opposed on principle.* Castro and others prevailed on him to remain in office, but Dr. Miró resigned a second and last time on February 13, and Castro succeeded him in the office. These six weeks might be considered a period of "dual power," if it were not for the fact that one power was real and the other was nominal. Also in February, just before Dr. Miró's departure, we now know, President Manuel Urrutia tried to resign for the first time, because the Cabinet refused his demand to close down the gambling casinos. He says that he presented a second resignation a few days later, when Castro made it clear that he did not wish the President to interfere in policy-making. And he tried to resign again on June 11 by feigning illness. After dissuading him three times, Castro went on television to attack him for having publicly denounced Communism and virtually drove him out of office on July 17.†

Whatever the merits of these cases, it is clear that they were tests of Castro's authority and power. When Miró told of his short term in office, he added sadly: "I resigned. Cuba did not protest. It accepted, it applauded."‡ Urrutia learned the same lesson: "Unfortunately, not until the dark night of Communism was well advanced would the Cuban people realize that I had striven only for their welfare and salvation."§ Castro toyed with them, knowing full well that they were aware of their own anomalous positions and that they were seeking a way out almost as soon as they had come in. All those cast out by Castro in 1959 and 1960 felt powerless to resist because everything he did was "accepted," everything was "applauded." And as he fed on

* Dr. Miró Cardona revealed the circumstances of these resignations, together with other important details of the next two years, in a long letter to the *Diario de la Marina* (Miami Beach), November 12, 1960.

† Manuel Urrutia, *Fidel Castro & Company, Inc.* (New York: Frederick A. Praeger, 1964), pp. 35–71.

‡ *Diario de la Marina*, November 12, 1960.

§ Urrutia, *op. cit.*, p. 70.

success after success, the "real" Castroist revolution began, more toward the end of 1959 than at the beginning.

All and None

If it was not a peasant revolution, a working-class revolution, or a middle-class revolution, what was it?

In the final stages of the Batista regime, it was none of these because it was, in part, all of them. A quite universal revulsion against Batista's rule took hold of Cuba in 1958 and gave the revolution a truly popular character. The intense desire for a change in which all the classes shared, and which gave the nation a temporary unity it had almost never before had, was recognized on all sides. When Batista's highest military official, General Francisco Tabernilla Dolz, was asked whether the army could have prevented Castro's forces from marching on Havana, he answered: "It could, but not for a long time, because by that time the people of Cuba were already against the regime of Batista, and there is no army, once the people get up in arms, that can suppress it." Questioned more closely whether the people supported the revolution, General Tabernilla replied: "Completely."* The Communists were equally impressed by the revolution's scope. "The triumphant revolution has not been the work of one party, of one class, or of one group," Juan Marinello wrote early in January, 1959. "The people have gained the victory."† In that first month in power, Fidel Castro spoke in the same vein. The battle had

---

* Testimony of General Francisco J. Tabernilla [Dolz], *Communist Threat to the United States Through the Caribbean*, Part 7, p. 421. Tabernilla, head of Batista's Joint Chiefs of Staff, broke with Batista in 1959 and wrote some scathing letters to and about his former chieftain (reprinted in Suárez Núñez, *op. cit.*, pp. 155–74).

† *Hoy*, January 8, 1959. The thesis of a *"révolution populaire"* is also put forward by Jacques Arnault, *Cuba et le Marxisme* (Paris: La Nouvelle Critique, Special Number, September–October, 1962, p. 113), the most interesting presentation of the "orthodox" Communist interpretation to date. Arnault also dates the turning point as October, not May, 1959 (p. 114).

been won, he said, "with the help of men of all ideas, of all religions, of all social classes," it "belongs to all," and it "had admirably united the people."* For about another six months, the virtual unanimity of the revolution was celebrated as one of its chief glories and claims to uniqueness; only later did Castro change his mind and charge that this was exactly what had been wrong with the revolution in its initial stage.

Thus, at least officially, the revolution was at first an all-class or a "classless" phenomenon. The class differentiation did not begin to take place, according to Castro's later version, until after the promulgation of the First Agrarian Reform, in May, 1959. In fact, however, the agrarian reform met with remarkably little criticism or opposition. Though it undoubtedly caused a great deal of perturbation on the part of those who were going to suffer from it, they were so isolated politically that they could do little but pretend to make the best of it.

The real trouble with the agrarian reform was caused by the application, not by the letter, of the law. The agrarian reform as carried out had little or no relation to the agrarian reform as enacted. The state lands, for example, were supposed to be the first to be redistributed;† no effort was made to do so. The seizures were completely arbitrary; the pledge of indemnification was utterly ignored; personal effects were left when a home had to be abandoned immediately, and not so much as a receipt was issued for them. The question here is not whether the law as carried out was better or worse than the law as written; the point is that the latter was never given a chance; we will never know how it might have worked out in practice.

It may be that Castro never intended to carry it out or that he changed his mind about the direction of his regime

---

* *Revolución*, January 22, 1959.

† Section 1, Article 5. The full text may be found in Selser, *op. cit.*, pp. 437–61.

by the time he came to carry it out. Again and again, in one form or another, these two problems arise: the amount of deception practiced by Castro, and the sharp shift in policy that took place in the second half of 1959.

By October, 1959, a curious incident gave Castro the occasion for making known that, in his own mind, the "class nature" of the revolution had changed. On October 21, the day after the arrest of Major Hubert Matos in Camagüey, Major Pedro Luis Díaz Lanz, the former head of the Rebel Air Force, piloted a plane over Havana and dropped anti-Castro leaflets from the air. The Cuban press reported that he had "bombed" the capital, killing two and wounding forty-five. Carlos Luis, one of the outstanding younger Cuban intellectuals, then a writer for the 26th of July organ, *Revolución,* later told what had actually happened:

"At the end of 1959, Major Díaz Lanz, head of the Revolutionary Air Force until his defection to the United States, dropped leaflets over Havana calling Fidel Castro a Communist. Anti-aircraft batteries opened fire, causing casualties among civilians. This was admitted in a radio broadcast, later suppressed, by Major Ameijeiras, the chief of police. But the next day, the newspapers announced that a plane from the north had bombed Havana. A major propaganda campaign started; the Foreign Ministry issued a pamphlet with photographs of the dead and an accusation against the United States. We intellectuals wrote a manifesto supporting without reservation the statements of the government. We did not question the discrepancies in the account of the incident; to have done so would have been to play into the hands of the counterrevolutionaries. Thus, in trying to maintain our revolutionary integrity, we unwittingly helped to prepare the ground for tyranny. The incident was used by the government to advance its own, still concealed, ends, facing us with a dilemma: either tell the truth, which meant siding with reaction, or, on the grounds of 'tactical needs,' become accomplices in a process whose ends we could not see. This dilemma would not trouble a Communist Party member or a reactionary, but it is decisive for the revolutionary."[*]

In effect, the exiles were so ineffectual in 1959 that they were capable of little more than stunts and pinpricks, and when Castro wanted to create a dramatic crisis in U.S.-Cuban relations, he had to transmute leaflets into bombs. On October 26, Castro delivered his first all-out oratorical attack on the United States before the largest demonstration ever organized by his regime to date, much of it made up of peasants brought in from the outlying countryside. He compared Díaz Lanz's exploit to Pearl Harbor, and held the United States jointly responsible for an "act of aggression" which, he said, "tried with inhuman fury, with inconceivable fury, to spread terror among our people." It was during this speech that cries of *"¡Paredón! ¡Paredón!"* ("The execution wall!") were heard for the first time publicly in response to Castro's excitation. Something happened on October 26 which signified a spiritual as well as a political transmogrification of the Cuban revolution. That Castro should have whipped up such a frenzy on the basis of what he knew was less than a half-truth—months before the oil crisis, the sugar-quota crisis, or the expropriations crisis—makes one skeptical of the view that he was always reacting to or striking back at U.S. provocations. It rather suggests that Sartre did not go far enough when he wrote: "If the United States didn't exist, the Cuban revolution would perhaps invent it."[†] He might have been less cautious.

Equally revealing was the "class content" of the October 26 speech. It indicated that Castro's revolution no longer

[*] "Notes of a Cuban Revolutionary in Exile," *New Politics*, Fall, 1963, pp. 143–44.
[†] Sartre, *op. cit.*, p. 113.

belonged to "all the social classes," and that the people were no longer "admirably united." The middle class was now pointedly excluded from the revolution's anointed. "We believe," Castro said, "that the best allies of the [revolutionary] soldiers are the peasants and workers," and that "the best fighting soldiers of the Rebel Army are the peasants." He implied that Hubert Matos and the officers arrested with him had "betrayed" the revolution because they had had the wrong class origin. Though he had made the point before, he dwelt at greater length than ever before on the revolutionary virtues of the Sierra Maestra peasants to whom he virtually attributed the revolutionary victory.*

As the middle class went down, the peasants went up. At the trial of Hubert Matos in December, Castro repudiated a position that he himself had taken only a few months before. As if he had never said that the revolution had been the work of "all social classes," he reproached Matos for having made exactly the same statement. "The different classes may have contributed more or less," Castro maintained, "but the revolution was principally the work of the dispossessed *guajiros* of Cuba."† Thus Guevara's *Guerrilla Warfare* appeared shortly after Castro had publicly espoused, in broad terms, the thesis of the "agrarian revolution."

In the next few months, Castro's studied exclusion of the middle class did not pass unnoticed. At the end of March, 1960, Castro himself brought up the subject in his verbal assault on Luis Conte Agüero, the last one who dared to call attention to the growing Communist influence. "There has been a complaint that we are always speaking of the

---

* *Revolución*, October 27, 1959. It should be noted that the cries of "¡Paredón!" did not come altogether spontaneously from the crowd. Castro incited the outbursts with a series of rhetorical questions and asked for a show of hands on whether "terrorists" and "traitors like Hubert Matos" should be shot.

† . . . *y la luz se hizo*, p. 37.

workers, of the peasants, of the students, and that we do not speak of the middle class," Castro said. After denying that he had always failed to talk about the middle class, Castro acknowledged that "a considerable part of the middle class supports the revolution," but then added: "What is happening in the middle class is that it is very vacillating, it is very confused. On the other hand, the truth is that the *guajiro* and the worker are always more clear."* In effect, the middle class had become the second-class citizens of the revolution, and *"clase media"* or *"pequeña burguesia"* was well on its way to becoming a term of shame and abuse.

To some extent, Castro was both right and wrong. He was right in the sense that the changing character of his revolution was bound to cause more concern in the middle class than in any other class. Unlike the working class and the peasantry, it had been immediately divided by Batista's coup, and it was just as likely to be divided by a pronounced change in the social order under Castro. As the omens and portents of some kind of Communist tie-up and even possibly Communist rule multiplied toward the end of 1959 and beginning of 1960, the greatest danger to Castro came not from the discredited and isolated vested interests but from the democratic-minded sector of his own movement. That is why the great crises, beginning with Hubert Matos' mute protest in October, 1959, to the stifled outcry of Conte Agüero in March, 1960, came from men who had helped Castro in his journey to power and who had swallowed everything but his transition to Communism. Castro preferred to beat off this threat by depicting it as a "class" phenomenon, the typical, inevitable "vacillation" and "confusion" of the middle class. It mattered little that he and his closest collaborators were as much middle

* *La Calle* (Havana), March 30, 1960, p. 11. This newspaper was published in 1959–60. The full text of this speech does not appear to have been published anywhere else.

class in origin as the men they were imprisoning or driving into exile.

Yet the "vacillation" and "confusion" in the middle class was double-edged. It worked for Castro as much as against him. One part of the middle class chose the traditional form of Cuban opposition—exile. Another part willingly or desperately decided to accommodate itself to the new order as long as possible. Only a small number, almost all disillusioned members of the 26th of July Movement, tried to organize anti-Castro underground movements at this time. The others voted with their feet, as the workers later voted with their "productivity." Those who did not go of their own volition were virtually driven out—sometimes quite unnecessarily, as in the case of the wholesale purge of the University of Havana in July, 1960.* The exiles took with them the greatest store of knowledge, training, and skills in Cuba, so desperately needed by the Castro regime that the loss was perhaps the single greatest factor in the economic decline that took place in 1961. Yet, instead of making some effort to stop or reduce the exodus, the regime acted with the maximum brutality or indifference to make it as large as possible. In retrospect, what is most striking about these months of transition from what was supposed to have been a democratic revolution to what was soon to become a certified Communist revolution was the relative paucity, rather than the magnitude, of the internal opposition.

The mass exodus deprived the awakening opposition of the very forces that would have been needed for any effective organization and action inside the country; and to that extent, its immediate effect was to strengthen rather than to weaken the Castro regime. Many of the exiles left thinking that they were going for months, not years; they as-

* The story has been told, with ample documentation, in Luis Boza Domínguez, *La Situación Universitaria en Cuba* (Santiago de Chile: Editorial Del Pacífico, 1962), esp. pp. 63–116.

sumed that no Cuban regime could long hold out against such human and economic losses or against overt U.S. hostility. But, for the time being, the exodus was tantamount to resignation and impotence. Much of this sense of helplessness was induced by the overwhelming forces of repression that Castro had built up in his army, police, and popular "militia." But the main factor, for many, was probably the social milieu in which the events of 1960 took place. For the masses of people, the choice was not whether they were for Communism or against it; all the charges that Castro was consorting with Communism, they were still being told, were a reactionary fabrication or an imperialist plot. They were given the choice of trusting in Fidel Castro or not. And, at this time, on this breaking point, Fidel Castro could not lose.

In 1961, it may be recalled, Guevara looked back at the course of the Cuban revolution and ascribed to it three "peculiar characteristics," of which the first one was "that telluric force"—Fidel Castro. He might have left out the other two peculiarities and still obtained the same result. For Cuba did not prove that a Latin American nation could deliberately choose Communism; it proved, if proof were still needed, that a charismatic leader can make a nation choose almost anything even in the act of denying that he is choosing it for them. Castro's "charisma" was not limited to any one class as, for example, the peasantry; if it had been a class phenomenon, it would have been much more limited and vulnerable. Castro cut across all classes; he established a mass relationship primarily with his person, not with his ideas, and so could change his ideas without changing the relationship. This was especially true of his appeal to the youth, always the vital force behind him. We are accustomed to "class analyses," but we have yet to devote enough thought to a "generational" struggle that cuts across classes and even wins converts from the

younger generation of the class marked out for destruction.
The continuing exodus showed that the anti-Communist
opposition was widespread, but it was weakest among the
youth who had always made up the "action squads" in
Cuban rebellions. Without a strong basis among the youth,
there was little the opposition could do but go into exile.

The New Wave

Their identification with the peasantry in 1959–60 did
not make Castro or Guevara into peasants any more than
at a later date their self-proclaimed "dictatorship of the
proletariat" made them into proletarians. Even to Guevara,
"agrarian revolutionaries" did not mean the same as "men
of the soil." The very image used by Guevara, *una especie
de angel tutelar*" ("a sort of guiding angel") suggested a
being that hovered above the class rather than one that
belonged to it. It may well be that authentic peasant or
proletarian revolutionaries would have been less emotion-
ally hostile to the middle class or at least more mindful of
how much longer they could use the middle class for their
own ends than *déclassé* middle-class revolutionaries like
Castro and Guevara were.

The problem of the ex-bourgeois, anti-bourgeois revolutionary was not new with Guevara. One hundred and
twelve years earlier, Karl Marx and Friedrich Engels had
observed, as if they had felt it necessary to account for
themselves, that a small portion of the bourgeoisie could
"go over to" the proletariat. But they had been primarily
concerned with intellectuals, or as they put it, with "a portion of the bourgeois ideologists, who have raised themselves to the level of comprehending theoretically this
historical movement as a whole."* The idea that the proletariat needed "guardian angels" from another class to

* "Communist Manifesto" (1848), in *Selected Works* (Moscow: Foreign
Languages Publishing House, 1962), I, 43.

lead them in the day-to-day struggle would have been utterly alien to their thought. It was Lenin who went a step further and maintained that the working class by itself was incapable of going beyond trade unionism and that its "political consciousness" as a class could be awakened only from the outside. The political task, he held, was the work of "professional revolutionaries," mainly recruited from "the young generation of the educated classes," for whom the distinctions between workers and intellectuals or between trade and profession would be "obliterated."* Rosa Luxemburg at the time severely criticized Lenin's proposals. She was sorely troubled by the concept of a revolutionary organization made up primarily of nonworkers who "joined" themselves to the proletariat. And she made a noteworthy distinction between the "ambitious failures from the bourgeoisie" who were attracted to the social-democratic parties of Western Europe and the revolutionary intellectuals in Czarist Russia: "The milieu where intellectuals are recruited for socialism in Russia is much more declassed and by far less bourgeois than in Western Europe." The *déclassé* milieu in Russia, she noted, tended to encourage "wide theoretic wandering," ranging from complete rejection of political methods to "the unqualified belief in the effectiveness of isolated terrorist acts" as well as total political indifference.†

The *déclassé* bourgeois revolutionary, then, has been an old problem in the Marxist tradition. What Rosa Luxemburg wrote in 1904 about the Russian milieu still has some bearing on the Latin American milieu. Indeed, the differences between Lenin and Luxemburg in the early years of the century were relatively narrow compared to the differences that have developed between the Castro-Guevara

---

* "What Is to Be Done?" (1902), in *Selected Works* (New York: International Publishers [n.d.]), II, 98, 104, 127.

† *The Russian Revolution and Leninism or Marxism?* (Ann Arbor: University of Michigan Press, 1961), pp. 89, 99.

type of revolutionary and both Lenin and Luxemburg. The earlier two disagreed on the relationship of the *déclassé* revolutionary to the proletariat; they did not disagree on the proletarian nature of the revolution. The new tendency, to which Castroism belongs, has changed the very terms of the problem. Its road to Communism is paved with a peasant revolution led by *déclassé* bourgeois revolutionaries. In this schema, the proletariat is expected to play a relatively passive, minor role in the struggle for power; it is not supposed to become the active, dominant force until after the assumption of power and, even then, at a later stage.

The new school may conceivably be justified or at least explained by the new conditions in the "underdeveloped" countries. But new conditions give birth to essentially new movements even when they are gestated in the womb of the old.

This process may be extremely confused and ambiguous even for its chief protagonists, let alone for onlookers. The former may think they are doing one thing while they are doing another; they may try to do one thing and succeed in doing another; they may go forward, backtrack, and go forward again. There seems little doubt that, in 1961, Castro thought that the fusion with the PSP had shifted him onto an "orthodox" Communist course. The order of the day was then "industrialization," accompanied by a flight from agriculture, and the urban workers obviously constituted the basic industrializing class.

In his "I am a Marxist-Leninist" speech of December 2, 1961, which was the fullest expression of the fusion, Castro tried to analyze the components of the new "united" party in class terms. The PSP, he said, represented "the most advanced elements of the working class, in the countryside as well as in the city." The 26th of July Movement, he continued, "represented, in the first place, the *campesinos*."

Then, he added, "many people" from the working class, both those who had belonged to petty-bourgeois parties and those without any party affiliation, had "united themselves around the 26th of July Movement." Only after these two categories did he mention "professional sectors, intellectuals, youth elements, students, and also elements of the petty bourgeoisie, the most progressive and revolutionary elements of the middle class and of the petty bourgeoisie." The Directorio Revolucionario, he concluded, represented "more or less the same sectors, but fundamentally the student sector."*

This "class analysis" told more about Castro's state of mind at the end of 1961 than about the make-up of the three movements, especially of the 26th of July Movement, before 1959. It was contrived to make the working class and the peasantry appear to be the preponderant forces in the revolutionary union, with the working class given precedence and the middle class holding up the rear. If all had gone well in 1961, if the industrialization plans had been more successful, Castro might have put the "agrarian revolution" phase completely behind him. The identification of the PSP with the "most advanced elements of the working class" entitled it to the prerogative of becoming the leading cadre of the united party. But all did not go well. As agriculture became his main preoccupation, Castro again had to turn to the countryside to save himself. And as the struggle for power in other Latin American countries became an increasingly controversial issue, Castro again had to fall back on the "Cuban example" of guerrilla warfare and with it the primacy of the peasantry.

A new revolutionary theory, which is none the less new because it calls itself "Marxist-Leninist" or "Communist," has been arising in countries with an overwhelming peasant majority, a puny proletariat, and a miniature middle class.

* *Revolución*, December 2, 1961.

The new theory and its accompanying international movement are based on the thoroughly un-Marxist and, to a somewhat lesser extent, un-Leninist ideas of what might be called the "forwardness of backwardness" and the supercession of the proletariat by the peasantry as the chief revolutionary social force. The Chinese Communists have expressed this theory in the form of a dictum that Asia, Africa, and Latin America constitute "the main focus of global contradictions" and the "storm center of the world revolution." They have even taken the position that the proletariat of the more advanced industrialized countries will not emancipate itself, as Engels put it,[*] but that it will be emancipated by the victory of the underdeveloped peoples. To the extent that the new theory and the new movement reflect the objective conditions in overwhelmingly peasant and truly underdeveloped countries, they may have some social validity, whatever the ultimate effect may be.

But Cuba was not such a country. Its peasantry, by any definition, constituted a minority of the population, and the allegedly "revolutionary" peasantry of the Sierra Maestra-type, a small minority. A large part of its working class was socially far more closely related to the middle class than to the peasantry. The whole promise of the pre-1959 form of the revolution had been to give Cuba the political and social prerequisites for the full utilization of the economic and technical resources that were already there. It is possible to make Cuba fit the Chinese pattern only by distorting the character of the pre-Castro Cuban society or of the anti-Batista struggle for power, weighting both of them inordinately on the peasant side. In a sense, the "semi" or "intermediate" level of Cuban economic development kept it from fitting into either the traditional revolutionary pat-

---

[*] "The emancipation of the working class must be the act of the working class itself" (Engels, Preface [1888] to *The Communist Manifesto*).

tern of the advanced industrialized countries or the new pattern of the underdeveloped countries, and this "intermediacy" is the source of its quandary not only in the capitalist world but in the Communist world.

Yet, times have changed. In Lenin's day, it was customary for the *déclassé* in relatively underdeveloped countries to identify himself with the proletariat. In Castro's day, it has become fashionable for the *déclassé* to identify himself with the peasantry. Until the outbreak of the First World War, however, the international Marxism that Lenin knew was a relatively stable movement, dominated by the strong German Social Democratic Party in the direct line of descent from Marx and Engels themselves. Castro and those in other countries like him have found themselves in a revolutionary world in conflict and in transition. They have no traditions in the working class, and the peasantry has no traditions for them.

The *déclassé* element, then, is rather more unhinged than it used to be. Castroism is not a peasant movement or a proletarian movement any more than it was a middle-class movement. The *déclassé* revolutionaries who have determined Cuba's fate have used one class or another, or a combination of classes, for different purposes at different times. Their leader functions above classes, cuts across classes, or maneuvers between them. He belongs to a leadership type, not unprecedented in this century, which establishes a direct, personal, almost mystical relationship with the masses that frees him from dependence on classes. It also frees him from what Lenin thought was indispensable for a Communist revolution—a party. If Castro had happened to make his revolution in a much larger and stronger country, preferably far removed from the United States, he might not have needed to attach himself to an older movement or to place himself at the mercy of its greatest national power. He belongs to the new revolutionary wave for which it is more important to go than to know where it is going. Since it contains the ingredients of several different and contradictory revolutionary traditions—pre-Marxist, Marxist, and post-Marxist—in a still-unresolved form, it poses questions that only time may be able to answer.

III

CASTRO'S ECONOMICS

THE CRUCIAL PROBLEM of Fidel Castro's regime, it is clear, has been economic. For about two years after he took power, in January, 1959, Castro seemed to enjoy a charmed life. Every crisis worked to his advantage, every enemy made him stronger. After his total, dizzying triumph at the Bay of Pigs—or, as the Cubans prefer to call it, the Playa Girón—nothing seemed impossible to him any longer. It raised Castro's prestige in Cuba and Latin America to its highest point. It led to the liquidation of the internal opposition, which had been growing in strength and militancy. It effectively paralyzed U.S. policy for more than a year.

Paradoxically, however, this triumph may have led Castro to overreach himself. Circumstances seemed so favorable that Castro speeded up the visible transformation of Cuba on the East European model. He authorized the first stage in the development of a single government party, which Cuba had hitherto lacked, in the form of the ORI (Integrated Revolutionary Organizations). New legislation, especially in the field of labor, prepared the way for a completely Communist economy. More than 90 per cent of Cuba's trade was tied to the Soviet bloc.

We now know that the purge of the old-time Communist leader Aníbal Escalante, in March, 1962, was part of an internal crisis far more serious than had previously been realized. This crisis came out into the open between April, 1961, and March, 1962. Its gravest aspect was hidden deep in the Cuban countryside. It amounted to nothing less than a rebellious Cuban peasantry. I would not use the terms "serious crisis" and "rebellious" if two of the foremost Cuban leaders—in the first case Minister of Industries Ernesto Che Guevara, and in the second former President Carlos Rafael Rodríguez of INRA, the "agrarian reform" organization—had not used them already.*

Both Guevara and Rodríguez agree that the crisis was generated in 1961. According to Rodríguez, who has given the most detailed account, "serious errors" were committed in the last half of 1961 and the first two months of 1962. In 1961, food production was still largely in private hands, and the crisis hinged on the right of the private peasants to sell their products. As Rodríguez put it, "the great mass of *campesinos*—even the poor ones—showed the class tendency with respect to profit." They wanted, in other words, to sell at the highest price instead of handing over their wares to INRA for much lower fixed prices.

* Che Guevara, *Siempre* (Mexico City), interview with Víctor Rico Galán, June 19, 1963; Carlos Rafael Rodríguez, *Revolución,* May 18, 1963.

It was a classic confrontation. Faced with this traditional peasant desire to take advantage of a sellers' market, the Cuban authorities cracked down. Rodríguez specifically blamed INRA officials, local political leaders, and even the armed forces. The peasants' goods were seized and in some cases their land confiscated. This was not a war against *latifundistas,* or large landowners, for there were no more. It was a fierce struggle against small and middle peasants, predominantly the former. The severity of the methods may be gathered from Rodríguez' observation that they violated "revolutionary legality" and made no distinction between rich and poor. The strength of the resistance may be inferred from his allusion to the peasants' "disagreement and rebelliousness" [*"inconformidad y rebeldía"*].

In effect, the peasants sold on the black market or they went on strike. They sowed less and grew less. In 1962, especially in the months of March and November, Rodríguez said, the peasants had their revenge in the country-wide shortages that developed. He himself had been brought in as the new President of INRA in February in a top administrative shake-up. Castro reversed INRA policy and temporarily gave way to the peasants by lifting all restrictions, but the damage had been done.

The Women of Cárdenas

The regime was so acutely worried that, in June, it ordered a parade of tanks and machine guns in the city of Cárdenas as a warning to housewives who had come out in the streets beating pots and pans to protest food shortages. President Dorticós was rushed to the scene to make a threatening speech. The entire country soon knew about the Cárdenas demonstration. No attempt was made to conceal or minimize the seriousness of the incident. On the contrary, the regime took special pains to blow it up by putting the parade of tanks and machine guns and the Dorticós speech on television.

Dorticós himself explained the military display "as a warning and a reminder to our enemies, a modest sample of the military strength of a people in arms." He blamed the "difficulties and scarcities" on the "imperialist blockade" but admitted that "our errors and our shortcomings" had aggravated the situation. He denounced the women's protest as a "miserable and counterrevolutionary provocation" inspired by "imperialism." At one point he tried to stir the crowd to take such matters into its own hands.

"Do not permit a single provocation by the counterrevolutionary parasites in the cities! We will not have to use those tanks or those machine guns against them! You yourselves, comrades, are enough to crush them every day! If they repeat the provocation, our armed forces will not fail! The people out in the streets! The people masters of the street! No retreat or cowardice!"*

Against women beating pots and pans!

If the "imperialists" had really been capable of provoking such a demonstration in the heart of Cuba, it would have meant that they had controlled forces on the island far greater than anyone had imagined or than Castro had ever admitted. But Dorticós' charge was not intended to be taken literally or even seriously. Since the end of 1961, there had not been any effective underground in Cuba because of the remarkable system of spies and informers that had succeeded in infiltrating every opposition group.†

* *El Mundo*, June 17, 1962.

† A pro-Castro writer, Maurice Zeitlin, who visited Cuba after the Cárdenas demonstration, has confirmed the essential facts: "*Organized* dissent is prohibited, if one can judge by the government's response to a recent demonstration of a group of housewives in Cárdenas who went marching through the streets banging pots to protest food shortages. The next day the government put on an impressive military display which included helmeted soldiers (a sight one rarely sees in Cuba) and tanks" (*The Nation*, November 3, 1962, p. 287).

Late that same June, another incident took place in the town of El Cano, near Havana. It was sufficiently important for Castro to spend about half an hour on it in a speech.* According to Castro, one of the townspeople was accidentally killed and another wounded when Cuban armed forces attempted to round up a group that had taken refuge in a thickly wooded area. Castro characterized the hunted men as "a group of elements," without definitely stating whether they were oppositionists.

In any case, the townspeople were outraged by the killings. All the stores shut down in protest. The grocery closed. The pharmacy closed. The bakery closed. The protest was treated as if it threatened the very foundations of the regime. The grocer, the druggist, the baker, and all the rest found themselves attacked as the incarnation of the "bourgeois counterrevolution." Almost without exception, the shops were confiscated. Cars, trucks, and even telephones were taken away.

I do not mean to suggest that Castro was threatened with a vast popular uprising in June, 1962. Mass popular resistance was still largely passive and burst into the open only sporadically. But there seem to have been other incidents such as those in Cárdenas and El Cano, and for this reason Castro decided not merely to crack down but to do so with maximum publicity.

Still, if we may trust Carlos Rafael Rodríguez, it may have been a rather close shave. "Only faith in the revolution, only faith in Fidel, prevented the peasantry from losing confidence in the revolution," he later acknowledged.†

Yet Raúl Castro had the effrontery to tell Mme. Anne Philipe, who had the innocence to publish it without further questioning: "We have never sent a single soldier, a single policeman to stop demonstrations demanding better food supplies, even when we knew that they were organized by the counterrevolution" (*Le Monde*, January 3, 1963).

* *El Mundo*, June 30, 1962.

† Carlos Rafael Rodríguez, *Revolución*, May 18, 1963. His fullest analysis of the crisis appeared in *Cuba Socialista*, May, 1963, pp. 12–14.

But the private peasants were not the only ones in trouble. The "cooperatives" were also caught up in the crisis. The essential reason was that they were cooperatives in name only. In practice, as Rodríguez later admitted, they had been transformed into *granjas del pueblo,* or state farms. INRA administered them from above without in the least taking their members' wishes into account, giving them any voice in their affairs, or even holding *pro forma* meetings. From the point of view of their members, the cooperatives had all the disadvantages of state farms and none of the advantages, the most important of the latter being a guaranteed wage. Here again the crisis built up in the last half of 1961 and burst out in the first half of 1962. In November, 1961, Castro himself remarked that the peasants had become so "allergic" to the cooperatives that they "feared" the very word.* In June, 1962, Rodríguez reported that the cooperatives had become "dead organisms" and their members had been shifting to the *granjas* and private farms.† And in August, they were officially transformed into *granjas.*

Not that the *granjas* had been doing too well. They were so badly run at the time, their chief administrator has revealed, that 80 per cent of the local administrators had to be removed.‡ Later, Castro gave one reason for the trouble: 60 to 80 per cent of the sugar farms' administrators had had no more than a third- to fifth-grade elementary-school education.§ According to one pro-Castro writer, each dollar's worth of product on the state farms has cost approximately $1.20.¶ In 1962, then, the Castro regime ran into

* *Revolución,* November 11, 1961.
† *Ibid.,* June 19, 1962. More details are given in *Cuba Socialista,* May, 1963, p. 12.
‡ Interview with Cristóbal Díaz Vallina, Administrador General de Granjas del Pueblo, *Hoy,* July 6, 1963.
§ Speech of November 13, 1964.
¶ Adolfo Gilly, *Inside the Cuban Revolution* (New York: Monthly Review Press, 1964), pp. 4–5.

trouble on all three of its agricultural fronts—privately owned lands, "cooperatives," and *granjas*. One of the more durable myths about Castro's Cuba is the idea that the "agrarian reform" has been the most successful aspect of the revolution. If this were true, the past two or three years would have been very different.

Gradually, the agricultural miasma settled over the entire economic landscape. It made rationing necessary, which in turn brought on inflation, because the urban population had more to spend but less to buy. The inflationary spiral infected the workers, who no longer had the incentive to exert themselves for what they could not get anyway. Workers' absenteeism began to reach alarming proportions because workers found they could earn enough in two or three days to buy the little that was available. The quality of work also suffered with declining morale and reduced effective purchasing power. From the viewpoint of the regime, the chief culprits were the skilled workers, formerly the hard core of the organized Cuban proletariat. Castro had complained bitterly about the attitude of the electrical workers as long ago as December, 1960, but his wrath with what he called "worker-aristocrats"—whom he grouped with the big and little bourgeoisie and imperialist monopolies—came out most forcefully in a speech addressed to party members in the construction industry in July, 1963. He assailed the drop in productivity in the construction industry and accused the workers of doing more under the capitalists than under his regime.* Guevara a few months later ascribed the "terrible loss of conscience for quality" to the "initial scarcity of raw materials, and the suppression of private property."†

Yet one of the most significant aspects of this crisis was the fact that the Cuban leaders were not prepared for it.

* *Obra Revolucionaria,* December 15, 1960; *Revolución,* July 2, 1963.
† *La Tarde,* November 11, 1963.

Nothing that had happened in 1961 had forewarned them because 1961 had been a relatively good year, so good that the former President of the Cuban National Bank, the late Dr. Raúl Cepero Bonilla, called it "the year of the highest agricultural production."* This was especially true of Cuba's key crop, sugar, which still provided more than three-quarters of its export earnings. The 1961 sugar crop was an exceptionally large one of 6.8 million tons, the second largest in Cuban history. But the 1962 crop was only 4.8 million tons and the 1963 crop was still less, only 3.8 million.† Between 1961 and 1963, the only negative factor beyond human control was the drought, which could not, however, by itself have accounted for such a drastic drop. All the other factors were man-made, and the results should have made the Cuban leaders happy.

But they did not. Why they did not is the economic key to Castro's first five years in power.

Politics and Economics

Guevara himself has revealed a small but essential part of what went on behind the scenes.

In 1959, he had been put in charge of INRA's Department of Industrialization. His group worked on the "first simple and tentative lines" for the future Cuban economy. As Guevara later told the story, they made lists of products that had for many years been imported chiefly from the United States, and then began a "search for offers" of long-term foreign aid for the development of Cuba's own "basic industry." The "search" ended with the arrival of Soviet First Deputy Premier Anastas I. Mikoyan in Havana on February 4, 1960, and the signing of the first Soviet-Cuban trade agreement on February 13 of that year. Then Guevara

* *Cuba Socialista,* January 1963, p. 89.
† Gerardo Bernardo, *Hoy Domingo,* August 11, 1963.

went on a junket of Eastern Europe, lining up Soviet-bloc commitments of large-scale credits "to build a good number of basic industries." The Soviets promised $100 million for a steel industry, electric plants, an oil refinery, and a geological survey; Czechoslovakia, an automobile factory; China, $60 million for twenty-four different factories; Romania, fifteen; Bulgaria, five; Poland, twelve; East Germany, ten. The offers were snapped up.*

Soon after Mikoyan's departure, Guevara and other top Cuban leaders began a campaign to prepare Cuban public opinion for a rupture of the traditional economic ties with the United States, especially the preferential sugar quota. Guevara initiated the drive on March 2, 1960, in a speech in which he answered those who had charged that the Soviet-Cuban commercial agreement would "enslave" Cuba by accusing them of refusing to see "how much slavery the 3 million tons which we sell at supposedly preferential prices represented for our country."† In this way, Guevara for the first time managed to get across the idea that the "supposedly" preferential quota of the United States was a form of "slavery."

The leading Cuban Communist, Blas Roca, went to Moscow in May for his first meeting with Nikita Khrushchev and, unable to restrain himself until his return, wrote a letter published in the official Communist organ: "Cuba cannot be blockaded economically by the U.S. imperialists. Our factories will not be paralyzed from lack of oil, neither will our homes run short of bread in case the U.S. monopolies decide to reduce the sugar quota and refuse to send what we need for our normal life." Fidel Castro boasted that Cuba could produce more sugar and get more for it if there were no U.S. sugar quota.‡

* Guevara, *Cuba Socialista*, March, 1962, p. 30.
† *Hoy*, March 4, 1960.
‡ Roca, *Hoy*, May 24, 1960; Castro, *Hoy*, May 29, 1960.

At this point, the Eisenhower Administration, against the better judgment of the U.S. Ambassador, Philip W. Bonsal, played into the Cubans' hands. In June, 1960, three U.S.-and British-owned oil refineries in Cuba, in consultation with Washington, refused a Cuban request to process Soviet crude oil. The Cubans promptly took over the oil refineries; the Eisenhower Administration suspended the remainder of the 1960 sugar quota; the Cubans expropriated all U.S.-owned properties; the United States retaliated with a trade embargo. In retrospect, it appears clear that only a Cuban Government which was already inwardly committed to, and had prepared the way for, a break would have pushed the matter of the oil to such an extremity; and only a U.S. Government which had grossly miscalculated the forces at work or did not care any longer for other reasons would have made the break so easy.*

The Cubans welcomed the U.S. embargo. "Now," exulted Blas Roca, "Cuba has freed her foreign commerce from the monopoly of an imperialist power. Now Cuba has won freedom of trade with every country in the world." Fidel Castro scoffed at the idea that the United States could hurt Cuba, since the Cubans could obtain all they needed and wanted from the "socialist countries" and "neutrals." Guevara assured the Cuban people that the U.S. embargo would have few serious consequences, that it would not imperil the revolution, and that the U.S. would be hurt even more than Cuba by its own action.†

* We now know that President Eisenhower authorized the training of a stand-by Cuban exile force in March, 1960.

† Roca, *Hoy*, October 13, 1960; Castro, *ibid.*, October 16, 1960; Guevara, *ibid.*, October 21, 1960. Apparently the notion that the United States could not do without Cuban sugar was deeply ingrained and partially accounts for the risks Castro was willing to take. In *La Guerra de Guerrillas*, written before the summer crisis, Guevara had assured the Cubans that it was "very dangerous [for the United States] to reduce the Cuban quota and *impossible* to cancel it" (*op. cit.*, pp. 198–99, italics added). This may be one more example of how the Cubans went wrong by believing their own propaganda that no one but the United States benefited from the preferential sugar quota.

There was, then, an important internal political side to Cuban-Soviet relations. Cuban-Soviet economic ties were closely coordinated with Communist-Castroist political ties. By October, 1959, as we have seen, anti-Communism had been made a counterrevolutionary crime with the arrest of Major Hubert Matos. This transition to anti-anti-Communism in public policy preceded the Cuban-Soviet economic agreement of February, 1960. After the agreement, the active process of Communist-Castroist fusion speeded up. Immediately after the suspension of the U.S. sugar quota, Guevara told a youth congress in Havana in July that the Cuban revolution was "Marxist," as if it had never occurred to him before. The following month, as U.S. businesses in Cuba were being expropriated, Blas Roca held out the perspective of "complete union" or "fusion" of all the revolutionary forces "in a single movement," as if such fusion had not already been taking shape in some minds on both sides. And the first formal manifestation of "the integration of the revolutionary forces," as Lionel Soto put it, was a meeting held on December 2 in connection with the Escuelas de Instrucción Revolucionaria, as the culmination of a single, continuous process which had included the "search for offers" in 1959, the Soviet-Cuban trade agreement of February, 1960, the expropriations, and the embargo.

Another major decision came up at the end of 1960. This one grew out of the suspension of the Cuban sugar quota by the Eisenhower Administration in July. The Soviet Union had committed itself to purchasing 1 million tons annually for five years, or one-third of the former U.S. quota. The Cubans could see no way, in the depressed world sugar market of 1960–61, to dispose of the remainder. Moreover, they were then obsessed by two main objectives —rapid industrialization and agricultural diversification. Sugar represented all that had stood in the way of industrialization and diversification in the past. Instead of facing the loss of the U.S. market with a certain trepidation, the Cuban leaders could barely repress their joy. They viewed more industrialization and less sugar production as opposite sides of the same coin, and embraced both causes with equal enthusiasm. When the U.S. quota was suspended, therefore, they considered it to be a positive good and, as Castro later put it, "took the decision to cut down on all that sugar cane and reduce sugar production."*

Drought or no drought, then, there would have been a much smaller Cuban sugar crop in 1962 and 1963 (not in 1961 because the preparations had been made the year before). The sugar acreage was deliberately reduced, replanting neglected, and weeding pursued halfheartedly; in general, the entire industry was given a very low order of priority. The drought hurt other crops but, in the all-important case of sugar, it might have been part of the plan. Between the drought and government policy, there was in the period 1961–63 a reduction of 14 per cent in sugar area cut, of 42 per cent in ground cane, and 33 per cent in unit yield.†

Nevertheless, as 1961 opened, Castro's mastery of events, helped along perhaps by more than a bit of luck, seemed infallible. He had freed himself from all economic and diplomatic ties to the United States in a manner that made him seem to many the aggrieved and innocent party. The Eisenhower Administration's decision to suspend the sugar quota had fallen in with his own desire not only to get rid of the quota but to cut sugar production. The Soviet bloc had apparently agreed to underwrite what Guevara had called "a process of accelerated industrialization."‡ A new Ministry of Industries was created in February of that year with Guevara in charge. And after the April invasion fiasco, the Cuban cup ran over.

* *Revolución*, June 28, 1963.
† Bernardo, *loc. cit.*
‡ *Hoy*, June 21, 1960.

The Critical Triangle

What had gone wrong?

The private peasantry, the cooperatives, and the *granjas* were not the only things that had gone wrong. When a Latin American sympathizer asked Guevara to name some of the errors which had been made in Cuba, his answer, only half in jest, was: "It will have to be only some, because we would need ten days to recount all the errors."*

Guevara's own program of "accelerated industrialization" was the source of some of the worst disenchantment. The original conception was almost childishly simple. Its aim was the substitution of homemade goods for those previously imported from the United States. Its method was the physical transplantation across half the globe of dozens of factories in the shortest possible time. Its financial basis was long-term credits or outright gifts from the Communist world.

By early 1962, Guevara knew that there was something radically wrong with the scheme. At that time, he analyzed the trouble as follows: "We failed to put the proper emphasis on the utilization of our own resources; we worked with the fixed purpose of producing substitutes for finished imported articles, without clearly seeing that these articles are made with raw materials which must be had in order to manufacture them."†

In short, the Cuban industrializers thought solely in terms of factories, not in terms of raw materials for the factories. They were stunned to learn that, in many cases, the raw materials cost almost as much as the imported finished articles. In order to free themselves from dependence on the importation of finished articles, they had made themselves even more dependent on the importation of raw materials which they could not afford. Guevara subsequently

---

* *Revolución,* August 21, 1963.
† *Cuba Socialista,* March, 1962, p. 33.

explained: "We began to acquire factories, but we did not think of the raw materials for them that we would have to import." In this way, he said, two years had been lost "installing factories for a series of articles which could be bought at almost the same price as the raw materials that we needed to produce them."*

This unforeseen, though hardly unforeseeable, relationship between finished products and raw materials led to a Cuban balance-of-payments crisis. In 1960, when the Soviet bloc was anxious to displace the United States in the Cuban economy, it had been lavish in promises and credits. Two years later, however, it was less interested in what the Cubans wanted than in what the Cubans could afford. Either the credits had run out or they had been used so badly that the bloc had balked at throwing good money after bad. Most of the promised factories were held up or forgotten.

At some point toward the end of 1961 or the beginning of 1962, it is clear, the Soviets called a halt and demanded an accounting. We know from Carlos Rafael Rodríguez that, by March, 1962, Soviet bloc "advisers," who had become ubiquitous in the Cuban administrative apparatus, had become highly critical of Cuban methods, especially in the Ministry of Foreign Trade. In the same month, Guevara published an article in which he warned that Cuba would have to pay for its raw materials through its own foreign trade and not with Soviet credits or handouts. To be sure, the Cubans did receive further credits from the Soviet Union, but as Guevara later explained, they were to cover the existing unfavorable balance of payments, not to build industries.†

At this point, though not for this reason alone, the for-

---

* *Revolución*, August 21, 1963.

† Rodríguez, *El Mundo*, March 25, 1962; Guevara, *Cuba Socialista*, March, 1962, p. 33; Guevara, *Hoy*, February 12, 1963.

tunes of the former PSPers began to decline. As a result of his meeting with Khrushchev in May, 1960, Blas Roca had been able to get the credit for telling the Cuban people that they could depend on Soviet Russia to replace the United States even in the event of a U.S. blockade. In the following year or year and a half, Cuba was geared to the Soviet Union economically and to the former PSP politically. But as the Soviets began to feel the pinch of their Cuban commitment and to make the first efforts to ease up on it, the former PSP leaders opened themselves up to the charge that they had oversold the Soviets' willingness to underwrite the Cuban economy. If Fidel Castro had to assure the Soviet Union of his "orthodoxy" to get its full support, and if the best assurance was his embrace of the "orthodox" Cuban Communists, the increasing reluctance of the Soviet Union to carry the full burden of Castro's costly economic vagaries was bound sooner or later to hit back at the old-time Cuban Communists who had acted as the middlemen.

After the purge of Aníbal Escalante that same March, Soviet-Cuban political relations hit their lowest point. Escalante's fate was soon shared by the Soviet Ambassador in Havana, Sergei Mihailovitch Kudryavtsev, who since 1960 had been a conspicuous figure in Cuban politics. Unlike many Soviet envoys, he had never bothered to conceal his power or limit himself to behind-the-scenes activities. Kudryavtsev's departure from Cuba was embarrassingly precipitate. He had just made known that he intended to take a vacation in Cuba. He left as if he had not been given enough time to pack his belongings. Castro did not see him off, and the Cuban press did not pay the slightest respects to his past services.

Castro did not see him off, it has been confirmed, because Castro had asked Moscow to recall him. Castro told an American correspondent in his favor that he had "expelled"

Kudryavtsev for having engaged in "open and excessive political activities."* Since Soviet Ambassadors do not carry out personal policies—though Kudryavtsev seems to have enjoyed an unusually free hand, testifying to the confidence the top Soviet leadership had in him—his abrupt departure could not have been without wider ramifications.

Kudryavtsev's contretemps was followed by a season of more or less open recriminations between the Soviet-bloc representatives and the Castro regime. European diplomats and journalists could scarcely believe their ears as they were suddenly treated by Soviet-bloc diplomats and journalists to an outpouring of bitter complaints about Cuban waste, disorganization, and unwillingness to work. Warehouses were said to be full of crates with Soviet-bloc goods and machinery that had never been opened or had been mishandled and permitted to rot or rust. At the same time, the Cubans grumbled audibly that what they were getting from the Soviet bloc was too little and too late, that machines broke down because essential parts were missing or could not be replaced, and that many Eastern products could not be integrated into Cuba's existing industrial plant.

As Soviet-Cuban relations began to show visible signs of strain, Khrushchev made a speech in Moscow for direct Cuban consumption. It was delivered on June 4 at a farewell meeting for 1,000 Cuban youths who had just finished a year's training as agricultural mechanics in the Soviet Union. Khrushchev compared Cuba's growing crisis with that which had confronted the Russian Bolsheviks after they had beaten off their enemies in the civil war. He put it to the Cubans bluntly: "There are some who begin to say: What is this? Fidel Castro calls on us to make the revolution; we follow him; we defeat Batista; and now meat is

* Lisa Howard, "Castro's Overture," *War/Peace Report*, September, 1963, p. 4.

lacking, rice is lacking, milk is lacking. What kind of revolution is this?"

Khrushchev advised the Cubans that it would take more than heroism and arms to overcome these difficulties. The road was "long and not easy." He promised to continue sending "arms and other things" to Cuba, but he stressed that the construction of socialism and Communism demanded "a high degree of consciousness, intelligence, and a great deal of work." He recalled that Lenin had solved the Soviet crisis by introducing in 1921 the New Economic Policy, which had "made concessions to capitalist elements within the country for the ultimate strengthening of the interests of socialism in the country." Lenin, he added, had also offered concessions to foreign capitalists. Some members of the Bolshevik Party could not understand the necessity for the NEP and had thrown away their Party cards, but he, Khrushchev, had marched with the Party.*

It is fairly clear from this and other indications that the Soviet leaders were counseling the Cubans to take it easy, to make some concessions to the Cuban middle class, and even perhaps to start mending their economic fences with the United States.

Castro himself had to offer public apologies to the Soviets for the reluctance of too many Cubans to take the "advice" of Soviet technicians. On June 29, at a farewell meeting for a group of Soviet technicians, he made this revealing statement:

"We know of our deficiencies; we know of many [Cuban] administrators who have no experience and, in some cases, do not even have a high political level; and in other cases, do not have a high or a greater feeling of hospitality.

"And so we know that a [Soviet] technician who went to a state farm administered by an experienced, hospitable comrade, conscious of his obligations, would be very well

* *Revolución,* June 4, 1962.

treated. But we also know that there was no lack of places where the administrator received them coldly or with indifference, or was not sufficiently responsible to utilize the knowledge which you possess.

"And so we have had reports when in some state farms the technicians were not well treated by the administrators, or when the administrators did not make use of the knowledge of the technicians; reports of various kinds, reports like those of administrators who thought the way to treat the technicians well was to take them out, to offer them girls [laughter]. . . ."*

The indications are that it took some time and not a little anguish for the Cubans to give up the view of industrialization as a simple, rather naïve, two-way process of factories–finished products and to think in terms of the far more complex, critical triangle of factories–raw materials–exports.

In a sense, the Cuban problem had come to resemble the Chinese problem—how far would the Soviets go to pay for their speedy industrialization? In both cases, the Soviets started to go part of the way, but then, for reasons of their own, not necessarily the same in both cases, they demanded a slowdown of the pace and payment for services rendered. Consciously or unconsciously, the Cubans had gone ahead after 1960 as if the Soviets had given them not a $100-million five-year credit but an unlimited account. There would have been no balance-of-payments crisis if the Soviets had not called for payments.

Once the Cubans had to face the realities of production costs, profit margins, and balance of payments, all their other problems came down on them too. If they had to pay for imports with exports, they were driven back to the key economic fact of Cuban life from which they had fled—that sugar made up more than three-fourths of Cuban exports.

* *El Mundo,* July 1, 1962.

But for about two years, the Cuban leaders had been denigrating the importance of sugar production and had deliberately cut it down. The resistance of the private peasantry,
the "disagreement and rebelliousness" in the sugar-growing
"cooperatives," and the mismanagement of the *granjas* were
not merely symptoms of an agricultural crisis; they were
not merely contributing factors in the vicious cycle of rationing, inflation, absenteeism, high costs, and low quality;
they were directly linked to the neuralgic points of Cuban-
Soviet economic relations—the trade agreements, the negotiation of credits, the balance of payments.

Thus what Guevara called the "two fundamental errors"
—the "declaration of war on sugar cane" and the desire for factories without "thinking of the raw materials
for them"*—intersected and interacted, exacerbating each
other.

Late in 1963, Guevara gave some examples of the blundering that brought the industrialization program to a
standstill. Two of the factories from Czechoslovakia were to
make picks and shovels. Cuba could just as well have
bought the finished products from East Europe. Instead,
the factories had to import raw materials, which depleted
the already extremely scarce monetary reserves. Another
Cuban factory made sacks; it required imports of jute,
which cost more than the finished sacks. The Cubans then
decided to buy another factory which would use a native
fiber. Guevara also lamented the fact that Cuba had factories to make metal containers—but no tin plate.† Judging
from the frequency and pain with which the Cuban leaders have mentioned their expensive education in the economics of raw materials, these miscalculations must have
been the rule rather than the exception.

In effect, Castro's first year in power, 1959, was one in

* *Revolución*, August 21, 1963.
† *La Tarde*, November 11, 1963.

which there was no "socialist" planning; in the second year, the "old order" was completely shattered but only the rudiments of a new order could be established; in the third year, the Castro regime was for the first time able to impose its basic ideas on the economy, and it thereby generated the subsequent crisis; in the fourth year, ironically called the "Year of Planning," the crisis erupted and caused a preliminary reconsideration of the policy; and in the fifth year, the crisis deepened in the first months and brought about a change of line.

"Culpa" but Not "Mea"

The Cuban leaders have tried to account for the crisis in characteristically different ways. The two who have done the most talking—namely, Castro and Guevara—have revealed not only a great deal about the crisis but also about themselves. Their main problem has not been to tell the people how bad the situation was, for this was common knowledge in Cuba; it has been to explain why it happened and who was to blame.

Castro spoke frequently and at great length in the last half of 1963 on what had been wrong in Cuba, and his emphasis was overwhelmingly on what the Cuban people had done that was wrong. Sometimes, as on June 4, he seemed to hold his own "Cuban revolutionaries" mainly responsible for the economic mess. He accused them of "agitating" and "mobilizing" too much, of building "in the air," blissfully oblivious to "the economic basis for everything." He was, he said, even "a little ashamed" of them. Sometimes, as on July 1, he complained bitterly that the workers did not work long and hard enough. "And we have to carry on this struggle," he said, "implacably, in all places, in all parts of the country, without a truce, without vacillation, one day demanding that the sugar workers, the agricultural workers, the shoe workers should produce more, should improve their quality." Or, on August 10, he turned on the "socialist administrators," whose waste, he said, was comparable to what the capitalists used to steal, who "consolidated" everything from garages to bars into nationwide bureaucratic monstrosities, who could not manage the former U.S.-owned lands as well as the "Yankee monopolies" had managed them. He made the broad generalization, on October 2, that "our weakness is principally in the lack of experience and ability of the people who have been in many places in agriculture." On October 21, he lit into the trade unions for accumulating funds by means of compulsory deductions and fund-raising parties, both of which were to be forbidden, and for their grievance committees, which he called an example of "illusionism" and "revolutionary infantilism." On October 30, he turned on most of his Cabinet ministers for spending too much money. On October 31, he incited a crowd, not for the first time, against "the bum [*"vago"*], the parasite, the *lumpen"* (the latter became one of Castro's favorite expressions after he officially adopted Marxism-Leninism).

The notable thing about almost all this criticism, scolding, and abuse is that they were directed at the people rather than at his own policies. The people were rarely in positions of any real power and most often totally without power. And by avoiding policies and power, Fidel Castro did not have to criticize, scold, or abuse Fidel Castro.

Guevara's emphasis, on the other hand, was refreshingly different. He made several attempts to analyze what went wrong, three of which are worth noting at some length. The first was his reply to a question from the French correspondent Jean Daniel on whether the U.S. "blockade" had endangered Cuba:

"We have serious difficulties in Cuba. But not from the fact of what you call the blockade. First, there has never been a complete blockade. We have not ceased increasing our trade with Great Britain and France, for example. . . .

"Our difficulties come principally from our errors. The greatest, that which did us the most harm, is, as you know, the underexploitation of sugar cane. The others involve all the inevitable gropings which the adaptation of collectivism to a local situation implies."*

But a speech by Guevara in Algiers on July 13, perhaps the most revealing confession of Cuba's misplanning on record, did not make the other errors seem so "inevitable." The fundamental trouble, said Guevara, came about because the Cubans tried to do two things that were contradictory. On the one hand, they "copied in detail the planning techniques of a fraternal country whose specialists came to help us," and on the other hand, they insisted on making their own decisions with "spontaneity and lack of analysis." He gave as an example of this planless planning the way they had arrived at their annual rate of economic growth. Instead of attempting to find out "what we had, what we should spend, and what we had left over for development," the Cuban planners had simply assumed a 15 per cent rate of growth and had made everything else in the plan conform to it. Cuba had never made more than 10 million pairs of shoes but the plan called for 22 million, and cattle and technical facilities were already inadequate. The chief of the forestry department had sent up such a fantastic estimate of lumber production that Cuba, traditionally an importer of lumber, had planned to export it. "Result: we continued to import lumber," said Guevara, "but we imported it late, badly, desperately looking around where to get it."

One can imagine the frustrations of the "fraternal specialists" in Cuba. According to Castro himself, the machinery that Cuba received up to the end of 1964 func-

* *L'Express* (Paris), July 25, 1963.

tioned at only 50 per cent of capacity owing to lack of maintenance, repairs, and organization.*

But even if the planning had been less "ridiculous," which is how Guevara characterized it, the major policy decisions, as Guevara described them, would have been near-disastrous anyway. "In industry," he said, "we made a plan of development based fundamentally on the idea of being self-sufficient in a series of durable consumption goods or intermediate industrial articles, which, however, could be obtained with relative facility from friendly countries. In this way we committed our investment capacity without completely developing our own resources of raw materials, including some intermediate products that we now make." And "in agriculture, we committed the fundamental error of scorning the importance of sugar cane, our fundamental product, trying to achieve quick diversification, as a consequence of which the cane stocks were neglected, and this, added to an extraordinarily intense drought that afflicted us for two years, led to a serious drop in our sugar production."

At the end of 1964, Guevara published a semiconfessional article in a British journal. In agriculture, he admitted, there had been "a general decline" as a result of the attempt to diversify too much and too quickly. "Serious agricultural problems" had arisen "immediately." Diversification should have been undertaken "by degrees" and "on a smaller scale" in traditional fields of cultivation "for a small number of new products." Because it tried to develop a great number of agricultural products "within a relatively few months," the change-over had produced a "greater weakness in the agricultural productive organization" than it had suffered from previously. "Many of us" had not been aware of the "basic economic fact" that "no other agricultural activity would give such returns as those yielded

* *Hoy*, November 20, 1964.

by the cultivation of the sugar cane." In industry, the fundamental errors had been caused "by a lack of precise understanding of the technological and economic elements necessary in the new industries installed during those [first] years." The elements most misunderstood had been the insufficiency of "technical efficiency" and the lack of nationally produced raw materials. The chief lesson learned from all this, according to Guevara, was Cuba's dependence on its "foreign trade." It could not afford to adopt a policy of "substitution of imports" until its exports could pay for an "industrialization program." And exports, until at least 1970, would mean more and more sugar.*

It would appear, then, that Guevara and others have been enrolled in one of the most expensive courses ever given in elementary economics. For at least a decade before Castro, agricultural diversification and expansion of manufacturing had gone forward in Cuba "by degrees" and "for a small number of new products," such as rice, coffee, and textiles. For a century and a half, sugar cane had spread over Cuba because it was so easy to cultivate and its "returns" were greater than a comparable effort put into other agricultural products. By attempting to force diversification and industrialization, the Castro regime had actually set Cuba back in both respects. In order to regain the lost ground, it was virtually retracing all the steps that Cuba had already gone through, beginning with the expansion of sugar cultivation. If there happened to be a slip-up in 1970, as there had been in 1960, Cuba would be left with little more than sugar in an already glutted market. Even if Cuba were to get moving again according to plan, the rise would begin not at the level of pre-Castro Cuba but at a much lower level. Whatever the future might bring, the first six years in power had taught the Cuban leaders the

---

* "The Cuban Economy: Its Past and Its Present Importance," *International Affairs* (London), October, 1964, pp. 593–96.

profound wisdom that there was no quick and easy road to diversification, that sugar was Cuba's "money crop," and that they could not get something for nothing, even in the socialist world.

In some ways, then, Guevara was far more candid than Castro. In fact, the reversal of Cuban policy at the end of 1963 was in large part a defeat for some of Guevara's favorite ideas. It was he who had first used the slogan of "accelerated industrialization." It was he who had played the leading role in negotiating the trade agreements with the Soviet bloc. It was he who had broached the theory that "Cuban socialism," unlike the other varieties, should be based predominantly on "moral" rather than on "material" incentives.

This last point is typical of what might be called "Guevaraism." As late as March, 1963, Guevara still insisted publicly that the "moral incentive" should take precedence over the "material incentive," which he scornfully described as a "residue of the past" to be removed from the popular consciousness with every advance of the revolution.* He told Jean Daniel in July: "For me, it is a question of doctrine. Economic socialism without Communist morality does not interest me."† Yet by August,

---

* *Revolución*, March 25, 1963.

† *L'Express*, July 25, 1963. A further point he made in this interview raises an interesting question about his Marxism. Guevara continued: "We are struggling against poverty, but at the same time against alienation. One of the fundamental objectives of Marxism is to eliminate interest—the factor of 'individual interest'—and profit from psychological motivations." But Marx located "alienation" in the capitalist system of production, in capitalist exploitation. The concept had nothing to do with counterposing "material" and "moral" stimuli in a *socialist* economy, which is itself supposed to do away with alienation. For Marx, the solution for "alienation" was a material one, in the economic order though its consequences would be moral or psychological. The very dissociation of "socialist economy" and "Communist morality" would be alien to Marx's thought. From a Marxist viewpoint, a "socialist economy" should have a "socialist morality," and a "Communist economy" should have a "Communist morality" (assuming that Guevara is making the traditional distinction between socialism and Communism). Guevara's viewpoint actually

even he had to recognize that the *"estímulo moral"* had not been very stimulating, and he grudgingly admitted that it was necessary "for the moment to give the material incentive the importance which it has."* This retreat, however, did not last very long. In 1964, Guevara went back with all his old zeal and fervor to the evangel of "voluntary labor" as the main method of developing a "socialist consciousness."† One can almost hear the debates in Cuba over relaxing or tightening the economic pressure on the peasants and workers in the guise of offering them more material or more moral "incentive."

In a sense, Guevara has represented both the most distinctive and the most dubious sides of this Cuban revolution. In the name of Marxism, he has identified himself with theories—the peasantry as the leading revolutionary class, the countryside as the main revolutionary battleground, the primacy of the "moral incentive"—that are far closer to the tradition of pre-Marxist Russian Populism and homologous movements elsewhere than to orthodox Marxism. He has embodied a peculiar doctrinairism of will and force to overcome all obstacles and enemies. His undoubtedly keen mind has invariably gravitated to the more extreme positions, which sooner or later, and more often than not, have turned out to be Fidel Castro's positions.

The Case of Professor Dumont

A well-known French agronomist and Castro sympathizer, Professor René Dumont, who was given unusual opportunities to study Cuban agricultural policy and practice,

---

implies that "alienation" can exist in a socialist as well as in a capitalist society, which may be true, but not in a Marxist sense. I am not suggesting that Guevara has no right to mix his categories; I merely question that it should be done in the name of poor, dead Marx.

* *Revolución*, August 21, 1963.

† These sentiments were clearly expressed in Guevara's speeches of March 14 and May 10, 1964.

has shed some light on internal Cuban differences. Dumont came to Cuba for the first time on his own initiative in May, 1960. At that time he was struck by the dangerously excessive tendency to centralize and socialize (a better term would be the French *étatiser*). He foresaw that the centralization would lead to a top-heavy, deadening bureaucracy and the "socialization" to macrocephalic, inefficient production units. Significantly, he confided his doubts to Carlos Rafael Rodríguez, then editor of the official Communist organ *Hoy,* who asked him to repeat them to Fidel Castro in person. Castro seemed most grateful to hear Dumont's criticisms, and a press interview was arranged for Dumont. Encouraged by Castro's seemingly favorable reception, Dumont publicly voiced his misgivings, but great was his astonishment when the entire Havana press failed to carry a word about the interview the next day.

He returned, however, three months later, in August, 1960, at Castro's personal invitation. As he put it, "my disquiet increased." He was taken by Castro on a personal tour of the Ciénaga de Zapata, a large swampland into which Castro had sunk millions of dollars in an extravagant reclamation project. His disquiet increased because Castro told him privately during this tour that he intended to set up the large-scale state-owned *granjas.* Dumont tried unsuccessfully to dissuade him. Not only did Castro go ahead with the *granjas* in 1961 but, as we have seen, they swallowed up the "cooperatives" the following year.*

In September, 1963, Dumont returned to Cuba for the third time. Most of his fears about the *granjas* had been realized. He encountered on a large scale what he called "bureaucratized anarchy." Again he recommended smaller and more controllable units of production with a view

* Dumont wrote about his first trip in *L'Express,* July 28, September 8 and 22, 1960, and in chap. vii of his book *Terres Vivantes* (Paris: Plon, 1961).

toward trying to do less and achieving more. Whatever may be the merits of Dumont's views, his insight into the different tendencies within the Castro regime is particularly important:

"The most realistic Cuban leaders, headed by President of the Republic Osvaldo Dorticós and president of INRA Carlos Rafael Rodríguez, have well understood these problems. The dogmatists in the Planning Board and the Ministry of Industries, on the contrary, continue to defend the dangerous thesis of *ultracentralized leadership of the economy, managed by means of budgetary credits.* The latter scorn the experience accumulated by the other socialist countries. Their justification is that Cuba is a small island endowed with good commercial media, where centralization will be easier than in the U.S.S.R.! Even more serious is the fact that they present the results of their system to the government with an overoptimistic slant and continue to make unrealistic, unattainable forecasts of production, even when the experience of the past years proves them to be wrong [*italics in original*]."*

In 1964, Professor Dumont put out another book on his experiences in Castro's Cuba.† It is one of the few indispensable works on the subject, not the least because it is written from a sympathetic rather than a hostile point of view. One need not share Dumont's political predilections to respect his determination to face reality without dogma or self-deception. As Dumont wryly notes, it was not easy in 1960 to give Castro any criticism, sympathetic or otherwise, because all the other sympathetic pilgrims, such as

---

* *France Observateur* (Paris), October 3, 1963. A slightly different line-up has been reported by the Argentine journalist Adolfo Gilly, who is pro-Guevara. Gilly confirms the dispute between the "materialist incentive" school represented by Rodríguez and the "moral incentive" school headed by Guevara. But he says that Blas Roca has "more or less openly" supported the first, Dorticós the second (*op. cit.*, p. 7).

† René Dumont, *Cuba: Socialisme et Développement* (Paris: Editions du Seuil, 1964).

Jean-Paul Sartre, had had nothing but praise for everything they had seen.* "All the foreign friends who visit us have nothing but compliments for us and you apparently only criticize us," Castro complained. "Why do you criticize us?" And, indeed, some of Castro's best friends had done him no good by being so uncritical. First the Cubans told their friends that they had virtually solved all their problems, especially in agriculture, and then the Cubans believed it when their friends gullibly told the rest of the world.†

Professor Dumont revealed:

"At the beginning of 1963, a report of the Dirección [top leadership] of agricultural production on the 1962 harvest clearly showed the problems and grave seriousness of the situation. On a national level, the sugar-cane replanting program had fallen back by 17.3 per cent, but this deficit reached 30.0 per cent for the people's farms [*granjas*]. In two years, the raw rice crop fell from 308,000 to 207,000 tons, and the yield per hectare [2.4 acres] fell from 17 to 14 quintals [1 quintal equals 220.46 lbs.].

"Corn fluctuated around 9 to 11 quintals, and the yield of the state sector fell in 1962, an average year, to 6.7

* One wonders whether M. Sartre knows that the First Conference of Teachers of Art, in Havana on October 24, 1964, officially decided "to fight against the manifestations and vices of the past, such as Existentialism."

† Examples:

"The Cuban revolution, unlike the Russian, has, in my judgment, solved the major problems of agricultural production by its agrarian reform" (Mills, *op. cit.*, p. 185).

"So far as agriculture is concerned, then, all the talk about declining production, imminent crisis, and the like is the exact opposite of the truth. Cuban agriculture is progressing with astonishing rapidity and gives every indication of continuing to do so" (Leo Huberman and Paul Sweezy, *Monthly Review*, December, 1960, p. 425).

"And so it came about that Cuba's Great Revolution followed the pattern of a 'permanent revolution,' passing rapidly from one stage of revolutionary struggle to the next, compressing more than a century of historical development into the narrow span of less than a year, and *solving within weeks problems which elsewhere and earlier have occupied entire decades*" (Paul Baran, *Monthly Review*, February, 1961, p. 519, italics added).

quintals per completely sown hectare. This corn production has been maintained, since 1959, only at the price of a
large increase of area, which went up from 175,000 to
231,000 hectares; this resulted in a great increase in the
cost of production per quintal of grain. The quantity of
sorghum fell by half in 1962, and the yield of state-
produced beans did not reach 400 kilograms [1 kilogram
equals 2.2 lbs.] per hectare. Private farmers obtained 880
kilograms of peanuts per hectare, less than in central and
southern Senegal, where the natural conditions are very
inferior. But the state sector fell to 540 kilograms (people's
farms) and even to 320 kilograms (sugar *granjas*). And
Oriente Province produced only 240 kilograms, which
Mestre [head of INRA's Department of Agricultural Pro-
duction] rightly calls 'a veritable scandal.' "*

And so he goes on, with growing indignation and con-
sternation. The quality of Cuban tobacco fell "cata-
strophically." The daily production of milk from cows
imported from Canada in 1961 often decreased, after only
three months in Cuba, by half. His report on Cuban industry is even more depressing. Much of the new machinery
could not function for lack of buildings or qualified personnel, or simply deteriorated on the piers in the hot and
humid climate. Since Cuban matches in 1963 had become
as poor as those of Soviet Russia in 1928, the Cubans jok-
ingly boasted that they had achieved as much in four years
as the Soviets had achieved in eleven! By trying to do too
much too soon, it became clear to Dumont, the Cubans had
merely succeeded in doing too little too late. He observes
that it would have been better not to have nationalized the
non-U.S. sector so quickly because nationalization merely
added the problem of administration to that of supplies.
Much of the blame, he feels, falls on Guevara, who took on

* Dumont, *op. cit.,* p. 70.

the problems of others but never worked out a satisfactory policy in his own ministry.*

Dumont concludes: "After progressing in 1959–60, due above all to a better distribution [of resources], the level of Cuban life stagnated in 1961; and it fell perhaps 15 to 20 per cent in 1962, with strict rationing." The low point, he says, came in 1962. Whatever the specific and concrete shortcomings may have been, he emphasizes, the greatest obstacle to Cuban development was "the general conception of the direction of the economy."†

Ironically, the Castro regime has suffered because it started from too high a general economic level, which it failed to maintain, rather than from a level so low that it could not fail to shine by comparison.

Grand Illusions

To a large extent, the Cuban leaders deceived themselves before they deceived others. It is almost cruel to recall what some leaders were saying in 1961 when, as we now know, the economy had already begun to backfire. In August, 1961, for example, Minister of Economy Regino Botí calculated that the rate of growth of the Cuban economy for 1962–65 would be between 10 and 14 per cent annually (a far cry from its decline by 15–20 per cent). "In 1965," said the hapless Botí, "Cuba will be, in relation to its population, the most industrialized country in Latin America and it will be at the head of production per capita in electrical energy, steel, cement, tractors, and refining of petroleum." As for five years more, he was even more euphoric: "I wish to emphasize that if we look further ahead and contemplate the future of Cuba in the next ten years, we must come to the conclusion that through the

* *Ibid.*, pp. 71–77.
† *Ibid.*, pp. 91, 95, 100.

work and efforts of the people Cuba will overcome the present transitory difficulties, and will reach within nine or ten years the highest standard of living in America by a wide margin, and a standard of living as high as almost every country in Europe."*

Guevara was equally incautious. In May, 1961, he gave assurances that Cuba would "double" its standard of living by 1965, "if the Americans do not trouble us."† Three months later, in August, at the Punta del Este Conference, he credited Cuba with the following achievements by 1965: "First place in America in per capita production of steel, cement, electrical energy, and, except for Venezuela, refining of petroleum; first place in Latin America in tractors, rayon, shoes, textiles, etc.; second place in world production of metallic nickel (until now Cuba has produced only concentrated nickel)," and more of the same.‡ The Cubans were so persuasive or so intoxicating that the late Mexican economist who worked with them, Juan F. Noyola, dazzled the readers of Mexico's distinguished economic journal *El Trimestre Económico* with the Cuban "projections." Early in 1961, he said: "In the next ten years, the Cuban economy is going to grow at a rate probably higher than 10.5 per cent annually, which it has registered in the last two years. It will attain a rate of 10 to 14 per cent annually, and the level of per capita consumption at the end of this decade will have a higher average, and in several specific fields a much higher one, than that of almost every country of Western Europe, in some cases as high as that of Canada."§

It should be noted that these extravagant forecasts were

* "Primera Reunión Nacional de Producción," August 26–27, 1961, *Obra Revolucionaria*, No. 30, 1961, pp. 18–19.
† *Revolución*, May 25, 1961.
‡ Quoted by Regino Botí, *Cuba Socialista*, December, 1961, p. 32.
§ "La Revolución Cubana y sus Efectos en el Desarrollo Económico," *El Trimestre Económico* (Mexico), July–September, 1961, p. 418.

made after the U.S. economic embargo had gone into effect. Indeed, Castroite theory and propaganda implied that the embargo was a precondition for Cuban progress and prosperity. If U.S. trade and investment had never done anything but hold Cuba back, as the most extreme "anti-imperialist" interpretation of U.S.-Cuban relations claimed, the inference seemed to be that it was necessary to cut them off to enable Cuba to move forward. If the United States was entirely exploitative and one-sided in its economic relations with Cuba, it was logical for those who held this view to welcome a break and even to do something to bring it about. The notion that the Cubans did not want to cut themselves off from the United States and reluctantly engaged in tit-for-tat reprisals in 1960 is totally inconsistent with the Castroite conception of U.S.-Cuban economic relations and with the wildly optimistic prophecies that followed the break in relations.

One might wonder whether the available evidence in 1960–61 lent itself to such optimistic forecasts. That this was hardly the case was shown by a critique of Noyola's article, published in the same Mexican journal, by Dr. Felipe Pazos, whom Guevara had replaced as head of the Cuban National Bank in November, 1959. Dr. Pazos, whose knowledge of the Cuban economy has few, if any, equals, subjected Noyola's article to a scathing analysis based on the known facts of the Cuban situation. In so doing, Dr. Pazos strikingly anticipated the conclusions reached by Professor Dumont two years later. In view of the "expert" misjudgments that were coming out of Cuba at the time, Dr. Pazos' criticism of Noyola's "predictions" was as courageous as it was prescient:

"The predictions do not in the least take into account the trauma suffered by the Cuban economy as a result of the radical and sudden change of its system of production and distribution; nor the massive displacement of the

directors of the country's economy—administrators, engi-
neers, accountants—without having the technical personnel
to replace them; nor the change in foreign commercial
relations, which has caused the value of exports to fall and
has enormously increased the difficulties of obtaining a
regular supply of many essential imports, especially spare
parts for U.S.-made machinery and equipment. How is it
possible to reach an annual rate of growth of 10 to 14 per
cent with a totally disorganized economy, with an absolute
lack of university-trained professionals, the immense majority of whom have left the country and whom the Cuban
universities in the present acute phase of revolutionary
radicalism are doing nothing to replace, and with 80 or 90
per cent of its capital plant manufactured in the United
States, which cannot be maintained or repaired with parts
and replacements made in the Soviet Union or in Czechoslovakia?

"To conclude: I believe that the propaganda of the Cuban revolution based on its alleged successes in the economic field is mistaken and self-defeating because the
reality is going to become known, a few months sooner or
later, and the difference is bound to give negative results.
Until a few months ago, the rise in the Cuban people's level
of consumption during the redistributive phase of the
revolution was useful to make socialist propaganda; but as
the revolution has entered the genuinely socialist stage
(state ownership),* the process of growth in production and
consumption has rapidly been reversed, and now it will not
be possible to continue making propaganda on the basis
of the well-being of the Cuban people. The Cuban revolution has ceased being an apparent example of the 'rational-

---

* Pazos here uses the term *"estatizadora"* for which there is a French
(*"étatisé"*) but not a good English equivalent. The nearest English term,.
"nationalized," loses the emphasis on the "state," which both the Spanish
and French terms convey.

ity and efficiency of the socialist system' and has been converted into a clear demonstration of the failure of totalitarian socialism in a Latin American country."*

This is exactly what happened, and it cannot be said that no one had foreseen it.

The Second Agrarian Reform

Fidel Castro brought back from Moscow in May, 1963, more than effusive praise for the personal virtues of Nikita Khrushchev and a *modus vivendi* with the other Latin American Communist leaderships. The Soviets and Castro had also agreed on a drastic shake-up of the Cuban economy.

In his report on his Soviet tour on June 4, Castro made known that an "international division of labor" was necessary, according to which Cuba would specialize in what she was best fitted for by nature—namely, agriculture. On June 27, he intimated that the "medium farmers," whom he accused of "sabotaging sugar production," were in for a bad time. On July 27, he announced that compulsory military service was coming. On August 10, he touched on a new "agrarian reform," but said that the final details had not yet been decided. On October 2, he publicly proclaimed the Second Agrarian Reform. And on November 12, his brother, Minister of the Armed Forces Raúl Castro, made the official pronouncement on compulsory military service.

Formally, the Second Agrarian Reform differed from the first in the proportion of privately owned to state-owned land it established. By 1961, the first one had established a balance of 29.16 per cent state-owned *granjas*,

* "Comentarios a dos artículos sobre la Revolución Cubana," *El Trimestre Económico*, January–March, 1962, pp. 17–18. The second article mentioned in the title was Paul Baran's "Reflections on the Cuban Revolution," translated from the *Monthly Review*, January–February, 1961, but Dr. Pazos devoted virtually his entire article to Noyola.

11.83 per cent "cooperatives," and 59.01 per cent privately owned.* After the first two were merged, the balance had become more simply about 40 per cent state-owned and about 60 per cent privately owned. This relationship was, in effect, the ultimate result of the First Agrarian Reform.

The privately owned 60 per cent had been divided into three categories: 140,000 landowners with less than 2 *caballerias* of land (1 *caballeria* equals 33 acres); 60,000 with 2 to 5 *caballerias;* and 10,000 with between 5 and 30 *caballerias.* The first two were classified as small farmers and the third as medium farmers.† The *latifundistas,* or large landowners, had been liquidated in 1959.

In its most elementary sense, the Second Agrarian Reform shifted the balance from 40–60 in favor of the private sector to 70–30 in favor of the state sector. The shift was accomplished by another great wave of expropriation, this time of the 10,000 "medium farmers." The remaining 30 per cent of small farmers, however, will also decline because those who drop out will not be replaced. In any case, the small peasants are totally dependent on the state and tightly controlled by an association closely linked to INRA. Gradually the state sector in agriculture will edge up to the 95 per cent of industry already owned by the Cuban state.

By increasing the "state sector" in agriculture to such a preponderant level, Castro did what Stalin had merely wanted to do. In his last work, *Economic Problems of Socialism in the U.S.S.R.,* published in 1952, Stalin had asseverated that full Communism demanded one more major structural change in the Soviet system—the conversion of the "collective farms" into "state farms." But he had died the following year without having done anything about it. His successors at first tried to carry out his final injunction.

* Report of Antonio Núñez Jiménez, *Bohemia,* May 28, 1961.
† Raúl Cepero Bonilla, *Cuba Socialista,* January, 1963, for the division of the privately owned lands; Fidel Castro, *Hoy,* August 11, 1963, on the classification of small farmers.

But as they discovered that every move in that direction was followed by a drop in agricultural productivity, they backed away from it. Faced with essentially the same problem, Castro plunged forward. Since Stalin had been in power for a quarter of a century without having considered it advisable to go so far, even he might have considered the Cuban action a little rash and premature.

Technically, the Second Agrarian Reform had another side. Administratively, it attempted to combine more state ownership with more decentralized operation. The plan called for more regional control and smaller productive units, with greater responsibility for local farm administrators. The regime counted heavily on youngsters sent to agricultural schools for periods of a few months to as much as two years to staff the new state farms. A larger and more effective bureaucracy was needed for the new system than ever before.

The new line was, in theory, not so much a clear-cut choice between agriculture and industry as a reversal of their previously allotted roles. The old line had encouraged industry at the expense of agriculture. The new one was based on the development of agriculture as the precondition of industrialization. In practice, however, agriculture was given such a high priority that not much was left over, at least in the foreseeable future, for industry.

There have been few ironies in recent history greater than the comeback of "monoculture" in Cuba. Before Castro, as we have seen, Cuba was not a sugar monoculture in terms of its entire economy, and even in the sphere of agriculture alone, the trend had been toward less land for sugar cultivation and more land for other crops. The sugar area had decreased from 227,806 *caballerías* in 1939 to 207,087 in 1953 to 184,362 in 1958.* But the cultivation of

* *La cuestión de la tierra*, Vol. III: *Las reformas agrarias en el mundo* (Mexico: Centro de Estudios y Documentación Sociales, 1963), p. 209.

rice had increased from 4,045 *caballerías* in 1945 to 8,185 in 1958, with an increase in yield of almost 500 per cent. Coffee, beans, fruits and vegetables, and other agricultural products, had also registered considerable gains.*

Under Castro, the sugar area continued to decline until 1963, when it reached a low of 87,153 *caballerías*.† But, as Cuba cut down its sugar production, the price of sugar rose, not stopping until it hit 13.20 cents a pound in December, 1963, the highest figure in forty-three years. As the price rose dizzyingly, Castro decided to gamble on a vast increase in sugar production at the expense of other crops, which, as Professor Dumont discovered, had been going downhill anyway. Despite the unusually low sugar crop of only 3.8 million tons in 1963, Castro announced in November of that year that his whole new economic policy was postulated on a spectacular increase in sugar production aimed at reaching 10 million tons by 1970.

Thus Castro's sugar policy went from one extreme to the other. Instead of taking away land from sugar production, new land had to be opened up to sugar. According to INRA's Carlos Rafael Rodríguez, the new sugar target made it necessary to add 37,000 *caballerías* of new land to sugar cultivation, an increase of more than 40 per cent over 1963. The figure, moreover, was predicated on a 50 per cent increase in yield per *caballería;* if the yield should be disappointing, as it has been, the area will presumably have to be increased.‡ In effect, the long-term pre-Castro trend in favor of agricultural diversification has for the time being been reversed, and sugar is reclaiming land that had been given over to other crops. In July, 1964, Castro disclosed that a decision had been made to concentrate on only three commodities, sugar, cattle, and tobacco, and not to attempt to recover the lost ground in coffee, rice, and

* *Un Estudio Sobre Cuba,* pp. 1046–62.
† Bernardo, *loc. cit.*
‡ *Hoy,* February 9, 1964.

other products.* By this time, however, the price of sugar was sliding downward, and it fell to 2.75 cents a pound in December, 1964. Nevertheless, Castro could not turn back, and early in the new year, he still proclaimed that "to win the battle of the *zafra* is to win the battle of the economy."†

Even the dreaded term "monoculture" has been somewhat restored to favor. A Yugoslav correspondent was told by the Vice Minister of Economy, Albán Lataste, at the end of 1964: "We have lost our fear of monoculture. We are now aware that we can overcome monoculture solely by developing that same monoculture further."‡ If, for some reason, Castro should lose this gamble, however, Cuban "monoculture" will be worse than ever. In theory, the Castro regime has adopted the principle that Cuba should grow what she is best fitted by nature to grow and buy whatever else she needs in the world market with the expected profits from her increasing sugar production. This was exactly the theory that had prevailed in the bad old days until a real effort to diversify was made in the decade before Castro. It is too early to tell whether more monoculture can really overcome monoculture, but meanwhile there can be no doubt that Castro has taken a step backward.

One wonders whether a revolution was really necessary to restore sugar to the place that it had had in the Cuba of the 1920's.

Arms and the Youth

The background of the compulsory military-service law is equally curious.

If Fidel Castro was on record unequivocally on any subject, it was on compulsory military service. One of his first

* Speech of July 26, 1964.
† Speech of January 2, 1965.
‡ Zarko Bozic, *Borba* (Belgrade), December 28, 1964, p. 3.

utterances after taking power had been: "We will not establish military service because it is not right to force a man to put on a uniform and a helmet, to give him a rifle and force him to march."* Four months later, he had repeated: "I wish to say one thing about what I think of compulsory military service: It should not be compulsory to be a soldier."†

In 1963, he had given little reason to believe that this policy was about to change. The Cuban military buildup was so great by the middle of 1963 that Castro saw fit to boast on June 4 that Cuba enjoyed a "situation of security," as far as any direct invasion by the United States was concerned. On June 27, he claimed that the last "counter-revolutionary infiltrators" were being wiped out and had been abandoned by those who had sent them. Thus, his first explanation on July 27 for compulsory military service was purely internal in character. He said that it was one of two measures—the other was compulsory junior high school (*Secundaria Básica*) attendance—to prevent "the parasitical element, the potential *lumpen* of tomorrow" from developing. He linked the military-service law solely with adolescents who dropped out of secondary school and became "uneducated, ignorant, parasitical."

It was apparently realized that it might be considered peculiar for "socialist Cuba" to solve social problems by military means. By the time Raúl Castro officially presented the compulsory military-service law on November 12, he found it necessary to make a special point of denying that it had been conceived "to do away with *los vagos*." He pointed out that the new law would mean a substantial saving in soldiers' salaries, because the recruits would get only 7 pesos a month and not what they had earned as civilians, as in the former system; he argued that it would enable the

* *Revolución*, January 14, 1959.
† *Ibid.*, May 12, 1959.

armed forces more easily to discharge troops who had served their terms of enlistment.* But he did not succeed altogether in disposing of the suspicion that the new law might have been far more important for economic and social than for strictly military reasons.

The unusually low age limit of seventeen put many youths in the armed forces. Most of the new recruits, Raúl said, actually came from the seventeen-to-twenty age group. They would spend three to four months a year cutting sugar cane or picking coffee beans. Raúl justified a three-year service period on the ground that it would enable the armed forces to cut more cane and pick more coffee. In fact, the future Cuban Army was curiously divided into two classes: those who would and those who would not be permitted to bear arms. The latter category was made up of "the *vagos,* the *lumpen,* the *gusanos*" and other undesirables.†

Whether it was the main reason or a most important by-product, the compulsory military-service law gave the Castro regime a cheap, militarized labor corps. This corps supplemented the "volunteer" system on which the regime had previously depended in emergencies. For some time, it had become clear that the "volunteers" were less and less

---

* In connection with this argument, Raúl Castro made an unexpectedly revealing reference to the arrival of Soviet troops in Cuba in August, 1962. He recalled that one unit on the Isle of Pines was supposed to be demobilized that month, and then gave this explanation for the delay: "At those very moments, the Soviet troops were arriving in our country. It was logical to think that, for one reason or another, difficult days might be approaching." Raúl used the expression *"la tropa soviética,"* or "Soviet troops," not technicians or instructors or some other circumlocution. Fidel Castro had previously made known that the Soviet-Cuban negotiations, which had resulted in "the strengthening of our armed forces and the dispatch of strategic missiles to our country," had taken place in June, 1962 (*Revolución,* April 20, 1963).

† *"Gusano"* ("worm") is the generic term of abuse in Cuba for "counter-revolutionaries." Thus, after the death of Dag Hammarskjöld, Guevara called him *"un servil gusano imperialista"*—"a servile, imperialist worm" (*Revolución,* October 30, 1961).

voluntary; they were, in fact, groups of workers hauled off in trucks from government offices and state-owned factories to perform agricultural tasks for which they were ill-fitted and ill-disposed. They were also highly inefficient; they cut the cane too high or picked unripe coffee beans. Worst of all, they were exorbitantly expensive. Fidel Castro admitted that the volunteer system had often resulted in an economic loss because, as he put it, "we pulled out a worker with a productivity of $10 and we probably set him picking coffee with a productivity of $1.50." Raúl Castro cited the case of fourteen electrical workers who cost $5,800 in salaries and other expenses and picked $304 worth of coffee.* Yet an alert Cuban exile economist, Dr. Carmelo Mesa Lago, has cast some doubt whether the Castro regime's stress on voluntary labor has been so unmaterialistic. From Cuban official figures, Dr. Mesa Lago has calculated that the Cuban state has "saved"—or the Cuban workers have been deprived of—$104.3 million from 1962 to 1964.†

When there is as much official propaganda and pressure for "voluntary labor" as there is in Cuba, the reality is bound to be more and more labor and less and less voluntariness. Except for a minority of idealists and zealots, it may be hard to draw a line between what is "voluntary" and what is merely unpaid.

But the main emphasis of the regime in 1964 was actually on the productivity of paid labor, which Guevara admitted at the end of 1963 was "our weakest point."‡ How weak it was he soon revealed statistically: Productivity per industrial worker had fallen from 11,200 pesos in 1962 to 8,598 pesos in 1963, a drop of 23 per cent in a single year. Guevara attributed this extraordinary decline to the incor-

* Fidel Castro, *Revolución,* October 22, 1963; Raúl Castro, *ibid.,* November 13, 1963.

† *Trabajo* + *Coerción* + *Gratuidad* = *Trabajo Voluntario Socialista* (Miami: Agencia de Informaciones Periodísticas, September, 1964).

‡ *Obra Revolucionaria,* December 30, 1963, p. 25.

poration of many inefficient little units in his ministry.*
A different reason for the infectious drop in productivity
was starkly stated by Professor Dumont: "There is nothing
to buy, for which reason there is no stimulus to work."†
The Cuban leaders, however, were not enchanted with
economic advice, even from "Marxist" sources, which told
them to increase productivity by increasing real purchasing power.

To break out of what was for them the vicious cycle of
purchasing power and productivity, they decided that they
could not depend on increased material or moral incentives, and they opted for an increase in an altogether different kind of incentive—compulsion.

For the youth, the new military law served as the most
direct and inescapable form of compulsion. Castro made
no secret of the fact that he counted on the armed forces
to do what education and social discipline had failed to do.
"We know of many cases of young men," he said to a meeting of Young Communists on October 21, 1964, "who were
a headache to their fathers, who were incorrigible, who
misbehaved, who stayed away from their classes." Happily,
he explained, "what could not be taught to them at home,
what could not be taught to them in elementary school,
what could not be taught to them in secondary school, they
learned in the army, they learned in a military unit." The
revolution, Castro also said, had made it "too easy" for the
young. They had been given important posts without the
necessary qualifications, and the "easy successes" had gone

* *Obra Revolucionaria*, February 26, 1964, p. 16.
† René Dumont, *Los Principales Obstáculos para una Expansión Rápida
de la Agricultura Cubana: Estructurales, Técnicos y Económicos* (Santiago
de Chile: Seminario de Liborio, April, 1964), p. 21. This is a report by
Professor Dumont that was made public by an enterprising group of
Cuban exiles in Santiago, Chile, which puts out a lively publication,
Liborio. Much of this report appears in Professor Dumont's previously
mentioned book in a somewhat attenuated form. The full report was is-
sued in two mimeographed sections by the Seminario de Liborio, dated
April and May, 1964.

to their heads. Under capitalism, life had been "very hard," but it had taught the older workers to appreciate the importance of their jobs. Castro implied that something of the sort was necessary under socialism, too, because "when the path is made too easy for men, it isn't good; when life is too easy, when things come too easily, it isn't good." On November 13 of the same year, his infatuation with military service had gone so far that he worried publicly that students exempt from military duty would "constitute an important segment of our youth without discipline, without training, without being organized, and without that conditioning which military instruction provides." As if "a disciplined and upright character" were impossible without military training, he triumphantly announced that he had found the perfect solution—military centers of technological instruction in which students could have their education and militarization at the same time.

Crime and Punishment

For workers, administrators, and officials, the Castro regime has revived the institution of "labor camps." Since the Cuban Government has refused to permit the International Red Cross or any other disinterested body to investigate these camps, most of the information about them has come from Cuban exile sources. At least one of these camps, however, has been mentioned in the Cuban press. It is located on the forsaken peninsula of Guanahacabibes at the westernmost tip of the island, and judging from remarks made to and by Guevara, who seems to be the only one willing or able to talk about it, this camp specializes in erring "bureaucrats." In an interview with Guevara at the end of 1963, one Cuban journalist suggested that this camp might have been responsible for producing "inhibitions" in the bureaucracy. Guevara did not encourage this line of questioning.* Four months later, Fidel Castro made a derogatory remark about this columnist; he was fired and has not been heard from since.†

In March, 1964, the subject of Guanahacabibes came up again at a gathering at the Ministry of Industries of industrial "vanguard workers" from all over the country. A reporter for the official newspaper, *Revolución,* gave the following account of the discussion with the Minister of Industries:

At one point, Guevara asked: "Which of you, with a sixth-grade education, would want, due to discontent or vocational interest, to study to become industrial managers?" Of about 150 present, only 3 or 4 replied affirmatively. Che smiled and commented: "Very few! What a fiasco!" One of the *vanguardia* explained that "no one likes to plant eucalyptus trees in Guanahacabibes." Guevara replied that the general impression of Guanahacabibes was wrong in two respects. There was not a single eucalyptus tree in the area, only "mosquitoes and other things." And all who made mistakes could not be sent there because "if all those who make mistakes went there, it would be a city full of skyscrapers." As an example of the kind of mistake that would send someone to Guanahacabibes, he cited a factory director who had "pirated"—as the Cubans call the practice

* This exchange appeared in the column signed "Siquitrilla," in *La Tarde* (Havana), November 11, 1963. At the end of February, 1964, the same columnist, referring to his previous interview, disclosed that Guevara had virtually threatened to send him to Guanahacabibes if Guevara did not like his work. This is the only demonstration of some journalistic independence that I have encountered in the Cuban press since 1960, and this journalist soon paid the price for it.

† *Bohemia,* April 3, 1964. A section of Castro's testimony at the Marcos Rodríguez trial was devoted to the Cuban press. After severely criticizing it, Castro revealed that the journalists had given the regime so much trouble that the School of Journalism had been closed. Adolfo Gilly writes: "The Cuban press is a national calamity. It is not just an information medium; it is a defensive wall against pressure from below, a uniform medium which allows discussions on art criticism or films but never dissent or criticism when it comes to a decision of the government" (*op. cit.,* p. 28).

of one organization "raiding" another—a managerial assistant. "Guanahacabibes is not so awful or so bad," Guevara assured them, "it is only a kind of moral punishment." Evidently, this "moral punishment" was terrifying enough to scare off not merely average workers but the most exemplary group of "vanguard workers." In any event, Guevara confirmed the fact that there is a form of administrative punishment in Cuba for "offenses" which are not "crimes" and, therefore, not legally punishable; these *"transgresiones,"* as Guevara called them, apparently fill the labor camps like Guanahacabibes instead of the old-fashioned prisons.*

The Inter-American Commission on Human Rights, set up by the Organization of American States, published a report in May, 1963, on political prisoners in Cuba. Much of this report reads like similar reports, similarly denied or ignored, of Nazi concentration camps in Germany thirty years ago, except that "conservative" opinion was then guilty of averting eyes and ears from the evidence and now "liberal" opinion is doing the same thing. According to this report, the Cuban concentration-camp system "shows many of the features that characterized and still characterize the concentration camps in some totalitarian countries —such as barbed wire fences, rudimentary barracks for shelter, and the infliction of corporal punishment and constant forced labor." The political prisons appear to be worse or at least no better than those used by the dictatorial Machado and Batista regimes. The report notes that "in the old colonial castles, such as El Principe and La Cabaña, the underground dungeons used during the period of Spanish rule have been rehabilitated as political prisons. These prisons are grim and damp, have dirt floors, and are infested with rats and insects; water seepage is often so

---

* José Vásquez, *Revolución*, March 6, 1964.

great that the floor is constantly flooded."* The pages of
evidence from former prisoners are filled with an all too
familiar horror and inhumanity.

The entire Cuban legal system under Castro has, in fact,
become little more than a crude machine of punitive compulsion. In this respect, the political course of the Castro
regime has had a legal counterpart. In the post-Batista
"Fundamental Law of Cuba" of February 7, 1959, the
regular courts were given jurisdiction over all legal and
criminal matters, except crimes in the armed services.†
But in May, 1962, a new category of "counterrevolutionary
crime," mainly for illegal trading, was established, to be
tried by "Revolutionary Tribunals" made up of politically
trustworthy "revolutionaries." The regular courts have
gradually been restricted to a few civil suits, and "justice"
has largely been meted out by the political Revolutionary
Tribunals. This "justice" has become increasingly severe
as the Cuban economy has gone downhill. On March 13,
1963, the almost incredible Law No. 1098 was enacted. It
provided for imprisonment of twenty to thirty years for
robbery or larceny of as little as $100, if minors were in-
volved, and the death penalty if committed in uniform; the
accused to be imprisoned as soon as charged and before
having been found guilty; brought to trial in twenty-four
hours; and sentenced within seventy-two hours.‡ The im-

---

* Inter-American Commission on Human Rights, *Report on the Situation of Political Prisoners and Their Relatives in Cuba* (Washington, D.C.:
Pan American Union, May 17, 1963), pp. 19–20. It should be noted that
this commission was headed by a distinguished Chilean jurist, Dr. Manuel
Bianchi. A previous report by the International Commission of Jurists,
Cuba and the Rule of Law (Geneva, 1962), contained sections on "Conditions in Cuban Prisons" and "Cruel, Inhuman and Degrading Treatment"
(pp. 204–25). A well-informed exile source, *The Cuban Report*, published
by the Directorio Revolucionario Estudiantil, in Miami, issued a study on
"The Plight of Cuban Political Prisoners," dated November 16, 1964,
which sums up what is known outside Cuba of the Cuban penal system.

† *Fundamental Law of Cuba 1959* (Washington, D.C.: Pan American
Union, 1959), p. 51.

‡ A commentary on the law by the Public Prosecutor, Dr. Santiago

mediate occasion for this law was an epidemic of house-breaking and robbery by militiamen in uniform, which the regime evidently could not suppress without resorting to methods no longer considered tolerable in civilized coun-tries.

The sentences handed out by the Revolutionary Tri-bunals may be gathered from news stories that have ap-peared in the Cuban press. On November 19, 1963, a routine news story in *Hoy* stated: "Revolutionary Tribunal No. 2 of the Havana District sentenced to twenty years' imprison-ment the accused Mario Sosa Hernández, who, with the aid of a minor, stole approximately 100 pesos' worth of fruits and vegetables from a store situated at Churruca 305, in El Cerro." An official Prensa Latina story in *El Mundo* of April 1, 1964, reported that one Ramón López Rosa had been sentenced by a Revolutionary Tribunal to *thirty* years in prison for stealing "a sack containing vegetables."

Self-professed Marxists rarely fail to see the connection between an increasingly repressive and retrogressive penal system, a deepening economic crisis, and deteriorating so-cial conditions—in the capitalist world.

How the Proletariat Dictates

But for the working class as a whole, the Castro regime has introduced still other methods of compulsion and coer-cion besides the military-service law, concentration camps, Law No. 1098 and the Revolutionary Tribunals. The chief pressure on the Cuban workers has been exerted through a new system of "wage scales and work norms."

After an experimental period beginning May 1, 1963,

Cuba, appeared in *Hoy*, March 29, 1963. This legislation in Cuba closely resembles the laws against "economic crimes" introduced in the Soviet Union in 1961–62 ("Economic Crimes in the Soviet Union," *Journal of the International Commission of Jurists*, Summer, 1964, pp. 5–12).

the system was adopted extensively at the end of the year. Essentially, it reorganized the whole system of wage scales into eight categories. This meant that 72.4 per cent of the working class was put in the lowest three categories and only 7.2 per cent in the highest three categories. Thus, about three-quarters of all Cuban workers were graded to earn from 85 to 115 pesos monthly. The new wage scale also served to reduce the average hourly wage from 90 cents to 75 cents. In every category, however, the actual wages were predicated on the fulfillment of "norms," or standards of productivity set by the government for each type of work or operation. To receive his full wage, it became necessary for a worker to fulfill his norm. If he failed to fulfill the norm, his wage would be reduced by the same number of percentage points as his drop below the norm. If he overfulfilled his norm, his wage would be increased by only half the number of percentage points of his rise above the norm, but he could not get more than the next category in the wage scale. Thus, the penalty for underfulfillment was twice as great as the reward for overfulfillment. Promotion from one category to the next higher was made dependent on an increase in technical qualifications. A worker could not get into a higher wage category without improving his technical rating, whatever the state of the labor market.*

But the Cuban leaders were apparently disappointed by the results obtained by this system of norms and wage scales. In 1964, Castro repeatedly returned to the subject of the Cuban workers' failure to work as hard, as long, or as well as he thought they should have been working. On October 30, for example, he developed the theory that the "rigor" of the capitalist system had forced the Cuban workers to work

---

* This system was fully explained, with figures and graphs, by Minister of Industries Guevara, Minister of Labor Martínez Sánchez, and others, in *Obra Revolucionaria*, December 30, 1963. I have given here the present percentages, not the projected ones.

more and better before the revolution. As soon as conditions improved, he said, "many began to produce less."
With the "pressures" of capitalism removed, and the revolutionary economy inefficient and disorganized, he went on,
"if anyone earned 10 pesos in four hours, it was logical that
he did not feel the need to work longer." The relative
merits of capitalism and socialism must have been very
much on his mind at this time for he discoursed on another
aspect of the subject twenty-four hours later. The capitalist,
he said, wasted money on luxuries and entertainment, but
he did not "throw away money in his business or manage
his money badly." Castro held up for admiration the fact
that the capitalist "employed the minimum persons necessary in certain types of work and the maximum persons
necessary in other types of work." Nothing was gained, he
admonished, "if the money which the capitalists spent in
one way, the socialists waste in another way."

Cuban capitalists might have differed with Castro on the
"pressures" that they had been able to exert on their workers. Since 1934, it had been practically impossible for an
employer to dismiss a Cuban worker without a long and
expensive procedure, and the "pressure" of the trade unions
on employers had been at least as strong as the "pressure"
of employers on workers. Indeed, rigid job-tenure regula-
tions and trade-union inflexibility had long been considered
among the chief obstacles to Cuban industrial and technical
development.* There used to be a saying in Cuba that it
was harder to fire a worker than to get rid of a wife—and
easier to find a new wife than a new job.

In any case, if Cuban workers no longer worked so hard
because capitalist "pressures" had been relaxed, as Castro
seemed to think, it followed that his regime needed substitute "pressures" to make them work harder. This was, in
fact, the rationale of Law No. 1166, the "Law of Labor

* *Report on Cuba,* chap. xvi.

Justice," promulgated on October 3, 1964, and put into effect on January 1, 1965. It was not, to be sure, the first of its kind but it was far more severe and extensive than anything the Castro regime had ever before attempted to enforce.

A crackdown on the Cuban workers had taken place in 1962 in the drive against "absenteeism." On August 29 of that year, Minister of Labor Martínez Sánchez had issued Resolution 5798, which consisted primarily of a table of penalties for "unjustified" absences from work. As he later recalled, "with this measure we opened an offensive against absenteeism at a time when labor discipline had relaxed extraordinarily, had weakened extraordinarily, when absenteeism had reached extraordinary proportions." Martínez Sánchez boasted that these "severe and firm methods" had successfully cut down the evil of absenteeism. But, he went on, the former codes on labor "indiscipline" had not worked out altogether satisfactorily. They had often exacerbated the relations of the workers, trade unions, and management. The "Work Councils" set up to enforce the rules contained trade-union officials who had been put in the embarrassing position of punishing workers instead of defending their interests.*

If an extraordinary epidemic of absenteeism had set off Resolution 5798, something similar must have accounted for Law No. 1166. The new "Law of Labor Justice" was designed to cover all possible "violations of labor discipline" and disputes between workers and managements. These violations now ranged from lateness, absenteeism, and "lack of respect for superiors" to damage of equipment, fraud, and "the commission of any delinquency or violation." Both the violations and penalties were classified into three grades—"light," "less serious," and "serious." The "light" penalties ranged from a warning to a wage deduc-

* Minister of Labor Augusto Martínez Sánchez, *Hoy*, October 28, 1964.

tion starting at 15 per cent for a period up to two months; the "less serious," from a wage deduction of up to 25 per cent for a period up to four months to transfer to a different job in the same place of work; the "serious," from a transfer to another place of work to a permanent discharge. The administration of this law was entrusted to five-member Work Councils, elected for three-year terms in every place of work employing twenty-five or more workers. To be eligible, members of these councils had to fulfill certain conditions, such as displaying "a good socialist attitude toward work," and they could be replaced if the Ministry of Labor ruled that they were deficient. To save the trade unions and managements from embarrassment, no trade-union official or member of the managerial staff could be elected to a council. Workers could theoretically appeal their cases as high as the Minister of Labor. In effect, the new law imposed a system of coercion more oppressive than anything the Cuban working class had known for about thirty years, in the guise of permitting the workers to coerce themselves. With party "nuclei" behind the elections of Work Councils, with a completely castrated trade-union movement, and with various safeguards to reorganize "unsatisfactory" councils from above, the form was likely to make very little difference in the application of the law.*

The "Law of Labor Justice" did not start off very auspiciously. The Work Council elections were held on December 2. At the unusual hour of 1:05 A.M. on December 8, Martínez Sánchez shot himself after having been dismissed from office for "grave administrative errors." The

---

* The full text of the "Ley de Justicia Laboral" appeared in *Revolución,* October 3, 1964. The most detailed official commentary was made by Martínez Sánchez, *Hoy,* October 28, 1964. An analysis of this law and its background by two Cuban exile economists, Dr. Carmelo Mesa Lago and Dr. Roberto Hernández Morales, "La Nueva 'Ley de Justicia Laboral' Castro-Comunista: Etapa Final de la Injusticia Proletaria Socialista," appeared in *Cuaderno de la Agencia Informaciones Periodísticas* (Miami), No. 45, November, 1964.

communiqué issued by Prime Minister Castro and President Dorticós described his condition as "at the brink of death." It did not require too much perspicacity to suspect that the results of the elections or the reactions of the workers to the whole scheme, the dismissal, and the attempted suicide were closely related.

Next to Martínez Sánchez, the old-time Communist labor leader Lázaro Peña has had the most unenviable job of holding the Cuban workers in line.

Back in 1939, Batista had paid off the Communists for their support by, among other things, permitting them to set up an officially recognized trade-union federation, the Confederación de Trabajadores de Cuba (CTC), with Lázaro Peña as its Secretary General. In 1961, Fidel Castro had paid off the Communists for their support by, among other things, permitting Lázaro Peña to come back officially as Secretary General of the CTC. But whereas Batista had to pay off the CTC, Castro did not. It was merely one agency of Castro's regime to get the workers to do what other agencies had decided. As head of the CTC-R (for Revolucionaria), Lázaro Peña had become, as a pro-Castro writer has put it, "the one leader who enjoys the unanimous opposition of the Cuban workers."*

Whether or not he enjoyed this singular distinction, Lázaro Peña tasted it to the full in the middle of September, 1963. The government had decided to cut wages in the construction industry by transferring workers to jobs in an inferior category, calling for less pay, whenever their equipment broke down. Since equipment was always breaking down, for reasons beyond the workers' control, such as the lack of replacement parts, the proposal was bitterly resisted by the construction workers. When their own leaders had exhausted all their powers of persuasion, Lázaro Peña took it upon himself to break the resistance. At the

* Gilly, *op. cit.*, p. 13.

meeting that he addressed, however, "a scandal broke out." Workers interrupted him, shouted at him to make sacrifices for the revolution by giving up his automobile, and indelicately reminded him of his old tie-up with Batista. The meeting was hastily adjourned before Lázaro Peña could finish, and the Cuban press denounced the recalcitrant workers as "counterrevolutionaries" and "confusionists."*

The next move was up to the government. Far from backing down, Castro decided to launch a general campaign against the workers' past gains—through the apparent initiative of the workers themselves. This was the setting for Castro's speech of October 21, 1963, in which he attacked the unions' grievance committees as "illusionism" and "revolutionary infantilism." In the next few weeks, one union after another "volunteered" on behalf of its members to surrender their hard-won rights and privileges. "WORKERS RENOUNCE GAINS WHICH TODAY CONSTITUTE PRIVILEGES," read a typical headline in *Hoy* of October 30, 1963. The story told of a meeting called by the Sindicato Nacional de Trabajadores de la Energía Eléctrica, the electrical workers' union, to propose that working hours should be increased, and seniority pay, paid vacations, Christmas bonuses, and overtime pay be eliminated or reduced in the state-operated electric company. Whatever may be thought of the economic necessity for such measures, it was probably too much to expect of the workers that they should approve of their own unions leading them to the slaughter of their benefits.

At this very time, the Cuban workers were told by Guevara that they were living in a "dictatorship of the proletariat," a term which does not seem to have been used

---

* Gilly, *ibid.*, pp. 18–19, has one version of this incident. It was reported, in a distorted form, in the Cuban press.

before the end of 1963.* Unfortunately, it is impossible to tell what the proletariat thought of the news that it was dictating to Fidel Castro and Ernesto Che Guevara.

At bottom, then, the Castro regime had faced the choice between getting workers to work harder by increasing their "material incentives" or by increasing military and other methods of punitive compulsion. To a large extent, the regime's leaders did not feel that they had much choice, inasmuch as their economic policies had resulted in such disorganization and deterioration that they could not hope to raise buying power and real wages in time to affect their immediate plans. In this sense, the increasingly militaristic and totalitarian trend in Cuba has been driven forward by economic as well as by political forces. For a minority, the Castro regime could make a virtue of a necessity and place even more stress on the "moral" nonmaterialistic motives for economic activity. But for the great majority, something more forceful and forcible was needed. Thus, Castro's economic policy has been increasingly marked by an apparent contradiction—an appeal to the most idealistic sentiments and a resort to the basest means.

Policy and Polemics

These decisions were not made without considerable policy disputes and personal conflicts, some of which came out into the open. The strains and tensions within the regime must have been considerable, judging only from the visible part of these internal antagonisms.

* *Hoy,* December 18, 1963. On October 3, 1963, Castro had discussed this point somewhat less definitely with former U.S. Representative Charles O. Porter: "Personally, I don't consider it a dictatorship, but if we are going to have a definition of our government from a Marxist-Leninist point of view, we can say that it is either a proletarian dictatorship or a proletarian democracy" (*Northwest Review,* Fall, 1963, p. 81). It appears that Castro did not identify himself with this term to a Cuban audience until his speech on January 2, 1965.

In February, 1964, the official theoretical organ, *Cuba Socialista,* published an article by President of the National Bank Marcelo Fernández on the history and functions of a "socialist" national bank. This seemingly innocent exercise brought down on his head the wrath of Minister of Industries Guevara the following month. Guevara charged that Fernández and his associates in the bank still thought in terms of "classical economics" and even "vulgar economics," that they sought to make the bank instead of the Treasury Ministry the financial center of the Cuban economy, and above all, that they wanted to control investments and credits through the bank. In the May issue, Fernández tried to argue, without daring to take issue with Guevara on any specific point or even to mention his name, that socialist planning could take a monetary form with the bank necessarily playing a prominent role.* But it did him little good. He was shifted from the bank to the Ministry of Foreign Trade at the end of June, 1964.

Behind this controversy between Guevara and Marcelo Fernández was really a much larger controversy between Guevara and recent Soviet economic theory and practice. This came out most clearly in a series of editorials which subsequently appeared in *Nuestra Industria,* the official organ of Guevara's Ministry of Industries. For some time, the Soviets had tended to stimulate production by giving individual enterprises and managers greater autonomy and by imposing greater financial responsibility on them. This system, which had been markedly encouraged in the Khrushchev period, implied a greater degree of economic decentralization and a more sophisticated system of financial controls. In order to check on the performance of each

* These articles appeared in *Cuba Socialista:* Fernández, February, 1964, pp. 32–50; Guevara, March, 1964, pp. 23–41; Fernández, May, 1964, pp. 79–97. A fourth article by Luis Alvárez Rom, representing Guevara's point of view, appeared in the issue of July, 1964, pp. 64–79.

factory or establishment, instead of dealing with the gross figures of an industry as a whole, it was necessary to give individual factories or establishments their own financial accounts in the Central Bank, which could thereby audit their credits, investments, and efficiency. The more efficient or "profitable" an enterprise, the greater were the material rewards for both the managers and workers. Thus, Guevara's war on the role allotted to the Cuban National Bank by Marcelo Fernández, who was clearly inspired by the Soviet model, was only part of a much larger war on the part of Guevara against decentralization, relative autonomy, financial controls, and greater material incentives. Guevara's organ explicitly expressed its disagreement with "the emphasis given to material interest" by the Soviet economist Y. G. Liberman, the leading exponent of the new economic thought, whom it charged with advocating a change in "the methods of collective incentive, abandoning the old formula of rewards based on the fulfillment of plans in order to move on to more advanced plans."* The new Soviet economic trend threatened Guevara's commitment to the "moral incentive" as the "predominant form" in the present Cuban stage of the "construction of socialism," and from this basic difference followed his objections to the other aspects of the recent Soviet experiments to increase productivity by increasing material incentives—and to increase material incentives by increasing production.

One notable feature of the polemical exchange between Marcelo Fernández and Che Guevara was a new style in Cuban political writing. In his first article, Fernández quoted Lenin twice and Marx and Engels once. As a quotation-monger, however, Fernández was no match for Guevara. Fully half of the latter's article was made up of quotations: eight from Marx, one from Lenin, and one

---

* *Nuestra Industria*, July, 1964, pp. 46–47.

from Stalin, the latter dating from 1931. Fernández' second article used only one quotation from Lenin and one from Marx. This typically Communist custom of arguing by quotation had never appeared in such Cuban writing before. In any case, the dispute with Marcelo Fernández was merely a warm-up for Guevara.

In April, 1964, *Cuba Socialista* carried an article on "Forms and Methods of Socialist Planning and the Level of Development of the Productive Forces," by Professor Charles Bettelheim, a French economist of Communist persuasion. Like René Dumont, Bettelheim had made several trips to Cuba at Castro's behest and had given the Cubans the benefit of his experience and advice. According to Dumont, Bettelheim's reports had helped to convince Castro in the latter half of 1963 that the Cuban economy should be based for the next decade on agriculture, and Bettelheim had also warned that centralization tended to reduce initiative.* Neither of these recommendations was likely to endear Bettelheim to Guevara, who had long been committed by conviction and self-interest to full-scale industrialization and centralization. Despite the apparent victory of partial decentralization in the fall of 1963, Guevara had never given up. By March of the following year, he had felt confident enough to say publicly that "it is supremely important for us to defend energetically on all fronts the principle of centralized organization of the economy in the conditions prevalent in Cuba."† For Guevara, "centralization" was a "principle" from which the Cubans could depart only at the price of betraying their political purity. For Bettelheim, centralization was a means to be prudently employed only to the extent that it was necessary for "planning."‡

* Dumont, *op. cit.*, pp. 95 and 105.
† *Obra Revolucionaria*, No. 10, March 19, 1964, p. 12.
‡ Dumont, *op. cit.*, p. 107.

In his article, Bettelheim lined up a formidable battery of quotations from Marx, Lenin, and Stalin, especially Stalin. He cited Soviet precedents and even summoned a quotation from Mao Tse-tung to his aid. With the help of these and lesser authorities, Bettelheim tried to get across to the Cubans some highly theoretical propositions with barely concealed practical implications. He went to great pains to establish that there were "objective economic laws" for socialism as well as for capitalism, as if his Cuban students had been remiss in the recognition and application of those laws. He chided those who confused "the level of development of the productive forces" with the "juridical form of property," and chose to cite Lenin to the effect that mere "nationalization" did not constitute real "socialization." As he developed this theme, several gently disconcerting hints emerged—that, as in the Soviet Union, true "collective farms" were more appropriate and efficient than "state farms" in the prevailing Cuban "level of development of the productive forces"; that more state ownership did not necessarily mean more economic progress; that a "certain liberty in local interchange" as well as "individual production" would be just as beneficial in Cuba as in the Soviet Union or even in Communist China; and that different factors in the "productive forces" should be developed differently. In effect, Bettelheim tried to tell the Cubans that they had nationalized and centralized too much, too far, and too fast.*

A month later, Guevara took on Bettelheim. After trading quotations from Lenin with the French economist, Guevara accused him of making two fundamental errors.

* "Formas y métodos de la planificación socialista y nivel de desarrollo de las fuerzas productivas," *Cuba Socialista*, April, 1964, pp. 51–78. In an interview in *France Observateur*, January 9, 1964, pp. 5–6, Bettelheim had professed to be optimistic on the score of excessive centralization. Evidently, after four visits to Cuba, he still did not know his Cubans, or perhaps one should say, his Argentine.

Theoretically, these concerned "the correlation between the productive forces and the relations of production" and between the juridical superstructure and the relations of production. On both counts, Guevara charged Bettelheim with a "mechanical analysis." But this disputation in Marxist exegesis need not occupy us as much as its practical implications. The problem at issue was basically the tempo and forms of the Communist transformation of Cuba at its existing level of development. Was it more efficient to stress "state farms" or "collective farms"? Was it more productive to nationalize only the large industrial units or should they also take over all the tiny *chinchales,* as the Cubans call their innumerable artisan-like workshops? Bettelheim had intimated that the "collectives" were a form of "socialist property" better adapted to the Cuban stage of development, and he had especially singled out the Ministry of Industries' system of *consolidados*—the grouping together of similar but otherwise independent units, such as garages, for state administration and operation—as a particularly flagrant example of inefficient and artificial "juridical" collectivization.

Guevara could not reconcile himself to the idea that there were objective limits to what the Cubans might efficiently or advantageously do. He argued: "The vanguard of the revolutionary movements, increasingly influenced by the Marxist-Leninist ideology, is capable of foreseeing in its consciousness an entire series of steps to carry out, and to force the march of events, but to force them within what is objectively possible." The essence of "Guevaraism" might be summed up in the words, "to force the march of events." His afterthought, "within what is objectively possible," was, of course, begging the question. When anything is "objectively possible," it is rarely necessary "to force" events. In another passage, however, Guevara explained more fully what he meant by the "objectively possible."

Bettelheim, he pointed out, had thought in terms of *Cuba's* "productive forces" and "relations of production." But Guevara contended that Cuba was not alone, that "in the present epoch of imperialism, consciousness also acquires world characteristics. And this consciousness of today is the product of the development of all the productive forces of the world and the product of the teaching and education of the masses of the entire world by the Soviet Union and the other socialist countries."

This latter theory completely changed the terms of reference of the problems posed by Bettelheim. The determining factor, according to Guevara, was not the conditions in Cuba but in the entire "socialist world." It was, in effect, permissible or profitable to nationalize every last little *chinchal* in Cuba because Cuba was part of the Communist world and the Cuban "consciousness" was a product of all the productive and propaganda forces of the entire Communist world. On this premise, Guevara struck back at Bettelheim: "To say that the *empresa consolidada* [consolidated enterprise] is an aberration is approximately equivalent to saying that the Cuban revolution is an aberration." As for the fact that the Cuban bureaucracy might not be capable of administering so much nationalized economy and centralized power, Guevara dismissed this consideration as relatively unimportant. "Whether the administrative method is or is not the most adequate," he maintained, "has little importance, in the last analysis, because the differences between one method or another are fundamentally quantitative. The hopes in our system are directed toward the future, toward a more accelerated development of the [human] consciousness and, through this consciousness, of the productive forces." In Marxist terms, then, it might be said that for Bettelheim, "productive forces" determined "consciousness," whereas for Guevara, "consciousness" would determine the "productive forces." And

Guevara concluded his polemic almost insultingly with the saying, "May God protect me from my friends, and I will protect myself from my enemies."*

Implicitly, then, Guevara could not justify Cuban policy in terms of Cuban conditions. His entire case rested on an abstract international Communist "consciousness" which would enable the Cubans "to force the march of events." He never made clear why, if this abstraction was so determining, the Cuban leaders were having so much trouble with the average Cuban's political "consciousness," or why so much coercion was necessary to combat the evils of absenteeism and declining productivity. Curiously, the most powerful segment of the Communist world, the Soviet Union, had not found it advisable, on the basis of the same international "consciousness," to go as far as the Cubans in the preponderance of state farms. It was also strange that the Cubans should have chosen to make such hazardous and costly decisions on the apparent premise of an international Communist consensus at a time when the various Communist countries were asserting their individuality on a greater scale than ever before and when the leading Communist powers could not agree on just what Communist "consciousness" was.

Not so long before, curiously, Fidel Castro himself had ridiculed the *consolidados* far more scathingly than Bettelheim had dared to do. "I don't know," Castro had said in August, 1963, "who was the first to get the idea of giving the name of '*empresa consolidada*' to anything here, because there is an *empresa consolidada* of this, an *empresa consolidada* of that, and an *empresa consolidada* of something else, Unit H here and Unit H there. It becomes something boring, tedious, intolerable. It would be better to have a garage that works well and gives people good service.

* "La planificación socialista, su significación," *Cuba Socialista*, June, 1964, pp. 13–24.

That is much more important than to go around putting up a huge sign to advertise that this place belongs to an *empresa consolidada*. Who knows how much paint has been wasted putting up names of *empresas consolidadas?*"*

The Guevara-Bettelheim controversy was even more revealing than the Guevara-Marcelo Fernández dispute had been. Both Guevara and Marcelo Fernández had been members of the 26th of July Movement. But Bettelheim was a foreign spokesman for a political tendency closer to the old-time Cuban Communists, who were no longer able to criticize any of Castro's policies publicly. If the old-time Cuban Communists had not outsmarted themselves and had not enmeshed themselves in a totalitarian party of their own making but no longer their own, some of them would almost certainly have in some way associated themselves with the point of view represented by Dumont and Bettelheim. Thus, curiously, it is necessary to read two Frenchmen to get an insight into the reservations and misgivings held privately by old-time Cuban Communists and their Soviet mentors.

The relationship of Fidel Castro and Ernesto Che Guevara is one of the main keys that unlock the innermost secrets of this Cuban revolution. The personal impress of Guevara on the revolution may prove in some respects to be the equal of Castro's, despite the fact that Castro alone can carry the burden of making the final decisions. For Castro has made different decisions depending on who has influenced him last, whereas Guevara has had the most lasting influence on him. While Guevara has been peculiarly single-minded in his objectives, Castro has had to maintain a balance of forces in his regime and has been far more keenly attuned to the sensibilities and moods of the Cuban masses. All that has been done had to be done in Castro's name, but this does not necessarily mean that

* *Obra Revolucionaria,* August 12, 1963, p. 37.

Castro has done it all. The Líder Máximo has been perfectly capable of watching as every last *chinchal* was gathered together into *consolidados,* and when the latter failed to work out satisfactorily, to ask who had been mad enough to get the idea of setting them up, as if he did not know that they belonged to Guevara's ministry.*

But while Castro's mind and interest have tended to flit from one subject to another, his past fantasies covered up by his latest enthusiasm, Guevara has devoted himself to the deadly game of infighting for the levers of power and to the elaboration of a theoretical mold for the unfolding revolution. I have been told by one of Castro's former ministers how, toward the end of 1959, Guevara had coldly remarked to him that "you are not going to last much longer," but he seemed so much in Castro's favor at the time that he could hardly take the threat seriously. Yet, within a matter of weeks, Guevara's prediction had come true. For five more years, that was the fate of all who crossed Guevara or whom he marked out for political destruction in his own good time. By 1964, Guevara could oust a President of the National Bank with an article and set himself up as the supreme theoretical authority in place of a leading European Communist mentor whose tutelage the Cubans had previously invited and accepted. The surest sign of the direction of the Castro regime has been Guevara's influence in it.

PSP—R.I.P.

Professor Bettelheim was not the only "orthodox" Communist casualty in Cuba in 1964. In March, two of the leading old-timers, Joaquín Ordoqui and his wife, Edith García Buchaca, were implicated in the trial of the in-

* Some *consolidados* were finally disbanded at the end of 1964, and Castro again ridiculed them as a "mania" on January 2, 1965.

former Marcos Rodríguez. As a student follower of the Communist line, Marcos had betrayed four members of the Directorio Revolucionario, then basically anti-Communist in tendency, to the Batista police in April, 1957. After fleeing to Mexico, Marcos was befriended by Ordoqui and his wife, and Ordoqui had helped him to become an official member of the Communist Partido Socialista Popular. The bizarre and novel-like details of this *cause célèbre* would take us too far afield, and it is enough to note that the Marcos Rodríguez scandal had such extraordinary political repercussions because the informer was not the only one on trial.*

In 1964, the elderly Ordoqui was a Vice Minister of the Armed Forces and Edith García Buchaca was Executive Secretary of the National Council of Culture. Through Marcos' connections with them and other top Cuban Communists, the former PSP was also put on trial. In her testimony, Edith García Buchaca hotly protested that "the record of the Partido Socialista Popular is being put on trial conjointly with a common informer." She complained bitterly that one of Marcos' chief accusers, Major Faure Chomón, a former Directorio Revolucionario leader and then the Minister of Transportation, had provided material "which is being utilized to create a whole anti-Communist climate, a whole climate of struggle against the old Communists." One old-time Communist after another took the stand to defend the honor of the old party. In his own intervention at the trial, Castro admitted that it had been "unexpectedly converted into a trial of a political character." Castro severely criticized Ordoqui, but not to make a bad situation worse, leaned over to exonerate Edith García Buchaca, to praise another old Communist effusively, César Escalante, brother of the previously disgraced Aníbal, and in general,

* The essential details were put together by Hugh Thomas, "Murder in Havana," *New Statesman* (London), May 29, 1964, pp. 838–40.

to soften the blow that the old Communists had received.*

Nevertheless, the Marcos Rodríguez affair could not be closed or forgotten. Eight months later, in November, 1964, Ordoqui was suspended from all his posts, including his membership in the National Directorate of the Party, pending a "full investigation" of his "political conduct" since 1957, the year of the fateful betrayal.

Ordoqui was no ordinary old-time Communist. He had joined the Cuban Communist Party in 1926 or 1927,† soon after its formation, and was, next to the mysterious Fabio Grobart, who had been a founding member, the oldest Communist still in the top leadership in point of service. For at least twenty-five years, he had been one of the five or even three chief Communists in Cuba, entrusted with the most critical, confidential affairs, including those relating to the Soviet Union. And now, whatever the merits of the case, it was his turn, after Aníbal Escalante, to be destroyed politically by Fidel Castro. In less than three years, with these two gone, the old-time Communist representation on the National Directorate had been cut by 20 per cent.‡ In fact, César Escalante, the only old-time Commu-

---

* The full text of the trial was published in, among other places, *Bohemia,* March 27 and April 3, 1964.

† Félix Pita Rodríguez, *Joaquín Ordoqui, Biografía de una Voluntad* (Havana, 1943), p. 15, gives the date as February, 1926. But in an interview with Nicolás Guillén, in *Hoy,* August 14, 1960, Ordoqui gave the date as 1927.

‡ The Dirección Nacional, originally of the ORI (Organizaciones Revolucionarias Integradas, or Integrated Revolutionary Organizations) and later transferred to the PURS (Partido Unido de la Revolución Socialista, or United Party of the Socialist Revolution), had been set up in March, 1962, with a membership of twenty-five, ten of them old-time Communists, including Aníbal Escalante and Joaquín Ordoqui. The order of precedence, strictly followed in listings of the leadership, together with the previous formal affiliations, of the remaining twenty-three follow: Fidel Castro (26th of July), Raúl Castro (26th of July), Ernesto Che Guevara (26th of July), Osvaldo Dorticós (26th of July), Blas Roca (PSP), Emilio Aragonés (26th of July), Carlos Rafael Rodríguez (PSP), Augusto Martínez Sánchez (26th of July), Faure Chomón (Directorio Revolucionario), Ramiro Valdés (26th of July), Severo Aguirre (PSP), Flavio Bravo (PSP), César Escalante (PSP), Lázaro Peña (PSP), Manuel Luzardo (PSP), Ramón Calcines

nist whom Castro had seen fit to praise at the Marcos Rodríguez trial, was constrained to send a letter to the former
Party organ, *Hoy,* of August 19, protesting the failure—
unprecedented in the preceding five years—of any Cuban
paper to mention the thirty-ninth anniversary of the founding of the Communist Party of Cuba.

The year 1964 was a bad one for the old-time Communist Manuel Luzardo, whose Ministry of Internal Trade
was publicly attacked by Raúl Castro in May; for the former Directorio Revolucionario leader Alberto Mora, who
was dismissed as Minister of Foreign Trade in June; for
Marcelo Fernández, who was shifted from the Presidency
of the National Bank to the Ministry of Foreign Trade in
June; for Regino Botí, who was dismissed as Minister of
Economy in July; for Ordoqui in November; and for
Martínez Sánchez, who shot himself in December. There
were more casualties in the top leadership in the last half
of 1964 than in the previous four years.

For Guevara, however, 1964 was a very good year. In
the last half of 1963, he had trimmed his pronouncements
on the role of force in Latin American revolutions, the
primacy of moral incentives, and the desirability of centralization, as if he had been forced to make some concessions after Castro's return from Moscow in May of that
year. On all these issues, he was his old, uncompromising
self again a few months later. Marcelo Fernández and Professor Bettelheim were not the only ones to feel his fangs in
1964. In July, a new Ministry of the Sugar Industry was
created, and Guevara's first deputy at the Ministry of Industries, Lieutenant Orlando Borrego Díaz, was moved
over to head it.

(PSP), Juan Almeida (26th of July), Armando Hart (26th of July), Sergio
del Valle (26th of July), Guillermo García (26th of July), Osmany Cien-
fuegos (26th of July), Raúl Curbelo (Directorio Revolucionario), Haydée
Santamaría (26th of July).

The new Ministry was the outgrowth of a bitter struggle for control of the sugar industry that had been going on for more than a year. Early in 1963, the question had arisen in the top leadership whether it might not be better, in view of the disastrous drop in sugar production, to take the industry out of INRA and transfer control of it to the sugar mills, the industrial side of the operation. If Guevara had had his way, INRA would apparently have been left with little more than an empty shell. According to Rodríguez, the decision was finally reached to leave the cultivation of the cane, the agricultural side of the industry, in INRA's charge. But Guevara, evidently not satisfied, soon denounced the lack of coordination in the industry and demanded "only one road, only one view, only one voice." Rodríguez came back with a gentle reminder that the top leaders, including Fidel Castro, had decided in favor of INRA, and nothing more was heard of this little squabble.* By the summer of 1964, however, the new Ministry of the Sugar Industry indicated that Guevara had found a way to cut in on Rodríguez' territory.

Six months later, Rodríguez was less successful in beating off an attack not only on INRA's sugar performance but on its entire agricultural record. At an INRA "congress" toward the end of January, 1965, Rodríguez reported a substantial increase in the cattle industry in 1964 over the preceding two years, but he had to admit that general agricultural production had continued to decline. For 1964, he confirmed an "enormous drop in corn and a big drop in rice"; coffee and beans had also done badly; fruits and vegetables had barely held their own; tobacco had fallen off by 87,600 quintals (1 quintal equals 220.46 lbs.). He was not able to do much more than promise that 1965 would be a much better year.†

* Guevara, *Hoy*, March 12 and 24, 1963; Rodríguez, speech of February 24, 1963.

† *Hoy*, January 28, 1965.

In his concluding speech, Rodríguez tried to make peace on the burning issue of material versus moral incentives. In the past, while Guevara had stressed the moral over the material, Rodríguez had cautiously advocated both. Now he felt it necessary to protest that there was "no basic difference in Cuba with respect to the fundamental character of this problem." In other "socialist countries," he said, managers were receiving special rewards for increasing production. But this practice, he declared, had yielded "negative results," and it behooved Cuba not to commit the same errors—probably the first time in more than three decades that Rodríguez, a Communist since 1933 when he was twenty, had publicly found fault with the Soviet Union.* The Cuban line had obviously hardened in favor of "moral incentives," and Carlos Rafael Rodríguez was not one to rebel against it, any more than he had rebelled when the Party had told him to become a minister in Batista's Cabinet back in 1944.

Two weeks later, on February 15, Fidel Castro announced that INRA had been presented with a new President—Fidel Castro. He intimated why he had made the change by saying: "Although we have a set of favorable conditions, it is not enough that they should exist, but we have to take maximum advantage of them."† And so, instead of INRA losing the sugar industry, Carlos Rafael Rodríguez lost INRA.

If a list had been drawn up of old-time Communists to be purged or even demoted by Castro, Rodríguez would undoubtedly have been at the very bottom. He had gone over to Castro during some of the darkest days in the Sierra Maestra; he had been considered the ideal mediator between the old and the new, the young and the old Communists; no other former top PSP leader seemed to have

* *Ibid.*, January 30, 1965.
† *Ibid.*, February 16, 1965.

merited so much and to have benefited so much from Castro's favor. That he should have been eased out of INRA—which, as he had once nostalgically put it, was "more than a product of the revolution; it was the revolution itself"—showed that the whole top leadership of the former PSP could not fall much lower.

Indeed, the old cadre, product of a quarter of a century of training in the hard Stalinist school, could not have suffered much worse blows at the hands of an open enemy. It had survived persecution, illegality, factionalism, a world war, alliance with and parting from Batista, all the twists and turns of Stalin's line, and then Khrushchev's line—but it could not survive Fidel Castro. One by one, the old Communist leadership had been dismembered, dishonored, and discarded—Aníbal Escalante put through the ringer of an old-fashioned purge, Joaquín Ordoqui in even worse disgrace, Edith García Buchaca removed from the National Council of Culture, Juan Marinello ousted as head of the University of Havana and sent off to a sinecure in Paris, Manuel Luzardo humiliated by Raúl Castro, Lázaro Peña described by a pro-Castro writer as the only leader whom the Cuban workers unanimously oppose, Carlos Rafael Rodríguez and Severo Aguirre let out of INRA, Blas Roca an object of scorn. The victims were not even able to cry out to the world; according to the rules of the game, they had to grin and bear it and even go to their political destruction singing Castro's praises.

In a curious way, the Communists' experiences with Batista and Castro resembled each other. In 1938, they had made a deal with Batista which had paid off quickly and handsomely. Party membership had jumped spectacularly from 2,800 in January, 1938, to more than 5,000 in September, 1938, to 23,300 in January, 1939.* Batista had

---

* Blas Roca, *Las Experiencias de Cuba* (Havana: Editorial Páginas, 1939), p. 8. These figures differ in different Communist sources, but there can be no doubt that Communist membership increased sharply in 1938–39.

enabled the Party to obtain full legality for the first time, to put out a daily newspaper, to gain control of the labor movement, to elect Senators and Representatives and dozens of municipal officials, to enter the Cabinet, to become a major national force. But all this had been achieved primarily as a result of a diplomatic arrangement on top, not a struggle below. Batista remained Batista, and when he seized power again in 1952, this time without the Communists, they had to pay dearly for their years of prosperity thanks to his indulgence.

The Communist Party that had emerged from the struggle against Batista was again a relatively small, weak, isolated organization. Morally, it had been so tarnished by its previous association with Batista and by its refusal until almost the last moment to engage in armed struggle against him that it could hardly win a trade-union election in mid-1959. Again its trump card was a diplomatic arrangement on top, and once more the fortunes of the old-timers seemed to improve miraculously. Castro gave them everything that Batista had given them, and more. But Castro, too, remained Castro. What he could give he could take away. In both cases, the Communists had not, so to speak, earned their way. In theory, they were the most devout votaries of the "class struggle," but they did not get ahead in 1937–38 or in 1959–60 through "class struggle." They owed their greatest gains to political deals that were the envy of bourgeois politicians, and a deal with Castro turned out to be not very different from, if more dangerous than, a deal with Batista.

The PSP, then, has suffered the fate of all those who helped Fidel Castro to power, who tried to use him, or who believed in his professions of faith, whether in "constitutional democracy" or in "orthodox Communism." It has paid the same heavy price for the lesson that Fidel Castro does not, in the end, share power. All who have tried to harness his "charisma" to their own purposes have merely enhanced it by giving him material and other assistance which he would otherwise not have had.

The world Communist movement as we have known it has been based primarily on ideology and organization. It has done quite well in some countries without inspired leadership. It has never before tried to assimilate a charismatic leader of the Castro type who seemed to present it with a ready-made revolution. The Castro phenomenon raises the question whether charisma and Communism can be faithful bedfellows. It may indicate that traditional Communism cannot effectively get to the masses through the charismatic leader. They remain "his" masses, stemming back to "his" guerrilla force, "his" Sierra Maestra peasantry, "his" 26th of July Movement, "his" agrarian reform. If the masses can be made to follow him into Communism, they can also let him decide what true Communism is and who the real Communists are. And internecine struggles are fought over these issues, not over abstract allegiance to Communism.

The Communist Dilemma

The political beheading of the old Cuban Communist leadership has not as yet settled anything for the other Latin American Communist parties struggling with their own problem of Castroism. Most of the older and larger parties have found that they cannot live with it, and they cannot live without it. They must admit that Castro's victory in Cuba set off a revolutionary wave of varying depth and force throughout Latin America. They wish to compete for the youthful *révoltés* most attracted to Castroism. They cannot deny that Castro, and Castro alone, has succeeded in doing what every Communist party considers to be its *raison d'être*—to capture power. And yet most of them cannot bring themselves to adopt the Castroist tactics for capturing power.

In 1964, the *World Marxist Review,* organ of the Soviet-oriented Communist parties, published a series of articles which indicated the variety of ways that the different parties tried to handle the problems raised by Castroism.

A Brazilian Communist leader warned that "the rate of radical social change cannot be predetermined at will." Writing before the overthrow of the Goulart regime in March, 1964, he explained that the Brazilian Party was interested in "structural reforms" of the existing order rather than its immediate overthrow. He envisaged the "possibility of a peaceful revolution" through building up "the national and democratic movements." He protested that these "reforms" had to be achieved by "mass pressure" rather than through class "harmony" or "agreement at the top." But anything resembling "armed struggle" or "guerrilla warfare" was not even worth mentioning.*

A Guatemalan writer reported that the leading role in the 1962 revolutionary activity had been played by "intellectuals and students, that is, the intellectual stratum of the middle class." The small working class still had far to go, and "the peasant movement is developing extremely unevenly." Armed struggle had begun in February, 1962, and was subsequently supported by the Communist Party. But this did not mean that other Latin American countries might not prefer "peaceful development," that rural guerrilla warfare "must be the main form of struggle everywhere," or that the Guatemalan situation might not change.† Another Guatemalan Communist related the guerrilla struggle to the Guatemalan army coup in March, 1963.

* Giocondo Dias, "Some Problems of the Class Struggle in Brazil," *World Marxist Review,* January, 1964, pp. 21–25.

† Hugo Barrios Klee, "The Revolutionary Situation and the Liberation Struggle of the People of Guatemala," *ibid.*, March, 1964, pp. 16–24.

He attributed the Guatemalan developments in large part to the Cuban influence, which, he claimed, was most marked on "a large section of the peasantry and the more radical urban middle sections." As of the middle of 1964, however, the guerrilla centers were only "in their formative, organizational stage." Despite its support of guerrilla warfare in Guatemala, the Party was still of the opinion that "the formula that the insurrectionary center is sufficient to create the conditions for revolution is incomplete and, therefore, incorrect." But no hint was given that this was Guevara's "formula."*

A Panamanian Communist called the Cuban revolution an "epochal" event and "an inspiration to the people of Latin America." But he held that "the entire course of developments at home and abroad shows that there is every chance of the revolutionary process in Panama developing without civil war." He spurned the "provocations of adventurists"—without identifying them.†

From Peru came the usual tributes to "the impact of the Cuban revolution throughout Latin America" and the "experience of the Cuban revolution." But it was quickly followed by assurances that the conditions in Peru were not the same as those in Venezuela or pre-Castro Cuba. The basic difference was the absence in Peru of sufficient mass support of a revolutionary struggle for power. "That is why we cannot accept the thesis that all that is needed to 'kindle the flame' of revolution in any place and in all circumstances is to 'ignite the spark' of guerrilla warfare," the author asserted. "Considering the demands of the present stage of the revolutionary process and contrary to the adventurist policy of the 'ultra-Lefts' who are causing con-

---

* Alfredo Guerra Borges, "The Experience of Guatemala: Some Problems of the Revolutionary Struggle Today," *ibid.*, June, 1964, pp. 12–18.

† Orso Alba, "Panama in the Fight for National Sovereignty," *ibid.*, April, 1964, pp. 15–21.

fusion and who follow the Chinese splitters, we uphold the tactic of actively gathering strength."*

Victorio Codovilla of Argentina, whom we have previously cited, gave a somewhat different reason for choosing between peaceful and nonpeaceful tactics. He made the choice dependent on "the degree of resistance offered by the reactionaries to the revolutionary changes." This could be interpreted to mean that the reactionaries would thereby determine Communist policy, to which the traditionalists answer that Communist policy is never made in a vacuum and always adapts itself to existing circumstances. Codovilla also gave his blessings to the Cuban revolution but interpreted it in such a way that it became an orthodox Communist textbook case. He claimed, or perhaps pretended, for he probably knew better, that the Cuban revolution owed its success to the "hegemony of the proletariat" and that it bore out the old principle that "the party of the working class must not relinquish leadership to the bourgeoisie."†

The Uruguayan Communist leader Rodney Arismendi, writing after Goulart's downfall in Brazil, tried to steer an almost mathematically equilibrated middle course. The Cuban revolution had "sounded the bugle call proclaiming to the world on behalf of our continent that Latin America had entered the lists in the decisive battles of the age." But, unlike Codovilla, Arismendi recognized that Castro's movement had departed from the "established rules." He even tried to use Castro against the Chinese Communists by alleging that the Cuban experience and Castro's statements had dealt "hard blows" to the Chinese Communist concepts. But he was cautious enough not to offer any details of this experience or examples of these statements to

* Jorge del Prado, "Mass Struggle—The Key to Victory," *ibid.*, May, 1964, pp. 11–18.

† "The Ideas of Marxism-Leninism in Latin America," *ibid.*, August, 1964, pp. 40–49.

back up this rather farfetched statement. As for Uruguay itself, he held out the possibility of a "peaceful path of revolution" if an anti-imperialist government established itself in Brazil or Argentina; he took no chances in warning against the twin pitfalls of "petty-bourgeois adventurism" and "loss of revolutionary perspective"; and he sermonized that the revolutionaries "must master all possible forms of struggle" without confining themselves to any "particular formula."*

Finally, an article from Venezuela revealed that the Communist Party in that country had decided on a policy of "armed struggle" in December, 1962. It acknowledged that the Venezuelan elections in December of the following year had been a "grave setback" for the Party. Nevertheless, the Party leadership decided to confirm the use of force "as the basic form of the development of the revolution" at a meeting in April, 1964. As in Cuba, the Venezuelans believe that guerrilla warfare in rural localities holds the greatest promise of success.†

These quite different approaches in seven different countries indicate the range of reactions to the problems posed by Castroism in the older Latin American Communist parties still faithful to Soviet leadership. At one extreme, the Peruvian and most other parties have rejected and are resisting the Cuban line. At the other extreme, the Venezuelan Party has fully committed itself to the Cuban line, and the Guatemalan Party has moved in that direction. All parties and leaders vow their utmost support, or at least pay lip service, to the Cuban revolution and to Fidel Castro's heroic role. If they criticize some of Guevara's more extreme formulations, they do so in the guise of denouncing the Chinese Communist line. But, as in the Peruvian

* Rodney Arismendi, "Some Aspects of the Revolutionary Process in Latin America Today," *ibid.*, October, 1964, pp. 10–19.

† Carlos López, "The Communist Party of Venezuela and the Present Situation," *ibid.*, October, 1964, pp. 20–27.

article, they paraphrase Guevara so closely that no one can be deceived.

The Soviets, then, would like to counter the Chinese threat not by having the parties loyal to them adopt a "right-wing" rather than a "left-wing" policy or a uniformly "peaceful" rather than a "violent" road to power. Rather, the Soviet strategy consists in tolerating and even encouraging a broad range of policies from the most peaceful to the most warlike. It seeks to put the Chinese in the position of advocating an "extremist," "adventurist," "ultra-left" line everywhere. The Soviets have tried to stake out for themselves a position extending from Codovilla to Castro, permitting individual parties maximum leeway in determining their own policies. The key to the Soviet response is multiformity, not "polycentrism." In practice, however, this flexible policy requires a "live and let live" attitude on the part of the different tendencies in the Soviet sphere of influence. They can all be "right" because no single one of them is "right" in all circumstances. A conference of Latin American parties was held late in 1964 to work out a program of "unity" on the basis of emphasizing the "points of agreement" rather than the "disagreements," or at least of keeping the open and latent differences within the family.*

For this anti-Chinese strategy, the Soviets need Castroism on their extreme left flank. They have been willing to pay a pretty ruble to keep it within the fold or even to prevent it from going over bag and baggage to the Chinese. The fact that Castroism in some respects parallels Maoism is not, from this point of view, a total loss. It suggests that the Soviets can live with a certain amount of Maoism so long as it does not claim to have a monopoly of Communist wisdom and virtue or the right to read the Soviet leaders

---

* This was the main message of the communiqué of the conference published in *Pravda*, January 19, 1965 (English translation in *The Current Digest of the Soviet Press*, February 10, 1965, pp. 15–16).

themselves out of the one, true world Communist movement. In 1963, when Castro was extolling Nikita Khrushchev as "a great leader and a formidable adversary of imperialism,"* he partially served as a Soviet buffer against the Chinese, even if he soon refused to sign the test-ban treaty (though not for the Chinese reasons) or to join in Soviet attacks. If the Soviets could back Castro, it implied that they were hardly as pusillanimous as the Chinese said they were. At different times, the Soviets have used Castro against the Chinese,† and the Chinese have used him against the Soviets. Obviously Castro could not play this role if he were merely a Soviet satellite or a Maoist disciple; those who make him one or the other grotesquely underestimate Fidel Castro's stake in Fidel Castro.

For its players, the game holds dangers whatever moves they make; and if they do not dare to oversimplify it, there is no reason why anyone else should do so. The changing relations of the old-time Communist leaders and the new Castroist "guiding angels" in Cuba have undoubtedly not been lost on the Soviet Union or the Latin American Communist parties. On the other hand, the well-disciplined Cuban old-timers must take into account the needs of the Soviet Union and the other Latin American Communists vis-à-vis Castroism. How traditional Communism and Castroism ultimately fare together will probably be decided from an international rather than a purely Cuban perspective.

For Soviet Russia and the Communist "Old Guard" in Latin America, Castro's Cuba represents an experiment

* *Revolución,* June 5, 1963.

† The first full-scale Soviet polemic of July 14, 1963, boasted of "the assessment that the leaders of the Cuban revolution themselves give to the policy of the government of the Soviet Union, which they call a policy of fraternal solidarity and genuine internationalism." In late June, 1963, the Cuban delegation to the World Congress of Women, in Moscow, headed by Vilma Espín, wife of Raúl Castro, voted with the Soviet bloc *against* the Chinese—but it was not reported in the Cuban press.

with no exact precedent.* At one time, it seemed to be one of the main factors in a new pattern adopted by them for Communist expansion. It has already taken them far from where they wanted or expected to go. It may become one of the main factors in a reconsideration of that pattern, at least in its Cuban form. Whether it is better than what they had before may be less important than whether it is better for them.

The Sierra Maestra Complex

In economics as well as in revolutionary tactics, then, Castroism has evolved a policy and authority of its own. From its very inception, it has had the same revolutionary tactics, but it has not had the same economic and social policy. In the latter sphere, the Cuban leaders have gone so far from their origins, and even from their first years in power, that they have given up trying to establish a continuity with their past and have decided to repudiate it.

Toward the period before 1959, they have adopted an attitude of worldly-wise estrangement. They have spoken of it as if they had become blasé grownups looking back at their innocent and somewhat brainless childhood. On October 30, 1963, for example, after discoursing on the necessity of avoiding "tedium, uniformity, and monotony" under socialism, Castro thought of saying: "It is possible that we ourselves could not have expressed these things to the people years ago, because we did not know; but we knew that we did not know." And he went on with even greater modesty to say that they still did not know any more than

* I would suggest that there is some analogy, by no means perfect, in the 1923–27 attempt of the Communists to take power in China through membership in the Kuomintang and later, on Stalin's orders, through acceptance of Chiang Kai-shek's leadership. The point here is the similarity of tactics, not the similarity of Castro and Chiang, though it is sometimes forgotten that Chiang, too, was once considered a "left revolutionary," albeit something short of a Communist.

they had known when they had landed in the "Granma," the yacht that had brought them from Mexico to Cuba in December, 1956. All he could claim seven years later was that they were far more aware than they had been of the "extraordinary possibilities." A year later, on September 28, 1964, he was still saying: "We began to construct socialism without knowing how socialism should be constructed. We knew what we wanted, but we did not know how to get it."

Of the period after 1959, Castro has become equally disparaging. In October, 1963, the month of the Second Agrarian Reform, he referred to the previous five years as "the era of spoiled children, of being tolerant around here, of mistakes, of infantilisms."* A few days later, he said that "we cannot go into the sixth year of the revolution with short kindergarten pants," and he asserted that it was necessary "to leave behind the stage of economic cretinism."† This harsh judgment of the revolution's immediate past, which is, after all, his own, did not prevent Castro from assuring the same audiences that he had at last found the right road and that the agricultural future was just as bright as the industrial past was to have been.

But the admission of ingenuous blundering was not without political purpose. It served, above all, to emphasize the sharpness of the break with the recent past, as if, in its sixth year, the Cuban revolution was entering not merely another stage but its first real stage and had to begin to take itself seriously. The Cuban leaders felt a need to tear down and poke fun at most of their first five years in power in order to free themselves of all past commitments. This revolution has been peculiar in that it has periodically required a *tabula rasa* to regain its momentum. Ironically, therefore, the very things about it that charmed and won over foreign

* *Revolución*, October 22, 1963.
† *Ibid.*, October 31, 1963.

sympathizers like Jean-Paul Sartre, C. Wright Mills, Waldo Frank, and others had to be repudiated and denounced in Cuba.

After "a few conversations and a quick look round" on the island in 1961, Mrs. Joan Robinson gushed: "This free-hand style of administration, which astonishes visitors from East and West alike, can work (and somehow it does work, errors and omissions excepted) because the country is small and the administrators know each other, having been under fire together in the mountains."* That "free-hand style of administration" was exactly what the Cuban leaders decided to wipe out because it did not work. Those little concrete houses for peasants that had gone up in the first year or two of Castro's regime came to be regretted as having been "unproductive." In the long list of errors that Guevara recited in Algiers in July, 1963, one was "too much emphasis at the beginning on the satisfaction of social needs."

If any democratic leader had confessed to the kind of errors made in Cuba, he would have risked making himself a laughingstock. But the Cubans have not been judged by ordinary democratic standards. They have enjoyed, in some circles, a special dispensation given to them by the old magic word "revolution," and in Latin America, the new magic word "Marxism." The first one has lost virtually all meaning, and the same thing seems to be happening to the second. As it is widely used in Latin America, as well as elsewhere, a better term might be "Magic Marxism," because it has little in common with the original. Socialism, after all, was not invented by Marx. He spent a lifetime trying to put the earlier utopian thought on a "scientific" foundation, that is, to determine the social and economic conditions necessary for its realization. Marx did not believe that everything was possible everywhere or all at once. There have been many "socialisms," but in our time some

* *The Listener* (London), August 24, 1961, p. 265.

of the old varieties, especially those impregnated with utopianism and anarchism, have tended to reappear in new guises under the single brand name of "Marxism." Thus, we now have Cuban "Marxists" who were capable of ordering factories and overlooking the little detail of raw materials; and who, when they could not make a success of 40 per cent nationalized agriculture, nationalized 30 per cent more.

As one looks back at Castro's first six years in power, the main thread of continuity seems to be Castro's power itself. This power has rested primarily on those—in the leadership as well as among the masses—who have supported him unconditionally rather than on those who have supported what he has stood for from time to time. His personal cadre has been loyal to him for over a decade through his different public manifestations, as a constitutional democrat, an anti-Communist and anticapitalist "humanist," a "socialist," a "Marxist-Leninist," and a Communist. It is spread throughout the government and the party, but its chief stronghold is the armed forces, which have become the virtually private preserve of the unconditional Fidelistas of longest standing. In his early period, Leon Trotsky observed that the party organization substitutes itself for the party, the Central Committee substitutes itself for the party organization, and finally "a single 'dictator' substitutes himself for the Central Committee." Castro has reversed the process. He started as the leader and only afterward felt the need for a Central Committee, a party organization, and a party. And though he talked much of the role of the party, which has been in formation since 1961, he had not yet, by the beginning of 1965, brought himself to call the first party congress to elect a party leadership which, at least formally, would not derive its powers solely from him.

Hence, Castro is both within and above the system of government that he has worked out. He does everything but cannot be blamed for anything. When Carlos Rafael Rodríguez told of the mistreatment of the peasantry in the last half of 1961 and first months of 1962 he found it necessary to add: "Many times the peasant showed his disagreement and rebelliousness against situations that were not just with these words: 'If Fidel knew about it.' "* But how could Fidel have failed to know? After all, he had in that very period been President of INRA, and the former Executive Director, Antonio Núñez Jiménez, had been directly responsible to him. If the peasants, including the poorest ones, had for at least eight months been provoked to rebelliousness by INRA officials, local political leaders, and even "comrades of the Revolutionary Armed Forces," as Rodríguez said, what was the Maximum Leader, the Prime Minister, the head of the party, and the President of INRA doing all that time? At the end of 1963, the same actors played out the same little drama. This time Rodríguez was on the receiving end of one of Castro's tantrums. On October 30, as a result of another agricultural shake-up, Castro cried out: "Enough of revolutionary theoreticians, enough of purely theoretical Marxists! The purely theoretical Marxist-Leninist is really an unproductive expense to society." Whom did he mean? Forty-eight hours later, Rodríguez and the entire staff of INRA signed a long, self-debasing letter, addressed to Castro, confessing to all the errors and misdeeds that Castro had inveighed against. Lázaro Peña, not Fidel Castro, has become the Cuban workers' Enemy No. 1 for carrying out Fidel Castro's orders.

In this system, there will never be any lack of enemies, internal and external. "The revolution," Castro has said, "needs the enemy; the proletariat does not flee from the enemy; it needs the enemy. The revolution needs for its development its antithesis, which is the counterrevolu-

* *Revolución*, May 18, 1963.

tion."* In different circumstances, Stalin had developed a related theory that the class struggle sharpens as socialism advances. If he did not have enough enemies, he invented them. Castro's frustrations have been taken out on a wider and wider circle of foes, until it embraces his own "bureaucracy."

In one of his most revealing speeches, on November 13, 1964, Castro blamed Cuba's troubles on the "socialist bureaucrats," some of whom he called "idiots" and threateningly accused of forgetting that "this is a revolution of workers and peasants, that this is a revolution of workers, for workers, and not a revolution of the workers for the petty bourgeoisie." As if he were giving up on anyone old enough to have an administrative or managerial job, he cried out that "we are going to sweep them away with the new generation that we are forging!" It did not seem to occur to him, or if it did occur to him it made no difference, that he and his closest associates had set up this administrative monstrosity, that he had been warned again and again that it could not work in the existing circumstances, and that a "Marxist" was supposed to adapt his practical goals to the material at hand. But this was the end of 1964 and not the summer of 1960, when one of Castroism's proudest boasts had been that it did not intend to "sacrifice" an entire generation, as Stalin had done.†

In economic policy as well as in revolutionary tactics, then, an uneasy equilibrium has been established between "traditional" Communism and Castro's Communism. The economic differences have been expressed most sharply in the areas of state ownership and operation, especially in

---

* *Hoy*, February 24, 1963.

† "Moreover, we Cubans have a responsibility we are well aware of—to show the possibility of a new way of economic development to the Americas without sacrificing a generation or more in the making of a decent economy. We revolutionaries have dedicated ourselves to this" (Mills, *op. cit.*, p. 82).

agriculture, centralization of industrial controls, and material-versus-moral rewards for workers and management. There is far more state operation of agriculture, centralization of industrial control, and emphasis on nonmaterial rewards in Cuba than anywhere in Eastern Europe. Castroism, in effect, has come to represent an "extremist" Communist tendency in both economic policy and revolutionary tactics. Men with an acutely short-range perspective of taking power could not adapt themselves to a patiently long-range economic program in power. In Communist terms, they have largely substituted the "subjective" element of revolutionary will or "consciousness" for the "objective" factor of the "productive forces" at their disposal. Just as they have maintained that armed struggle would create the objective conditions to justify it, so they have decided that revolutionary "consciousness" will bring forth the "productive forces" to fulfill it.

In both cases, Castroism has tended to return to its origins. It has been obsessed by what might be called a "Sierra Maestra complex"—the legend of the twelve who with the help of a few hundred or a few thousand "illiterate, uneducated, and technically untrained" peasants allegedly overthrew a "regular, disciplined army." In his speech of January 2, 1965, on the sixth anniversary of his taking power, Castro saw fit to evoke this legend more starkly and threateningly than ever before. Faced with declining material support from the Soviet bloc, he told the Cuban people that they would not be "completely revolutionary" until they could do with "absolutely no aid" whatsoever from the outside. To warn them of what they might have to expect, he asked them to imagine themselves confronted with a "total blockade." At this point, he invoked "the man of the Sierra Maestra," his old hero with the "virgin mentality," into whose mouth he put the following words: "Good, I have lived all my life without fuel, without electric light, without transport, without medicines, without everything." That, he exhorted, was the proper attitude for the workers of Havana to take.

In effect, Castroism has oscillated between two extremes: to make a Cuba out of all Latin America or to make a Sierra Maestra out of all Cuba. The supreme paradox of the Sierra Maestra complex is that it bases the most advanced Communist "consciousness" on the most backward part of Cuba. In this speech, in which for the first time he officially pronounced Cuba to be a "dictatorship of the proletariat," Castro held up what Guevara had called the most "petty-bourgeois"–minded peasants in Cuba as the exemplars of the revolution.

This peculiar *mésalliance* suggests what is difficult and different about Castroism. At this critical moment, in the very act of affirming the Communist present, Castro had to seek strength in the pre-Communist past. His past differs from that of all other Communist leaders and repeatedly insists on injecting itself into the present. Castro has had a most variegated past, but the only parts of it that he is truly proud of and chooses to relive again and again are the Moncada and Sierra Maestra episodes. At one time, it seemed as if he were trying to adapt himself fully to the Communist tradition and write off a good deal of his own former "petty-bourgeois prejudices and defects" of the Moncada–to–Sierra Maestra years. If all had gone well in 1961, he might have gone further in this direction. But all did not go well, and in his pushing and pulling at a recalcitrant reality, he found the past far more inspiring and sustaining than the present. A movement which had developed its ideology within itself would not have had to reconcile these contradictions. But there was Communism long before there was Castroism; there was Communism in conflict with essential aspects of Castroism during the latter's very gestation; Castroism could only attach itself to a much larger, older, canonical movement and, having done so, strive to retain its individuality within it.

In a previous era, such incongruities might not have been permitted within the framework of world Communism. But in an era of unprecedented schisms within that world, the ingredients that have set Castroism apart do not seem so exotic. In any case, there has been a tacit agreement on the part of all the Communist states, no matter how great the differences between them, not to look the Cuban gift horse too closely in the mouth. The fact remains that Castroism has chosen to become an adopted member of the Communist family, that the rest of the family has accepted it, and that a large part of the family has supported it at very considerable cost. The decision to do so in 1959 or 1960 was undoubtedly a calculated risk, primarily on the part of Nikita Khrushchev and his closest associates. As long as this situation remains, it is hard to see how Castroism can be considered outside the spectrum of the Communist world. It is equally hard to see how it can be denied its own special place in that spectrum.

When one reflects on the distance that Castroism traveled in its first six years in power, its future holds the gravest foreboding for the Cuban people, for Latin America, and for the world at large. Its most distinguishing characteristic has been an immanent violence which turns inward as readily as outward. And this excess of violence may well prove to be its undoing.

APPENDIX

SENATOR FULBRIGHT
AND U.S. POLICY

WHATEVER OTHER MERITS it may have had, Senator J. William Fulbright's speech of March 25, 1964, provided a much-needed occasion for a full-scale reconsideration of the United States' Cuban policy.* Though the speech covered much more ground, perhaps too much ground, it probably had more direct, immediate, and practical relevance to Cuba than to any

* The full, original text of this speech was published in the *Congressional Record*, March 25, 1964, pp. 6028–34; a somewhat abbreviated version appeared in *The New York Times*, March 26, 1964.

other part of the Communist world. When the Chairman of the Committee on Foreign Relations advised us to distinguish between different Communist regimes elsewhere, one wondered why he should have bothered to kick in an open door. The distinction between China or Russia on the one hand and Yugoslavia or Poland on the other has been recognized for quite some time. But his views on Cuba, to which I wish to limit myself, represented a far more concrete challenge to U.S. policy. A fair test of his entire position may well be how right or wrong he was about Cuba, though I do not mean to suggest that all of his other observations did not need to be discussed on their own merits. I happen to be largely in agreement with him, for example, that "it is not unreasonable to expect the United States to go a little farther than halfway in the search for a fair settlement" with Panama.

Senator Fulbright called on us to base our policy on "objective facts" rather than on "cherished myths." The trouble is, of course, that one man's facts may be another man's myths. The first step, in such cases, is to define the point or area of disagreement as sharply and clearly as possible. Then we will at least know what we are disagreeing about.

Senator Fulbright's entire argument rested on the fundamental premise that "the boycott policy is a failure." He evidently considered it a failure, without reservation or qualification, because it had not by itself brought down Fidel Castro's regime. And if this were the sole criterion of success or failure, he would have been right. But was it?

Before trying to answer the question, it may be well to go back and put the boycott in some historical perspective. For this purpose, I must recapitulate some of the essential points that have already been made in previous pages:

A turning point took place in Cuba in the fall of 1959, marked in October by the arrest of Major Hubert Matos, who had protested Communist infiltration of the Rebel Army, and in November by, among other things, a shake-up in the Cabinet and in the Cuban National Bank, as well as the first stage of the Communist takeover of the Cuban Confederation of Labor. These events did not come to pass overnight; they had been in gestation for at least five or six months. At this point, Guevara's Department of Industrialization, then a part of INRA, went on a "search for offers" to displace the United States in the Cuban market. This "search" led to Soviet First Deputy Premier Anastas I. Mikoyan's visit to Havana and the signature of the first Soviet-Cuban trade agreement in February, 1960.

A few weeks later, Guevara, by then President of the Cuban National Bank, initiated the open crisis of 1960 by calling in the oil companies' representatives and delivering an ultimatum to them, without any possibility of negotiation, for the processing of a large percentage of Soviet oil, starting with two bargeloads that were already on the way. The Cuban Government had not been paying the oil companies for over two years and had piled up a huge debt of $16 million for oil imports and $60 million for previous refining. The companies had given this large credit to the Castro regime to show that they were not without good will or at least a sense of accommodation. But, as usual, when Guevara was ready to strike, he struck decisively and brutally. He did not ask for negotiations; he confronted the companies with an accomplished fact. It was one of those moves which the Castro regime has repeatedly made to get a desired hostile reaction, which it then uses to carry out an aggressive policy as if it were a defensive one.*

* New light on the oil episode has been provided by former Venezuelan President Rómulo Betancourt. In *The Reporter* of August 13, 1964, he revealed that Fidel Castro had asked for a $300-million loan from Venezuela, as part of "a master play against the gringos," during his visit to Caracas in January, 1959. In *Cuadernos* (Paris) of December, 1964, Betancourt filled out the Venezuelan side of the 1960 events, including the fact

Then followed the Cuban expropriations which, in October, 1960, resulted in the U.S. embargo on virtually all trade with Cuba. The significant thing for our present purpose was the Cuban reaction to the embargo. The Cuban leaders, it will be recalled, did not cry out that the U.S. was trying to ruin their country. They cried out that now the U.S. had finally made it possible for Cuba to flourish and to be free. The boycott, paradoxically, was hailed as Cuba's Declaration of Independence, the long-awaited economic liberation of Cuba.

It would be a mistake to think that the Cubans greeted the embargo with joy in order to hide their grief. For years, a "revolutionary" school of thought had taught that the United States was responsible for all of Cuba's ills, and that Cuba could get rid of them by getting rid of every vestige of U.S. influence and investments. The Cuban reaction to the embargo was the logical outcome of this intellectual conditioning. Rarely has a historical interpretation had more profound political consequences or such a clear-cut test of its practical implications.

It was now up to Castro to prove that, without the United States, Cuba could leap into the promised land of "accelerated industrialization," diversified agriculture and increased productivity. It was up to the Soviet Union to demonstrate that Cuba would be better off as part of a Soviet-bloc "international division of labor" than as an economic appendage to the U.S. It was up to the Communist world to show how Communism could be successfully applied to a Latin American outpost.

The methods used were almost naïvely simple. To recapitulate again: The Cubans imported experts who proceeded to make Cuban copies of East European techniques.

---

that the Cubans never once made any effort to get in touch with the Venezuelan Government in a matter that, after all, involved Venezuelan oil and Venezuelan interests (p. 4).

Within a matter of months, however, the new order failed to live up to expectations. A rebellious peasantry developed in the middle of 1961. The program of "accelerated industrialization" virtually came to a halt by the end of the year. The sugar crop took a sharp drop in 1962 and an even sharper one in 1963. Agricultural diversification went backward instead of forward. For example, rice production had advanced to a high point of 181,000 tons in 1957, two years before Castro, and plunged to 95,400 tons in 1962, after three years of Castro.

Ironically, Guevara made an important speech on February 25, 1964, exactly one month before Senator Fulbright's address in the Senate, in which the Cuban Minister of Industries discussed subjects of the greatest relevance to the question raised by the Chairman of the Committee on Foreign Relations.

Among other things, Guevara emphasized that "supplies" (*"abastecimientos"*) had been the weakest link in the Cuban system. Imports from the Soviet bloc had fallen short of expectations by as much as 30 per cent, making it necessary to dig into the reserves of raw materials in 1963. According to Guevara, "almost all the factories depend on imported products," the shortages of which were, therefore, responsible for "the shutdowns, the periods of low productivity, the mechanical breakdowns which cannot be repaired in time owing to lack of spare parts."

The next great problem, Guevara went on, was the state of Cuba's industrial equipment. The new technicians, he said, were able to keep the factories going but were not able to take care of their equipment properly. "Today," Guevara added, "we are experiencing a very great strain in a number of factories which are already in difficult condition to operate, because the equipment has rapidly deteriorated, and we do not have the specialized technical equipment to enable us to change the situation, that is, to make new spare parts, to maintain the most complex units of production so that they would function perfectly." Guevara also confirmed that the U.S.-made machinery in Cuba had broken down to the point of "very little efficiency."

All this added up to one thing in 1964: Castro desperately needed a breathing spell of at least two or three years.* That was the purpose of all his maneuvering and diplomacy. He had worked his way into an economic corner, and he could not get out of it with Soviet aid alone. More than anything else, he needed time, and he was willing to buy it from those whom he considered his worst enemies—if they would sell it to him on terms acceptable to him.

Senator Fulbright was overly impressed by the deals which the Castro regime had made with some Western countries in the first quarter of 1964, especially the Cuban purchase of 400 British Leyland buses. The real question, in March, 1964, was whether the relatively small-scale British, French, and other deals would open the way for relatively large-scale U.S. deals. That is where Senator Fulbright came in.

It has been necessary to sketch in the background of the boycott because I do not think that it can be profitably discussed in a historical vacuum. What did the Senator mean when he said that he was "not arguing against the desirability of an economic boycott against the Castro regime but against its feasibility"? He seemed to mean that it was not "feasible" as a way of bringing down the Castro regime. If that is all he meant, he could have been permitted to score an easy victory. But was the boycott ever given such a mission? Obviously not, since—for one thing—there would have been no Bay of Pigs adventure if the

---

* Charles Bettelheim has stated that he does not expect the "turning point" in the "equilibrium" of Cuba's foreign trade to come until 1968 (*France Observateur*, January 9, 1964, p. 6).

boycott was supposed to have accomplished the same thing. It would seem elementary to point out that the fact that the boycott has not by itself overthrown Castro does not mean that it may not have done other things of vital importance.

Unfortunately, Senator Fulbright's contribution to the debate over U.S. policy suffered from imprecision. He suggested far more than he said and refused to carry his thought to its ultimate conclusion. His key word—"feasibility"—was curiously ambiguous. It implied that we no longer had to decide whether or not to maintain the boycott because the decision had already been made for us by events. We did not have to decide any longer whether the boycott was desirable; if it was not "feasible," why torment ourselves over its desirability? He stopped short of telling us what to do if, as he insisted, the boycott was no longer feasible. He seemed to believe that our allies' decisions had deprived us of all power of decision in this matter, as if the basic effectiveness of the boycott depended primarily on them rather than on us.

This was one way of begging the question. It provided a nice, pragmatic pretext for absolving us of responsibility for our own actions. It transmuted a hard problem of policy into the easy solution of an accomplished fact. It constantly played with words that concealed as much as they revealed. When Senator Fulbright told us that the Castro regime was "not on the verge of collapse," was he trying to tell us that it was also on the verge of stabilization or had already stabilized itself? When he told us that it was not likely to be overthrown by our policies, was it not also true that our policies could prevent it from being overthrown?

If the Castro regime was not on the verge of collapse, it was surely not on the verge of stabilization. It had rather entered a dangerous period of transition which would determine its ultimate collapse or stabilization. The economic miracle that Castro and the Communists had promised in Cuba had become an unmistakable mirage. If nothing else, the boycott had left Cuba wide open to the Soviets and had given them a chance to show what they could do. The United States may have been guilty of many things, but it could not be held responsible for the missing 30 per cent of Soviet imports, the "difficulties" which Guevara had sportingly admitted had come "principally from our side," the increase of workers' "absenteeism" and decrease of their "productivity."

Indeed, Senator Fulbright could not have chosen a more unfortunate moment than March, 1964, for his pronouncement on Cuba. Ever since Castro's long pilgrimage to Soviet Russia in May of the year before, Cuba had been forced to reorganize its entire economy to lessen the burden on the Soviet Union. The new conscription law at the end of 1963 had militarized Cuba beyond anything in its history. At the very moment that Senator Fulbright was speaking, the trial of the former Communist informer Marcos Rodríguez had ripped through the façade of monolithic unity and had revealed top Cuban leaders at each other's throats.

The one thing that could pull Castro through every danger threatening him would be U.S. "acceptance of the continued existence of the Castro regime," as Senator Fulbright recommended. The Senator seemed to think that the critical question was whether Castro was a "distasteful nuisance" or an "intolerable danger." I do not wish to get entangled in the semantics of Castro's exact classification, but if he had become more of a "nuisance" than a "danger," it must have been because he had made serious mistakes at home and had suffered serious setbacks abroad. Thus, first we are told to be nice to Castro because he is so strong that we cannot hurt him, and second we are told to be nice to him because he is so weak that he cannot hurt us.

Every time a Communist power needs a breathing spell,

it begins to make cooing sounds and dangle offers of trade. Just as predictably, a strange alliance of sympathizers and businessmen springs up. The *quid pro quo* is usually, as Professor Hans J. Morgenthau put it, "idiotic." The Communist regime obtains the means of long-term survival and power; the West obtains short-term profits, if there are any, for a few entrepreneurs.

This shortsighted view of the national interest was also implicit in Senator Fulbright's remarks on Cuba. In the case of Communist China, he stopped short of demanding immediate recognition and posed at least one condition— "the abandonment by the Chinese Communists, tacitly if not explicitly, of their intention to conquer and incorporate Taiwan." Whatever one may think of this condition, it was something beyond a scramble for trade. But, in the same speech, the possibility of a *quid pro quo* in the case of Cuba never even arose. Senator Fulbright treated the boycott not as if giving it up were a deliberate political decision with serious consequences but as if it had already been decided for us by forces beyond our control. Consequently, we were asked not only to make a gratuitous gift to Fidel Castro's stability but to do so in the worst possible way.

It is hard to believe that the Chinese or the Cubans take their own "paper tiger" propaganda literally. But if the tiger is stupid, however strong, he will be, in the long run, a "paper tiger." It is frequently necessary, therefore, to prove that the United States is not a stupid tiger. In no area is this demonstration more necessary and more difficult than in the utilization of Communist conflicts, contradictions, and crises. In some quarters, the "utilization" of such conflicts seems to mean little more than a rationing of U.S. largesse—some Communist states get more, some less, and some nothing at all. It is peculiarly characteristic of the U.S. politico-economic make-up that the least dangerous and most negotiable opportunities should be frittered away by

permitting foreign trade and investment to take precedence over foreign policy. The Soviets ruthlessly use foreign trade and aid as an instrument of foreign policy; we more often use foreign policy as an adjunct of foreign trade and investment.

Ever since Castro declared himself publicly a Communist, his regime has hammered away at the thesis that all Communist revolutions are "irreversible." The mass acceptance of this idea would be more important to the Communist world—and its rejection more important to the non-Communist world—than any other stake, in Cuba or elsewhere. If it could be unshakably planted in enough people's minds, the ultimate victory of world Communism would be ensured whatever the outcome of the struggle in that world. It would, in effect, mean that Communism can only go forward, never backward.

Yet, if there is one place in the world where Communism can be "reversible," it is Cuba. It is the most brittle of existing Communist regimes for several reasons: It is separated from its source of supplies and other Communist powers by thousands of miles; it is located in a zone of overwhelming U.S. military superiority; and, above all, its leaders, unlike the traditional school of Communist leadership, operate on the basis of an extremely short-term perspective of revolutionary dynamism, a characteristic that tends to create an ambiance of permanent crisis. Those who may be willing at this stage to give up all hope and effort to bring down the Castro regime should take into account the total magnitude, the full enormity, on a world scale of this decision.

To some extent, Senator Fulbright evaded the larger issue by the simple expedient of overlooking the fact that Cuba is and considers itself to be an integral part of the Communist world, whatever other formula some of Castro's fellow travelers may prefer for home consumption. When

Senator Fulbright assured us that the Castro regime was a "distasteful nuisance" rather than an "intolerable danger," he must have been thinking of that regime *in vacuo* and not as the far-flung and dependent outpost of a Communist world that is both a nuisance and a danger. Indeed, Senator Fulbright could sustain this distinction only by dissociating Cuban Communism from the Communist world and by insulating the United States from Latin America. For in almost the same breath that he argued that "Castro is a nuisance but not a grave threat to the United States," he admitted that "Cuban Communism does pose a grave threat to other Latin American countries." Though Senator Fulbright added that this grave threat could be dealt with by "the inter-American system," an assurance no Latin American could take seriously, the fundamental questions were begged: Was not an admittedly grave threat to Latin America *for that very reason* far more than a mere nuisance to the United States? If the United States accepted the continued existence of a Communist regime in Cuba, would it not in the long run increase the gravity of the threat to Latin American countries?

Despite all this, I fully agreed with Senator Fulbright that the time had come to stop clinging to "old myths" and to face "new realities," though his myths and realities were not mine. A reconsideration and reconstruction of our Cuban policy were long overdue.

Which Fulbright?

Before going on to such a reconsideration, it is necessary to do justice to all of Senator Fulbright's Cuban positions in 1964. In the above section, I have been concerned solely with the Cuban portion of the Senator's much-discussed speech of March 25. But there is reason to believe that

Senator Fulbright soon changed his mind about some of the main propositions and implications in this speech.

In an article in the *Saturday Evening Post* of May 16, 1964, Senator Fulbright caught some of his readers unprepared by writing: "I believe that the United States under present conditions should maintain its own political and economic boycott of the Castro regime."

It is hard to see how such a conclusion could be drawn from the position previously taken in the speech. If the boycott was not "feasible," as he had argued, why maintain it? How could we continue the boycott and "accept" Castro's regime at the same time? Surely Senator Fulbright did not mean to maintain an unfeasible boycott or to accept Castro with a policy totally unacceptable to Castro.

Senator Fulbright made no effort to reconcile the arguments in his speech of March 25 and the policy recommendation in his article of May 16. His rethinking of the whole problem was, however, more clearly evident in his book *Old Myths and New Realities,* which soon appeared.

The first chapter of this book is presented as a "revised and expanded" version of the March 25 speech. One of the most revised sections was certainly the Cuban section.

In the original speech, Senator Fulbright had said: "I should like to make it very clear that I am not arguing against the desirability of an economic boycott against the Castro regime but against its feasibility." In the book, he wrote: "I should like to make it very clear that I am not arguing against the desirability of a concerted free-world economic boycott against the Castro regime, but against its feasibility." And the book followed with the sentence from the May 16 article about maintaining the U.S. boycott of the Castro regime.*

Obviously, "an economic boycott" in the original speech

* J. W. Fulbright, *Old Myths and New Realities* (New York: Random House, 1964), pp. 29–30.

had referred to a U.S. boycott. If it had not done so, it would have had little bearing on the present policy of the United States, which was the aspect of the speech that gave it immediate significance and resonance. By inserting the words "concerted free-world" into the book's version of the same sentence, Senator Fulbright explained away one of the weakest substantive points in the speech but so blunted its political edge that he was able to withdraw its one important policy implication.

Nevertheless, events soon demonstrated that Cuba's trade with Western countries was not so well-founded as it had seemed to be at the time of the March 25 speech. The economic basis for these deals had been a financial windfall in the form of inordinately high prices for sugar in 1963. Despite the disastrous drop in the size of the 1962 and 1963 Cuban sugar crops, Castro could claim on January 2, 1964, that Cuba had accumulated a reserve of $100 million in foreign exchange. It was this reserve and the promise of future high earnings from inflated sugar prices that Castro could dangle before the Western powers. But the exorbitantly high prices for sugar at the end of 1963 could not last more than a few months. So much new acreage had been converted to sugar production all over the world, not least in Latin America, that the market was soon glutted, and the price of sugar plunged from about 11 cents a pound in January, 1964, to 3.7 cents a pound in the fall of 1964. As a result, on September 28 of that year, Castro was forced to admit publicly that the unforeseen, but not unforeseeable, drop in the price of sugar had created new difficulties for the Cuban economy in general and the trade offensive in particular. The new buses and much of the new equipment from Europe, he explained, had been bought largely on credit, and the decline in *divisas* (foreign currency) had brought on a credit crisis. The acuteness of the crisis may be gauged from Castro's words that "we will make any sacrifice before we fail to pay a single *centavo*" and that "a year of strong restrictions [in consumption] is preferable to failure to pay" future installments on the credit deals.

In fact, by the end of 1964, the great hopes of the Castro regime no longer rested on countries like Britain and France but rather on economic relations with Franco Spain. Cuban-Spanish trade rose from $8.4 million in 1962 to $37.1 million in 1963, with a $9.0-million balance in favor of Cuba. Cuban-Spanish trade in the first four months of 1964 amounted to $21.0 million, compared with only $4.2 million for the same period in 1962.* Curiously, the State Department, which had not concealed its extreme displeasure at the British-Cuban and French-Cuban deals, was able to restrain its indignation at the Spanish-Cuban deals, though the United States was capable of putting far more economic pressure on Spain than on Britain or France. The whole Spain-Cuba-U.S. triangle was almost too ironic to bear, with "Communist" Castro being bailed out by "fascist" Franco, and the United States being undercut by one of its most expensive and unnecessary "allies," Spain. One would imagine that this would have brought forth yelps of pain from Washington and the U.S. press. But nothing of the sort happened.

In any event, to come back to Senator Fulbright, what one thinks of some of his ideas on Cuba depends on which Fulbright one has in mind. This is especially true of what he has said about the kind of threat that Cuba holds out to the United States and Latin America. In his March 25 speech, he merely said that "Castro is a nuisance but not a grave threat to the United States." This is also how he puts it in his book.† But in his May 16 article, he protested: "There has been considerable inaccuracy on another point. I did not say that the Castro regime is not a 'grave threat' to

* *The New York Times,* September 29, 1964.
† Fulbright, *op. cit.,* p. 33.

the hemisphere. I said that it is not a 'grave threat' directly to the United States. I did say that it is a 'grave threat' to the Latin-American countries, but one which should and can be dealt with through the procedures of the Organization of American States."

Though some of the words are the same, a somewhat different note has been introduced in this formulation of the problem. If Senator Fulbright believes that the Castro regime *is* a "grave threat" to the hemisphere, it is hard to see how he could exclude the United States, which we may assume can still be found in the Western Hemisphere. But Senator Fulbright gets around this problem by introducing for the first time the word "directly" after "grave threat." The implication here is that Cuba may be a direct threat to Latin America, but only an *indirect* threat to the United States. This is, to my mind, a tenable position, but an "indirect threat" is a far cry from a mere "nuisance." In trying to correct his critics, whoever they were, Senator Fulbright more nearly corrected himself in his May 16 article. But, unfortunately, that correction does not appear in his book.

Clearly, the Cuban threat to, let us say, Venezuela, is vastly more grave and more immediate than to the United States. If this were all that Senator Fulbright had tried to say, there could be no dispute with him. But if we may imagine a hemisphere in which Venezuela has been taken over by Castroite terrorists and guerrillas—that is, one in which the admittedly grave threat has become an even graver reality—there can be no doubt that the interests of the United States would be seriously involved. The hysterical approach to the Cuban problem, which Senator Fulbright rightly deplores, might very well come over us if a country like Venezuela should be subverted (the last Venezuelan election, in 1963, showed that it could not be taken over in any other way). It would seem to be a counsel of elementary prudence, then, to try to prevent such a disastrous eventuality by making Venezuela's cause our own rather than by drawing distinctions which would tempt us to adopt a different policy from Venezuela toward Castro. A policy based on the distinction between a "nuisance" to us and a "grave threat" to Venezuela would only increase the threat to Venezuela by ensuring Castro's survival and stability.

At the bottom of this distinction is really the difference between thinking of Castroism as if it were purely or primarily a Cuban phenomenon and conceiving of Castroism as a much larger, more amorphous Latin American phenomenon.

Finally, Senator Fulbright decided to operate on a key thesis in his speech—the "three options open to the United States with respect to Cuba." These options were, in his own words: "First, the removal of the Castro regime by invading and occupying the island; second, an effort to weaken and ultimately bring down the regime by a policy of political and economic boycott; and, finally, acceptance of the Communist regime as a disagreeable reality and annoyance but one which is not likely to be removed in the near future because of the unavailability of acceptable means of removing it."

When I originally criticized Senator Fulbright's position, I wrote on this score:

"The question arises whether Senator Fulbright has presented his options accurately. According to him, the first two, invasion and boycott, are merely different methods of achieving the same end: Castro's overthrow. Historically, however, they came into existence as complementary rather than as alternative policies. In March, 1960, former President Eisenhower took the first step toward an invasion by authorizing the training of a small standby force of Cuban exiles. In October, 1960, the boycott was started. In the following period the boycott obviously was intended to operate side by side with the proposed invasion, not apart from it. After the Bay of Pigs failure in April, 1961, the boycott willy-nilly continued, as the Kennedy Administration futilely sought other means of action. It could not be given up without helping Castro, and this alone gave it, and still gives it, a *raison d'être*.

"This suggests that something is also wrong with Fulbright's third option—'acceptance.' That seemingly innocent, disarming word does not begin to convey the hard reality which he repeatedly tells us to face. The hard reality is that giving up the boycott means giving Castro the supplies, the equipment, the spare parts, and all the rest that the Soviet bloc has not been able to provide adequately. It is not merely a negative act; it is a thunderously positive act. 'Acceptance,' in Fulbright's sense, does not merely mean recognizing the Castro regime's existence; it means actively, materially, unceasingly, helping that regime to survive. I am not trying to suggest that Castro's regime may not survive without our help; I am simply pointing out that our help, especially at this time, will ensure its survival.

"The boycott surely is not sacrosanct. But if we are going to give it up, let us call things by their right names and truly think 'unthinkable thoughts.' The real issue is not whether we should accept the reality of Castro's continued existence or the unfeasibility of the boycott, but whether we should give him what he wants and needs through the medium of trade and all that it implies. The 'unthinkable thought' in this case is nothing less than the shift from an anti-Castro trade policy to a pro-Castro trade policy.

"In fact, therefore, Fulbright's three options are not all of the same kind. He really has only two major options, invasion and 'acceptance,' and one minor option, boycott. The latter is by its very nature a limited measure with a limited objective, a *faute de mieux* type of policy. Keeping it or giving it up may hurt or help Castro, but it was never capable of deciding his fate."*

In his book, Senator Fulbright apparently rethought the options available to us and presented them in a quite different way. He cut the speech's three down to two, and even the latter did not come out the same:

"Broadly speaking, there are two ways to deal with this threat [of Castro]: The first possibility is the forcible overthrow of the Castro Government, which would deprive the Soviet Union of its most important base in the Western Hemisphere—although not its only base (Soviet Embassies in Mexico City and Montevideo, for example, are important centers of propaganda and similar activities). The overthrow of Castro might be accomplished, in theory at least, either from within or without, either directly or indirectly. The second approach is the isolation of the Castro regime, combined with efforts to insulate and strengthen the rest of Latin America against its subversive efforts."†

It may be noted that the first option in the speech had merely envisaged a U.S. action to remove Castro's regime "by invading and occupying the island." The first option in the book broadened the sense of this alternative to take in an internal as well as an external overthrow. The second option in the speech—the boycott—became something less specific in the book: "isolation." And the third in the speech—"acceptance"—was dropped altogether as one of the options, though it reappears five pages later as the conclusion which Senator Fulbright continued to arrive at in the book.

By making this operation on his speech's three options, Senator Fulbright could with more reason come out for a continuation of the boycott. To my mind, the changes in

* *The New Leader*, April 27, 1964.
† Fulbright, *op. cit.*, p. 27.

his book were all for the better, and testify to an open-mindedness rare in the political world.

Unfortunately, Senator Fulbright's treatment of Cuba in his March 25 speech received vastly more publicity than the second thoughts on the same subject in his book. Senator Fulbright himself has not repudiated the speech and apparently regards the Cuban section of his book as a clarification of the speech, though it seems to me that he has clarified some essential portions of it out of existence. As a result, the speech has tended to live a life of its own, and it may haunt both the Senator and U.S. policy for some time to come. If I have paid so much attention to the speech, it is because I think that it represents a kind of thinking which extends far beyond Senator Fulbright and continues to be expressed in different ways.

After the Bay of Pigs

I would like to come back to the speech for the last time in order to get into the larger subject of U.S. policy.

The most significant and striking thing about the three original options was not what they took in but what they left out. In none of them was there the slightest allusion to, or place for, the Cuban people.

This extraordinary oversight was also characteristic of the Eisenhower-Kennedy policy of 1960–61. It was one of the chief contributing factors to the Bay of Pigs disaster, which has been criticized mainly for military reasons, such as the lack of air cover. The political neglect of the internal Cuban resistance in the operation is worth at least as much attention.

If ever the internal situation in Cuba had begged for attention, it was in the spring of 1961. The split in Castro's 26th of July Movement on the issue of Communism was wide open by the summer of 1960. An anti-Castro guerrilla operation in the Escambray Mountains had been attempted and abandoned that fall. A far more widespread and promising anti-Communist movement had then taken shape inside the Rebel Army, especially in Camagüey Province. In December, 1960, Castro and other Cuban leaders had made worried speeches about the state of mind in Havana and elsewhere. None of these anti-Castro manifestations owed much to U.S. help or encouragement.

Yet all the planning for the Bay of Pigs invasion discounted the internal resistance. This would have made more sense if the planners had expected the small invasion force to bring down Fidel Castro's regime as if it were a house of cards; or if, as the Cuban members of the force believed, they could count on U.S. armed support. But the "authoritative" U.S. version now is that the invasion force was not expected to do the job by itself and that any commitments of U.S. armed support were unauthorized. Instead, the plan merely expected the force to gain a beachhead on which to establish a *"de facto* anti-Castro government"* that the U.S. would recognize. What then? The answer is that the planners, at least on the U.S. side, calculated on "pockets of resistance" springing up throughout Cuba in support of the beachhead. The Cuban people were thus supposed to finish what the invasion had started.

I do not wish here to refight the battle of the Bay of Pigs. I merely wish, for my present purpose, to point out that the plan could make sense only if the landing were followed up either with direct U.S. intervention or with popular Cuban resistance. What actually happened during the invasion was, of course, something else. President Kennedy ruled out the first choice, and nothing was done to help bring about the second. Castro, ironically, was warned of the approaching blow by the air attack forty-eight hours earlier. The existing anti-Castro underground was permitted to await events passively in utter ignorance and confusion. As a result, the entire underground was smashed—in Camagüey, it is claimed, on the verge of staging a rising—by the mass roundup of thousands of real and suspected oppositionists on the morning of the invasion. The dangerous and painstaking work of months was undone in hours.

The anti-Castro resistance inside Cuba never recovered from this misfortune, which was not of its own making. Unmourned, unacknowledged, unransomed, it was the hapless victim of U.S. policy. And, consequently, we are still paying for the Bay of Pigs.

At that point, U.S. policy might have made a fresh start. We should have profited from the expensive lesson of ignoring the Cuban people. But, by and large, nothing of the sort happened.

For two more years, the chosen instrument of U.S. policy continued to be the Cuban Revolutionary Council. This organization had been formed as a united front of various Cuban exile groups in March, 1961, as the basis for the *de facto* government the CIA intended to set up the following month. After the military setback, however, the more independent members of the Council, who felt that they had been humiliated and misled, resigned. The split reflected the growing dilemma which plagued the exiles: If an external U.S.-backed intervention could not "liberate" Cuba, how could a recently disrupted internal resistance succeed?

The strategists of the reorganized Council, still headed by Dr. José Miró Cardona, believed more fervently than ever before that only a U.S. invasion could overthrow Castro. The opposition rejected this position but did not have the means to pursue a meaningful internal Cuban strategy. And U.S. policy necessarily expressed itself mainly through one or the other of these exile tendencies.

By 1962, the exile community was not at all what it had been in the first months of 1959. As a study by Richard R.

Fagen and Richard A. Brody of Stanford University has shown, "by 1962 a considerable proportion of the refugees were neither rich, well-educated, occupationally advantaged, nor in any sense members of the pre-Castro 'establishment.' "* Nevertheless, most of these refugees were so desperately anxious to go home that they were more interested in getting there than in how they would do so. Despite the changed composition of the exile community, which might have offered political opportunities for a new orientation, the Council continued to embody the deepest yearning of the exiles because nothing else seemed to offer the slightest practical prospect of homecoming.

The Council was made up of professional and amateur politicians, mainly of an older generation, who, by themselves, would not have attracted a much bigger following than their immediate families and intimate friends. Its only real source of power was its line to Washington. The only Cuban exile leader regularly received by the President of the United States was the President of the Cuban Revolutionary Council. Only the Council could afford an annual expenditure in six figures. Only its officials and staff received checks regularly from a mysterious source known to everyone. In order to hold onto its desperate constituency, however, the Council had to maintain a permanent state of tense expectancy. Breathless rumors, winged gossip, inside information for the outside emanated regularly from Miami, always bearing the same glad tidings—the imminence of U.S. "action."

The high point of this intelligence came, of course, during the missile crisis in October, 1962. The Cuban leaders understood the recruitment of exiles into the U.S. armed forces only as an earnest of U.S. military intentions. On October 22, when President Kennedy ordered the U.S.

* "Cubans in Exile: A Demographic Analysis," *Social Problems,* Spring, 1964, pp. 389–401.

"quarantine" of shipments of offensive weapons to Cuba, the Cuban recruits at Fort Knox were alerted; Council leaders alerted key members of the Cuban exile community that an invasion was only hours away; and the key members alerted their friends and associates, until every Cuban exile seemed to be packing, or thinking of packing, for the short journey home. The peaceful deflation of the crisis was actually the Council's deathblow. In April, 1963, on the eve of the second anniversary of the Bay of Pigs, Dr. Miró Cardona resigned as President of the Council with a long statement implying that the U.S. had let him down by failing to use force to overthrow Castro. From Miró's own story, it is not clear that President Kennedy ever gave him any real commitment, but it is clear that Miró interpreted the President's reiterated support as an implied confirmation of his own well-known hopes and expectations.

I think it is safe to say that future historians will not regard the resolution of the missile crisis as the perfect, grandiose triumph that has sometimes been claimed for it. It rather resembles a hill that stands out so sharply because the plain in front and behind it is so flat. President Kennedy, after all, did not simply demand the removal of the missiles and a return to the *status quo ante;* he offered to give Nikita Khrushchev "assurances against an invasion of Cuba," which, however unobjectionable in other circumstances, had never been broached before. In the end, the anti-invasion pledge, despite the conditional form which it took, gave Khrushchev the out that he was looking for and enabled him to agree to the withdrawal of the missiles in an equally conditional form.

I do not wish to gainsay that the missile crisis was handled, in its essential, in an admirably controlled and discriminating fashion (though, on this occasion, it is said, Senator Fulbright came out for immediate invasion). It is noteworthy, however, that the confrontation was wholly military; that it was deliberately limited to Soviet Russia and the United States; and that this time, all of Cuba, from Fidel Castro to José Miró Cardona, was, for better or worse, left out completely.

Thus, for two years, and ultimately to the disillusionment of both sides, U.S. support of the Council artificially distorted the internal development of Cuban exile politics. It sponsored and subsidized a Cuban exile leadership which had its base of power not in Cuba, not even among the exiles, but in Washington. In effect, Washington had been faced with a choice of backing those exile leaders who looked primarily to the United States for a solution or those who wanted to make the Cuban people the principal factor in their own salvation, without refusing help from any source, including the United States. By choosing to back the former in the period between the Bay of Pigs and the missile crisis, U.S. policy caused one invasion fiasco to be followed by another—different in kind and far less spectacular, but no less demoralizing and avoidable. The exile leaders may have much to answer for, but they did not make their mistakes alone.

Between Bankruptcy and Adventurism

This is not the first time that I have tried to express some of these thoughts. Before the missile crisis, in an interview which appeared in the July 8, 1962, issue of the Cuban exile magazine *Bohemia Libre,* I made an effort to speak to the Cuban exiles with candor and concern. At one point the interviewer, Dr. Andrés Valdespino, asked me what role I thought the Cubans themselves should play in the overthrow of Castro. I seized the opportunity to say:

"The great majority of Cubans, especially those in exile, have to base their struggle fundamentally on the principle that Cuba will be liberated in Cuba, not in Miami, New

York, or Washington. Miami, New York, and Washington can and should help substantially, of course, but they cannot take the place of the struggle inside Cuba or decide by themselves alone the destiny of Cuba. The decisive struggle will take place inside Cuba itself, and the exiles will influence it only to the extent that they help, encourage, and inspire those who are risking their lives in Cuba. To put it rather crudely: A dollar spent to help the Cubans in the underground in any way is worth more than a hundred dollars spent to help exile politicians."

Shortly after the missile crisis, I was asked to write a memorandum for the President of the United States. Again I tried to use the occasion to get across a warning on the policy then pursued with respect to the Cuban exiles. In that memorandum, dated November 13, 1962, I wrote in part:

"The time may also have come, if it is not long overdue, to re-examine the relationship to the various tendencies and groups among the Cuban exiles. The question might be put in a practical fashion: If we wish to help and encourage the still largely passive resistance in Cuba to become active, and to widen the cracks and splits in Castro's regime, what exiles are likely to contribute most to the accomplishment of these ends?

"Certainly not those who live only for the day of U.S. military intervention. Yet, to an outsider like myself, this appears to be the peculiar contradiction in our present policy vis-à-vis the exiles. Those who claim our support, and are able to produce the most impressive visible evidence in support of their claims, can do least for us to implement any effective policy not based on full-scale military invasion. They are men of an older generation who represent the pre-Batista past; they insist on separating the political and social components of a healthy democracy; they cannot conceivably inspire a popular movement inside Cuba.

"It is not necessary, and it would be unwise, at this late date, to upset the whole apple cart of Cuban exile politics. But is it not advisable to broaden the base of our support and sympathy? In a sense, among Cubans today (and not only Cubans), only the young can speak to the young, only the disillusioned to the disillusioned, only the 'revolutionary' to the 'revolutionary.' We have, if appearances do not deceive me, given little or no aid and comfort to the young, the disillusioned, the 'revolutionary' in the anti-Castro struggle. We have precious political capital in these young Cubans who have gone through the fire of Fidelismo, who have in the past few years undergone an incredible range and depth of political experience, who have ventured up to the edge of Communism and turned back in revulsion. There is no comparable group in all Latin America.

"Yet they have been largely ignored. They do not even have a means, an 'organ,' to express themselves, though the Batista crowd in this country is able to put out an expensive, slick-paper publication. They have gone a long way from some of their earlier preconceptions of 'American imperialism.' It cannot be emphasized too strongly that they—and only they—can be a bridge to the internal struggle inside Cuba because those who will break with Castro tomorrow must go through the same process they went through yesterday. How we treat them now will be a test for those like them still in Castro's camp."

It should be clear that I have always rejected the choice between political bankruptcy and military adventurism.

Yet this has been the frame of reference in the United States for the past five years. The Eisenhower-Kennedy policy of 1960–61 opted for invasion. Though former President Kennedy was in his last months obviously rethinking the whole Cuban problem, he died before he had come to any firm decision. The Republican candidate in 1964, Barry Goldwater, had nothing more original to offer than a rewarmed version of the Bay of Pigs debacle—a U.S.-backed exile operation to "recapture" Cuba.

The idea that any exile force, without direct and massive U.S. participation, could overthrow Castro's regime today is almost not worth discussing seriously. It has been professionally estimated that a minimum of three to six U.S. divisions would be required to invade and occupy Cuba. In order to save U.S. lives, it would be necessary to take more Cuban lives. Landings would have to be prepared and followed up by the heaviest bombardments. The bombs would not distinguish between Castro's troops and the Cuban people as a whole.

Moreover, the political bond that has held together the diverse elements in Castro's regime is hostility toward the United States; the disintegrating force has always been Communism. Within days of an invasion, the casualties would bring on curses against U.S. bombs, not Communist bombs. It might be argued, of course, that Castro had invited the invasion and should be held responsible for it. But such logic would do far more, I dare say, to relieve some U.S. consciences than to console the Cuban dead and wounded. According to the distinguished Cuban exile Dr. Justo Carrillo Hernández, in a dawn meeting with him and other members of the Cuban Revolutionary Council, President Kennedy explained his opposition to U.S. participation in the Bay of Pigs by exclaiming: "Americans shooting Cubans? No! No! No!"

I do not mean that U.S. military action in Cuba can be ruled out under all circumstances. Conceivably, an extreme international situation might require extreme measures in Cuba. Thus, while I may disagree with Senator Fulbright on whether or in what way Castro's regime is a "danger," I still think that it is necessary to ask whether the present danger justifies such extreme measures. Indeed, some time before Senator Fulbright, I wrote in connection with the Bay of Pigs:

"An invasion force which succeeded in overthrowing Castro without a demonstrative show of popular support could only have ruled Cuba in a state of perpetual civil war or as a thinly disguised American occupation."* A few months later, in preparing that article for my book *Castro's Revolution,* I added: "The true liberation of Cuba could not be achieved behind the backs of, and without the active participation of, the Cuban people in Cuba, and their participation could not be artificially manufactured or arbitrarily delegated."

That is still true. It is still the starting point for any consideration of a Cuban policy that seeks to avoid the complementary follies of invasion and capitulation. Senator Fulbright rightly rejected invasion, so he flirted with a euphemism for capitulation; Senator Goldwater rightly rejected capitulation, so he edged toward a thinly disguised form of invasion. Since, in reality, we are not likely to capitulate or to invade, this kind of debate was little more than shadowboxing. Is there, at this late date, an alternative? I think there is, but there is no miracle in the offing and no button to push.

There is, rather, an already extended historical process which must be envisaged as a whole. In Cuban history, as it happens, the struggles for freedom have been long ones, with many ups and downs, repeated setbacks, and ultimate victories. The fight for independence against Spain is often called the Thirty Years' War; it broke out in 1868, raged openly for ten years, flickered intermittently for the next seventeen years, and entered its final stage in 1895. The resistance to dictator Gerardo Machado started soon after he took office in 1925, flared up in 1927, rose in 1930, broke loose again in 1931, and brought him down two years later.

---

* "Cuba and United States Policy," *The New Leader,* June 5, 1961.

It took almost seven years until Batista was overthrown at the end of 1958.

In each case, the Cuban people found within itself the resources of heroism and sacrifice to start the struggle, to carry on largely by itself in the darkest hours, to produce new leaders. The tragedy of Cuban history has not been the lack of will to struggle against the greatest odds; it has been the failure to gain the full benefit of those struggles, partly as a result of inner Cuban weaknesses and partly as a result of U.S. policies.

More and more Cuban exiles, however, have come to recognize that the Cuban people, not the exiles, not the United States, represent the principal factor in the present struggle. It is not that the Cuban people can win by themselves; they need all the help they can get from the exiles, from the United States, and from everyone else. But the struggle cannot be won without them or against them. This simple proposition may seem fairly modest in its potentialities. Yet the course of the past six years would have been very different if it had been taken seriously. In the spring of 1961, the Cuban underground would not have been totally ignored and uselessly sacrificed in favor of a U.S.-controlled invasion force. Exile leaders committed to an even larger scale U.S. invasion would not have received for so many more months such unguarded and unconditional backing. Cubans in Cuba would not have been discouraged from risking their lives unnecessarily because they were told that the exiles or the Marines were soon coming to the rescue.

If we had done nothing more than avoid these gross miscalculations, we would be far better off today; if we do not repeat them, we will be far better off tomorrow. A great deal can be gained simply by letting Castro make more mistakes and by making fewer ourselves.

Exiles have always played an outstanding role in Cuban

struggles. The greatest Cuban of modern times, José Martí, was an exile most of his life. The exiles have invariably failed, however, whenever they have been obsessed with their own conspiracies and have lost touch with or faith in the mass of people at home. This has happened, with U.S. encouragement, to a considerable part of the present exiles. But there are those—and their numbers have been increasing—who recognize the futility of waiting for the United States to overthrow Castro by force; who put the internal struggle in Cuba in the forefront of their plans and activities; who seek aid wherever there is any hope of getting it, including the United States, but not as the subordinate instruments of U.S. policy.

Fundamentally, three courses are open to Cuba and the Cuban exiles. The first might be called "restoration." It is the policy actually followed by most Cuban exile politicians and the vested interests, both U.S. and Cuban, of the past. It may be expressed openly or more surreptitiously by refusing to say anything unpleasant about pre-Castro Cuba. The second is Castroism, as it has evolved in power. These two extremes feed on each other. The best argument in favor of the past is the evils of Castroism, and the best argument in favor of Castroism is the evils of the past.

The third course might be called "reconstruction." It rejects both the evils of the past and Castroism. It has no illusions about pre-Castro Cuba and no apologies for Castro's Cuba. It recognizes that if there had not been uninspiring leadership in the regime of former President Prío Socarrás, there would have been no Batista in power a second time, and if there had been no Batista, there would have been no Castro. It seeks to find its way back to the historic currents of Cuba's democratic idealism and social reformation. These currents, as embodied in the original ABC program, the original Auténtico program, the original Ortodoxo aspiration, the 26th of July Movement's original promise, and other manifestations of political renovation, have always been frustrated or betrayed. But there is a living tradition out of which new vistas and new forces can come forth. Like the phoenix, such movements rise out of the fire and ashes, eternally old and eternally young.

INDEX

INDEX